Front cover:
Silent features like *Bavu* (Universal, 1923) were shipped via railway express in bulky tin boxes, plastered with stickers reading 'Notice to Express Employees/CAUTION/ Keep Fire and Lights Away'. Universal destroyed the negative of *Bavu* and hundreds of other silents in 1948. [Richard Koszarski Collection.] (page 8)

This issue:
Silent Cinema

Edited by Richard Koszarski

Editorial office:

Richard Koszarski
Box Ten
Teaneck, New Jersey 07666 USA
E-mail: filmhist@aol.com

Publishing office:

John Libbey & Company Pty Ltd
Level 10, 15–17 Young Street
Sydney, NSW 2000
Australia
Telephone: +61 (0)2 9251 4099
Fax: +61 (0)2 9251 4428
E-mail: jlsydney@mpx.com.au

© 1997 John Libbey & Company Pty Ltd

Other offices:

John Libbey & Company Ltd
13 Smiths Yard, Summerley Street
London SW18 4HR, UK
Telephone: +44 (0)181-947 2777
Fax: +44 (0)1-947 2664

John Libbey Eurotext Ltd, Montrouge, France
John Libbey - CIC s.r.l., Rome, Italy

Printed in Australia by
Gillingham Printers Pty Ltd, South Australia

An International Journal

Volume 9, Number 1, 1997

This issue:

SILENT CINEMA

The *Canadian Journal of Film Studies / Revue canadienne d'études cinématographiques* is available to all members of the *Film Studies Association of Canada / Association canadienne d'études cinématographiques*. The Journal can also be obtained through individual subscriptions at the cost of $35.00 per volume in Canada, and US $35.00 in all other countries. Postage is included. Back issues are available at $15.00 per volume.

Don't miss the upcoming issue of the

Canadian Journal of Film Studies
Revue canadienne d'études cinématographiques

On the

CENTENARY OF CINEMA IN CANADA

(vol. 5 no. 2, Fall 1996)

This issue of the *Canadian Journal of Film Studies / Revue canadienne d'études cinématographiques* will include:

"Querying or Queering the Nation: the Lesbian Postmodern and Women's Cinema," by **Jean Bruce**; "Exile on Hastings & Main Streets: The Vancouver Films of Larry Kent," by **Dave Douglas**; "The Introduction of the Lumière Cinematograph in Canada," by **André Gaudreault and Germain Lacasse**, translation by Madeleine Beaudry; "Alterity and Nation: Screening Race, Sex, Gender and Ethnicity in *Back to God's Country*," by **Christopher Gittings**; "Cinema, Theater and Red Gushing Blood in Jean Beaudin's *Being at Home with Claude*," by **André Loiselle**; "The Crisis of Naming in Canadian Film Studies," by **Brenda Longfellow**; "The Challenge for Change in the Alternative Public Sphere," by **Scott MacKenzie**; and "Hags, Nags, Witches and Crones: Reframing Age in *Company of Strangers* by **Angela Stukator**. Also "J. Booth Scott, A Personal History (1966)," introduced by **Blaine Allan**. Plus *Book Reviews* by Gene Walz and Lianne McLarty.

For subscription information and complimentary issues and to order back issues and single copies, please contact the Editorial Office:

SCHOOL FOR STUDIES IN ART AND CULTURE:
FILM STUDIES
Carleton University
1125 Colonel By Drive Ottawa, Ont. K1S 5B6
Tel. (613) 520-2600 Ext. 6693 Fax (613) 520-3575

Film History, Volume 9, pp. 3–4, 1997. Copyright © John Libbey & Company
ISSN: 0892-2160. Printed in Australia

Silent cinema

One thing is certain: the farther silent cinema recedes into the past, the more activity it seems to generate on library shelves, at festival programs, and in the catalogues of non-theatrical distributing agents.

This is the opposite of what logically should be happening. After all, as each year goes by, the silent period occupies a proportionately smaller slice of film history. The fixed number of titles produced in the silent period fails to grow, and surviving silent filmmakers, whose published memoirs or presence at retrospectives might be expected to spark audience interest, diminish to almost nothing. (And as Gregg Bachman points out in this issue, surviving members of the silent film audience are themselves growing scarce.)

In 1950, when 52-year-old Gloria Swanson played Norma Desmond as some sort of relic from the Jurassic period, the number of college classes on silent film could be counted on the fingers of one hand, while the other hand could comfortably heft all the books on the subject still in print. James Agee's landmark essay on 'Comedy's Greatest Era', which had appeared in *Life* magazine not too many months earlier, attracted the attention it did precisely *because* the work of Keaton, Lloyd and Ben Turpin (*Life's* cover boy that issue) had been so rapidly forgotten.

The story of how silent film dropped from popular consciousness as quickly as it did, and how (and why) it managed to struggle back, would make a fascinating study in cultural history. A complete answer is certainly beyond the scope of this *Film History* issue, although David Pierce's essay offers some clues. Nevertheless, anyone affixing a W.K.L. Dickson postage stamp to their first-class mail must understand the 'sea change' in public awareness that has occurred here (the Theda Bara, Lon Chaney, and Zasu Pitts stamps, among others, now unfortunately belong to the 29-cent era).

During the 1940s, great collectors like John E. Allen and Gatewood Dunstan could acquire silent films by the carload, often simply for the service of carting them away. Yet the silent titles on their shelves were generally scattered and miscellaneous, with low-budget states-rights releases over-represented, major studio productions nearly invisible, and few foreign titles other than those circulated by the Museum of Modern Art. What would be their reaction if they could drop in at a neighbourhood Blockbuster video outlet in 1997, where they could find not only *The Phantom of the Opera*, but *The Wedding March*, *Pandora's Box* and even Carl Dreyer's *The Master of the House*? The catalogues of some of today's more adventurous distributors reveal elegant laser disc releases of titles which the founders of the Theodore Huff Memorial Film Society would have killed to possess.

The presentation of silent films with elaborate and imaginative musical accompaniments has lately become the most fashionable international manifestation of this revival. Today the success of these events goes beyond the concert or screening-room audience to a new marketplace defined by broadcast, home video, and compact disc technologies. What even in the 1960s was only a niche market composed of scholars and buffs has now broadened to such a degree that it risks becoming a victim of its own success.

Perhaps the most remarkable evidence of this was the appearance on the front page of the *New York Times*, 17 September 1996 (true, still below the fold) of an extensive story on the restoration of Frederick Warde's 1912 production of *Richard III*. While the political manoeuvrings behind this story are at least as interesting as Warde's film, the fact that the event was judged to be front page news is in itself extraordinary. Just wait until those missing reels of *Greed* turn up!

By comparison, there seems to be less interest at the moment in such crucial periods of film history as the 1940s or the 1970s, despite the far greater availability of films and documentation. Papers submitted to this journal, for example, are as likely to be about the silent period as about all the other seventy years of film history put together.

This issue of *Film History*, even though it deals with the silent feature period and not the early cinema era (an especially active hotbed of inquiry), suggests why researchers find the silent years so fruitful. Such topics as censorship, nationhood, or the roles of women and minorities within the industry are not simply the concerns of silent movie antiquarians, but active issues of compelling interest to a wide range of contemporary commentators: the advantages of dealing with these issues in their earliest state are obviously attractive to researchers across the methodological spectrum.

The supply of silent films might be limited, but the analytical potential of the cinema's earliest years, it would seem, is endless. ♦

Richard Koszarski

UPCOMING ISSUES/ CALL FOR PAPERS

Non-Fiction Film
edited by Mark Langer

Sreenwriters and Screenwriting
edited by John Belton

International Cinema of the Teens
edited by Kristin Thompson

Cinema Pioneers
edited by Stephen Bottomore
(deadline for submissions
1 September 1997)

Film and Television
edited by Richard Koszarski
(deadline for submissions
1 December 1997)

Red Scare
edited byDaniel J. Leab
(deadline for submissions
1 March1998)

The editors of *FILM HISTORY* encourage the submission of manuscripts within the overall scope of the journal. These may correspond to the announced themes of future issues above, but may equally be on any topic relevant to film history.

Film History, Volume 9, pp. 5–22, 1997. Text copyright © 1997 David Pierce. Design, etc. copyright © John Libbey & Company.
ISSN: 0892-2160. Printed in Australia

The legion of the condemned – why American silent films perished

David Pierce

Of the approximately 10,000 feature films and countless short subjects released in the United States before 1928, only a small portion survive. While some classics exist and are widely available, many silent films survive only in reviews, stills, posters and the memories of the few remaining audience members who saw them on their original release.[1]

Why did most silent films not survive the passage of time? The current widespread availability of many titles on home video, and the popularity of silent film presentations with live orchestral accompaniment might give the impression that silent films had always been held in such high regard. Instead, for many decades after the coming of sound, silent films had all the commercial appeal of last week's weather report.

This article will explore the factors that contributed to the loss of such a large number of silent films in a seemingly random fashion. There is no single villain: an unstable storage medium and an extended period of no commercial value were contributing, but not decisive, factors. The loss of most silent films resulted from shortsighted decisions by their owners and a combination of happenstance and neglect.

Not many copies in existence

Although it might seem remarkable that not a single print survives for most silent films, usually there were not many copies to begin with. While newspapers or magazines were printed and sold by the thousands, relatively few projection prints were required for even the most popular silent films. In the earliest days of the industry, producers sold prints, and measured success by the number of copies sold. By the feature period, beginning around 1914, copies were leased to subdistributors or rented to exhibitors, and the owners retained tight control. The distribution of silent features was based on a staggered release system, with filmgoers paying more to see a film early in its run. Films opened in downtown theatres, moved to neighbourhood theatres and finally to rural houses. This process was controlled by a system of clearances that dictated rentals and when a picture would be available to each class of theatres. In the 1920s, a film would normally require two years to work its way from

David Pierce is an independent film historian and copyright consultant with a special interest in the feature period of the silent film. He received a Masters Degree in Business Administration from George Washington University. Mr Pierce has written for *American Cinematographer* on the Kodascope Libraries, *American Film* on why some films are in the public domain and *Film Comment* on ownership of major film libraries. His Internet site, *Silent Film Sources*, is located at http://www.cinemaweb.com/silentfilm. Correspondence: PO Box 2748, Laurel, MD 20709, USA.

premiere to final performance. Since the prints were in continuous use, this demand could be satisfied by a modest number of copies. In 1926, Paramount was making 150 prints for domestic release and an additional 50 copies for foreign use.[2]

Periodically, prints would be returned to the distributor for repair. Inspectors would fix splices and torn sprockets, sometimes cannibalising several prints to create one showable copy. By the end of their run, pictures would be circulating to theatres that changed their program every day, in prints that were often in very poor condition. Exhibitors were constantly complaining about the poor condition of the copies they received. A small town theatre running MGM's *Show People* (1928) was typical: 'We were rather surprised at getting a poor print after paying the golden price we did. Parts of it were quite rainy and scratched.' Theatres learned to expect well-worn prints, as with a complaint about *Our Dancing Daughters* (MGM, 1928): 'Naturally we would draw a slovenly inspected print for a night when we had a houseful of particular and critical people.'[3]

Most remaining prints were destroyed

Regardless of the number of prints, almost all of them shared the same fate. The value of a film declined rapidly following its opening engagement. Producers wrote off the production cost of their films quickly, usually by 90 per cent in the first year. Rental for a feature might be $3,000 per week for the first run in a downtown theatre, and bottom out at $10 per day by the end of its run. After theatres no longer wanted a film, the only residual value for the heavily worn prints was the silver content of the celluloid.[4]

In *Suds* (UA, 1920), Mary Pickford saves an old horse from its fate at the glue factory. In real life, Pickford and her contemporaries ensured that all excess copies of *Suds* and their other films were accounted for and sent to their cinematic doom. In 1918, Kodak established a silver recovery centre in Rochester, New York, to process junk prints. Silver salvage of excess projection prints served two purposes: certifying destruction of the copies, while returning a final sliver of income to the owner. United Artists was a typical Kodak customer when they cleared out some of the older Mary Pickford releases from their distribution depots in 1925. United Artists sent 130 well-worn prints of *Suds* (1920), *Little Lord Fauntleroy* (1921), *Rosita* (1923) and other older Pickford titles to Rochester. The resulting income was a modest, but undoubtedly welcome, $302.74.[5]

After a film was no longer in active distribution, the studio would retain the original negative, the original work print and a projection print or two. Other than a copy for the studio library, these materials were usually stored outside California, because that state taxed old and new negatives on their full production cost. As a consequence, negatives were shipped to the east coast upon completion and most release prints were manufactured by laboratories in New York and New Jersey. Storage vaults for studios, laboratories and private storage companies were located throughout Manhattan, Brooklyn, the Bronx and Queens and in northern New Jersey at Fort Lee, Bound Brook, Little Ferry and Woodridge.

Destroyed for legal reasons

When these materials were pulled from storage, it was more likely for inspection or destruction than for preservation. When a film was sold to another company for a remake, the contract often required that all copies of the original be destroyed, with the occasional exception of a reference print. Paramount sold George Melford's *The Unknown* (1915) to Universal, agreeing 'to destroy the negative ... and all prints thereof in possession of the seller, except one print which the seller shall retain for library purposes'. Mary Pickford's *Little Annie Rooney* (UA, 1925), remade with Shirley Temple, still exists despite such a clause. Other titles were not so lucky.[6]

Some story contracts obligated the producer to destroy the negative at the end of the license period to leave the author free to make a new agreement. The agreement with novelist Rafael Sabatini for King Vidor's *Bardelys the Magnificent* (1926) with John Gilbert required that 'at final determination of contract, [MGM] must destroy all negatives and positives and render statement or proof thereof to owner'.[7]

Little perceived value

Before the introduction of sound, some older films retained value as a small number of reissues could be offered to theatres along with new releases. Independent producers lacking new films to offer with their old ones found that their old films were not in demand. Thomas H. Ince had been a successful independent producer before his death in 1924, and his estate was actively trying to realise as much income from his old films as possible. In 1928, a prospective reissue distributor wrote the Ince estate that:

> In view of the cost of preparing a series of reissues for the market and the expenses of selling, the outright purchase of a reissue is almost out of the question. Charles Ray, Dorothy Dalton and Enid Bennett pictures do not mean much on the market, unless the pictures themselves were outstanding specials in their time.[8]

Once silent film theatres converted to sound or closed, silent films lost their audience and became worthless. *Civilization* was a big success in 1916. Anxious for income from a reissue distributor, the Ince estate sold the film outright in 1929 for $750. Reissues were rare, so the only remaining value of most pictures was their remake potential. In 1930, the Ince estate sold a group of eight Charles Ray films at $500 each, and in 1932 managed to get $1,000 for Henry King's 1919 hit *23½ Hours Leave* from its star Douglas MacLean. Other independents had more success, though the US$40,000 price that *Tol'able David* fetched in 1930 was for the story, not the 1920 film that came with it.[9]

The assets of the failed Triangle Film Corporation included rights to as many as 2500 films and stories. The films included productions from 1915 to 1917 that were supervised by D.W. Griffith and Thomas H. Ince and Mack Sennett, with stars Douglas Fairbanks, Norma Talmadge, William S. Hart and Gloria Swanson. The library sold at bankruptcy auction in 1924 for $55,000. By 1937, three owners later, the films and stories were purchased for a rock bottom $5,000.[10]

After leaving Triangle in 1917, Mack Sennett was a prolific independent producer of shorts and occasional features, but by 1933 his company was bankrupt. The inventory of prints and negatives was sold at auction to a speculator for $875, which was about the value of the silver salvage, while Sennett purchased the copyrights for $75. In 1939 Warner Bros. released a two-reel condensation of Mack Sennett's *A Small Town Idol* (1921), and Jack L. Warner weighed purchasing the Sennett material outright. A studio attorney wrote to his counterpart in New York: 'I understand the picture is doing well, and thus J.L.'s desire to make this present deal.'[11]

In 1940, Warner Bros. bought all rights and materials to the Sennett comedies, acquiring nine tons of nitrate negatives and prints for $10,000. The 330 properties included the original negatives to *Yankee Doodle in Berlin* (1919), *The Shriek of Araby* (1923) with Ben Turpin in a spoof of Rudolph Valentino, and three features starring Mabel Normand: *Molly O'* (1921), *Suzanna* (1922) and *The Extra Girl* (1923). This footage was used to produce a handful of additional Warner Bros. shorts.[12]

Storage costs

An inactive film library requires a lot of storage space, but that was not usually a problem for studios that could use their own film vaults or rely on laboratories. Companies generally continued to hold their silent material until they had to pay storage fees or began to run out of room. RKO Radio Pictures stored their negatives and prints in vaults in Albany, New York. This included the films produced by RKO's predecessor companies, R-C Pictures Corporation and FBO Pictures. Reportedly, after the company ceased production in 1957 and sold its production lot in Los Angeles, RKO periodically destroyed silent negatives whenever they needed shelf space for reissue and television prints.

The situation was different for independents who kept their negatives and prints in laboratories or commercial storage facilities. Following the introduction of sound, owners began to question why they were paying storage fees on films that would probably never again provide any income. In 1930, Lloyds Film Storage in New York was charging 20 cents per reel per month for storage. The owner of a seven-reel silent feature would be paying $35 per year in storage fees for an asset with virtually no earning potential. Many owners junked

Fig. 1. Silent features like *Bavu* (Universal, 1923) were shipped via railway express in bulky tin boxes, plastered with stickers reading 'Notice to Express Employees/CAUTION/Keep Fire and Lights Away'. Universal destroyed the negative of *Bavu* and hundreds of other silents in 1948. [Richard Koszarski Collection.]

their materials, or simply stopped paying storage charges.[13]

Intentional destruction

Numerous owners evaluated the commercial value of their silent libraries and made a business decision. Producer Sol Lesser junked all of his silent productions in the 1930s when his production company needed storage space for newer films. Less verifiable, but just as credible, is the story that in the late 1940s, Columbia Pictures was presented with a significant increase in their fire insurance premiums. The decision made by Columbia executives was to reduce the material in storage by junking unneeded footage, including all of their silent films.[14]

After becoming an independent producer in 1923, Samuel Goldwyn produced seventeen silent features, including ten starring Ronald Colman. Goldwyn's wife and business partner, Frances Howard Goldwyn, ordered the destruction of almost all of his silent films. She told historian Robert S. Birchard that it was a business decision because the company needed the vault space. The only title she intentionally kept was Henry King's *The Winning of Barbara Worth* (1926) because it featured Gary Cooper and she felt it might have some commercial value.[15]

Nitrate film stock

The decision by these owners to destroy their silent films merely anticipated the inevitable disintegration of the films, because the film used a base of nitrocellulose that was not chemically stable. The 'nitrate' film base provided a luminous image, and was sufficiently flexible and resilient to withstand hundreds of projections. Eastman Kodak notes that this nitrate film stock 'had excellent physical properties', but suffered from 'poor chemical stability and high flammability', which meant that the film would rot if it didn't catch fire first. Nitrate film chemically deteriorates over time, and this process is accelerated by the symptoms of poor storage conditions: moisture and heat.[16]

Most silent negatives and prints were premature victims of decomposition due to poor storage conditions. Properly kept in a cool and dry environment, nitrate might outlast improperly stored safety film. While there were recommendations for ideal temperature and humidity available, there were no regulations to enforce them. Since nitrate materials were often stored in far less than optimal conditions, they became more susceptible to accelerated deterioration and fire.[17]

Outdoor vaults without air-conditioning can reach extreme temperatures in the winter and summer. A visitor to a nitrate vault in Fort Lee, New Jersey, in late October 1972 noted that although the outside temperature was 50 degrees, inside the vaults it was 20 degrees warmer, musty and damp. Most of the film stored in the vault was deteriorating. This type of storage would be damaging for safety film; for nitrate film it would rapidly accelerate decomposition that might otherwise take decades to occur.[18]

In the first stage of decomposition, the image starts to fade as the base emits gases that affect the film emulsion. The surface then becomes sticky, attaching itself to the adjacent film. Next, gas bubbles appear near the tightly wound sections of film, where the gases are unable to escape. The film softens and welds into a single mass with an overwhelming noxious odor before degenerating to a rust-coloured acrid powder.[19]

The life expectancy of a reel of nitrate film depends on any number of factors including the chemical composition of that batch of film stock, how the film was developed and washed, and the type of storage. Trace amounts of chemicals remaining from when the film was originally developed play a part as the decomposition often starts in a particular portion of the negative (often the intertitles) that was insufficiently washed. Once started, the decomposition transfers throughout the roll, and storage cans often trap the gases inside, accelerating the process.

Some nitrate from the turn of the century remains in excellent condition, while other films decomposed or fell apart after only a few decades. The original negative to D.W. Griffith's *The Avenging Conscience* (1914) was unusable ten years after its production due to improper handling and wear. Griffith sent the negative to Europe in 1923 to make prints for release in Germany. The German lab reported that the negative was heavily deteriorated and 'the destruction and decomposition through hypo had already advanced so far that the emulsion was destroyed and came off the celluloid'.[20]

Even before decomposition set in, a negative could experience shrinkage beyond the capabilities of standard laboratory equipment. MGM reported in 1954:

> The Consolidated Laboratories have just reported to us that they cannot satisfactorily print *Sally, Irene and Mary* (1925) as the negative titles have shrunk 1.75% and the picture has shrunk 1.40 per cent. The shrinkage that they can stand is 1.20%.[21]

When negatives were no longer able to produce prints, they became candidates for disposal. In April 1948, Universal ordered the destruction of all but a handful of their silent negatives. The comprehensive order required eighteen single-spaced pages to list the titles, stored in Woodridge, New Jersey and at Pathe Labs on East 106th Street in Manhattan. The memo excluded a number of titles from immediate destruction including *The Virgin of Stamboul* (1920) and *The Goose Woman* (1925), noting that 'it will be necessary for you to have the above seventeen negatives inspected. It will then be in order for you to junk what ever negatives that are not printable'. As one Universal executive wrote to his counterpart at Kodak in 1950, the Universal library of silent films was destroyed 'due to the fact that they had all deteriorated to the point where the retention of the "remains" was considered dangerous by the Pathe Laboratory in whose vaults they were stored'. An additional incentive to destroy the films might have been Universal's ownership of the Cellofilm Corporation, a silver reclamation company.[22]

Indifference and benign neglect

The principal reason for the loss of such a high percentage of silent films was general indifference. As there was seldom a demand for older material, inspection of the materials was erratic, and they were subject to increased danger as the nitrate aged. Many films were not destroyed before their time; they simply did not last long enough for anyone to be interested in preserving them.

Owners who could afford it would continue to store their films and periodically check their condition. As soon as a print or negative displayed the symptoms of nitrate decomposition, it would be destroyed. Evidence of decomposition in any reel would be justification to junk the entire film, since a rotting film was a much greater fire hazard, and an incomplete print or negative would be of no use.

A review of various studio records shows many silent films did not survive twenty years after their production. A 1935 vault inventory of Pathe Exchange, Inc. documented that the negatives for *Mary's Lamb*, George Fitzmaurice's *At Bay* (both 1915) and *Ruler of the Road* (1918) had been 'scrapped'. Holdings on *Carolyn of the Corners* with Bessie Love and *Prince and Betty* (both 1919) were non-existent beyond the story files. A 1937 inventory of films from the 1910s produced by the Triangle Film Corporation showed that of 60 features with remake rights, a negative or print existed for only twenty.[23]

Films held by studios still in operation fared no better. The negatives to *Broadway After Dark* (WB, 1924) with Adolphe Menjou and Norma Shearer and *Bobbed Hair* (WB, 1925) with Marie Prevost were junked on 12 November 1936. *Wolf's Clothing* (WB, 1927) with Monte Blue and Patsy Ruth Miller was destroyed on 14 September 1938. Because of decomposition in reel 5, the entire negative to Erich von Stroheim's *The Devil's Passkey* (Universal, 1920) was destroyed on 8 May 1941. Four reels of the six-reel negative to Mary Pickford's *Johanna Enlists* (Artcraft, 1918) had rotted and were junked upon inspection in November 1946. Pickford's *Rosita* (UA, 1923) was already incomplete. Von Stroheim's last film for Universal, *Merry-Go-Round* (1923), was junked on 1 December 1949.[24]

The negative for von Stroheim's *The Merry Widow* (1925) was examined by MGM in November 1950, and showed so much decomposition that it was scrapped. A year later, when the negative for *He Who Gets Slapped* (1924) with Lon Chaney was pulled from dead storage, the first four reels had decomposed and were junked. Parts of the negative to Greta Garbo's first American film, *The Torrent* (1926), were 'very badly decomposed' upon inspection in July 1953. Reel three of the negative to Merian C. Cooper and Ernest B. Schoedsack's *Chang* (Paramount, 1927) was reported as 'slightly decomposed' in May 1956. The entire negative was destroyed after a visit by the Los Angeles County fire inspector. *The Lucky Devil* (Paramount, 1925) with Richard Dix lasted long enough to decompose in 1960, and Ernst Lubitsch's *Lady Windermere's Fan* (WB, 1925) survived to be junked on 24 January 1961. The negative to Frank Capra's *Submarine* (Columbia, 1928) was destroyed in the mid-1960s due to decomposition.[25]

Prints frequently outlasted the negatives that generated them, but not always long enough. 'In the four years preceding Paramount's gift of about 90 feature films to [the American Film Institute], they had scrapped about 70 silent pictures', the AFI's Associate Archivist David Shepard said in a 1970 interview. 'In November 1968, Paramount gave the Library of Congress 90 [silent] features', he continued, but 'between November and April when the films were finally shipped, 13 of them had deteriorated'.[26]

In 1971 after the American Film Institute asked to borrow the last known print of James Cruze's *The City Gone Wild* (1927) from Paramount, the copy was pulled from storage and an inspection showed deterioration in one reel. The print was placed in a barrel of water and carted off by a salvage company while the AFI archivist was driving over to pick it up.[27]

Movies were not always junked, of course. Sometimes they succumbed to something closer to a natural death. In October 1969, Harold Lloyd buried 27 reels of deteriorating film in the yard adjacent to his estate's nitrate vault. The film laid to rest included odd reels of the original negatives to Lloyd's features *Why Worry* (1923), *Girl Shy* (1924) and *Hot Water* (1924) and negatives to a number of his one-reel short comedies. Had Lloyd not made safety negatives for most of his features and a single safety print for most of his shorts, the comedian would have barely outlived his life's work.[28]

Nitrate film fires

Films were usually junked by placing them in a barrel of water due to the risk of fire. At its best, nitrate film has a relatively low ignition temperature; decomposition lowers the flash point so rotting nitrate film can spontaneously combust at temperatures as low as 106 degrees Fahrenheit, emitting toxic fumes while burning. Once ignition begins,

Fig. 2. James Durkin, who directed John Barrymore that year in *The Incorrigible Dukane* (Famous Players, 1915), stands in the ruins of the 26th Street Studio, 11 September 1915. [Richard Koszarski Collection.]

internal oxidising agents accelerate the combustion so that tightly wound film will continue burning underwater.

The flammable nature of nitrate and careless handling led to many well-publicised fires with loss of life. A fire in a Pittsburgh film exchange in January 1909 killed ten people. In 1914, a courier carried four reels of film wrapped in paper into the smoking car of a Chicago commuter train. The package caught fire, killing two and badly burning 38 people, and destroying the interior of the car. A 1919 film-exchange fire injured 30 people.[29]

In the early 1910s, the Lubin Film Manufacturing Company laboratory in Philadelphia supplied release prints for the Jesse L. Lasky Feature Play Company and other producers. An explosion and fire in a storage vault on 13 June 1914 destroyed numerous negatives including *The Sea Wolf* (1913), produced by Bosworth, Inc. The Thomas Edison plant in New Jersey burned on 9 December 1914 when a fire started in a vault in the film inspecting building and quickly spread. The fire that burned the Manhattan studios of Famous Players on 11 September 1915 also destroyed the negative to *The Foundling*, an unreleased Mary Pickford film directed by Allan Dwan.[30]

These and other well-publicised disasters forced the industry to consider shifting to a safer film stock. Kodak had developed a nonflammable cellulose acetate film stock by 1909. Unfortunately, it was less durable and more expensive, with a grainier image, so a brief experiment with acetate release prints ended in 1911. Prints would warp and buckle under the high intensity open arc lights used in projectors, and distributors recognised that because of the rapid wear, the adoption of safety film would require a fourfold increase in the number of release prints. The National Fire Protection Association launched a major campaign for safety film in 1918–19 and again in 1923 with support from the International Association of Fire Engineers, but each effort was defeated by strong lobbying by film distributors and Eastman Kodak.[31]

Eastman Kodak began a rigorous fire safety

program in 1919, and in 1922 the Motion Picture Producers and Distributors of America assumed administration. Because of the risk to employees, tighter building codes and stricter handling procedures were introduced for laboratories and theatres. Fireproof projection booths, storage rooms and film vaults were equipped with sprinkler systems. Since all the prints being sent to theatres were new, the risk of fire was minimal if the reels were handled carefully. Existing or specially constructed buildings in each city were certified for storage and handling of nitrate film. MPPDA field agents reviewed the work of local film safety inspection committees. Each reel was inspected upon return from a theatre, since broken sprockets or bad splices might cause film to catch in the projector and ignite. Reels of film were stored in cans placed in fireproof containers, withdrawn only as needed for projection or inspection.[32]

Proponents of safety film continued their unsuccessful crusade. A 1923 bill to allow widespread use of 35 mm acetate film in schools and churches in New York state was vetoed by the governor following the vigorous opposition of the national projectionists' union. The professional standing of the projectionists was based on quality projection and safe handling of dangerous film. The wide availability of nonflammable film and portable projectors would endanger the dominant role of the projectionists within the industry.[33]

With air-conditioning and automatic sprinkler systems uncommon until the 1970s, film vaults were often little more than storage sheds. MGM had better storage than most and a higher proportion of MGM silent films survive than those produced by any other company. Roger Mayer, MGM's studio manager in the 1960s, recalled:

> None of the vaults had sprinklers. They were concrete bunk houses on what we called Lot 3, and there was a little fan in the roof. No air conditioning, no sprinklers. And that was considered good storage because [the films] couldn't be stolen.[34]

Several big fires in the early twenties destroyed many of the early Universal releases. A huge fire burned fifteen acres of the forty-acre Warner Bros. Burbank studio backlot on 4 December 1934. The *Los Angeles Times* reported that 'six film vaults also went up in flames, destroying hundreds of stock shots of foreign scenes and many valuable and irreplaceable films of the Vitagraph era'.[35]

Most of the Fox Film Corp. library was destroyed in a disastrous fire in Little Ferry, New Jersey on 9 July 1937, during a period of 100-degree temperatures. The storage facility was only two years old, and although built in a residential neighbourhood, the vaults were not equipped with automatic sprinklers. The building's 42 vaults held 40,000 reels of Fox and Educational prints and negatives produced from 1914 to 1932. Gases from decomposition built up due to faulty ventilation, and spontaneously ignited. The fire in the first vault led to the successive explosion of the others. One explosion emitted a sheet of flame from a vent that killed a 13-year-old boy running from a nearby house. Every reel of film in the building was destroyed, and the 57 truckloads of scrap removed from the site returned $2,000 in silver salvage. Besides destroying the best and often only material on every pre-1932 Fox picture, the toll included the original negative to D.W. Griffith's *Way Down East* (1920), which Fox had purchased for a remake.[36]

In the late summer of 1938, a fire destroyed the foreign negative to Charlie Chaplin's *The Kid* (1920). In 1939, Harold Lloyd bought the negatives of the short films he made at the beginning of his career. On 5 August 1943, one of the film storage vaults on his estate exploded, and Lloyd lost a third of his original negatives and prints. Rushing to investigate, Lloyd collapsed in the doorway of the vault, and seven firemen and a Lloyd employee were taken to a local hospital after breathing noxious fumes. [37]

In 1965 television producer Rudy Behlmer was walking with his editor from Lot 2 to Lot 1 at MGM's Culver City studio when he 'heard this loud noise – we later discovered it was one of the vaults blowing up'. Roger Mayer recollected:

> Someone was killed in that explosion. Somebody was working on the film at the time and as far as anybody could tell, it was an electrical short of some sort igniting the film.

The explosion in vault 7 destroyed the entire contents, including the original negatives to *A Blind Bargain* (1922) with Lon Chaney and *The Divine Woman* (1928) with Greta Garbo. Mayer noted that the MGM vaults were spread out so that a fire would not reach nearby vaults, and 'a sprinkler system would not have made that much difference because the amount we lost by fire was minimal'.[38]

Fate unknown

The known factors – intentional destruction, decomposition, fire – do not account for the loss of such a large proportion of the films produced during the silent era. Many mysteries remain. For example, there is uncertainty about when the Warner Bros. and First National silent features were destroyed, but there is no doubt about their fate.[39]

In 1952, Warner–Pathe short-subject producer Robert Youngson began producing a series of one-reel condensations of Warner Bros. silent films. Youngson 'was given the run of the vaults', recalled his friend William K. Everson, 'except there wasn't that much inside'. Youngson was limited in the films he could abridge because Warners had 'very very little left', according to Everson. 'I remember I saw a list of it and there were only about 30 silent titles.'[40]

Youngson condensed Warner's surviving big-budget silent features *Don Juan* (1926), *Old San Francisco* (1927) and *Noah's Ark* (1929) into ten-minute short subjects. With so many films no longer in existence, Youngson turned to the Rin-Tin-Tin vehicle *Tracked by the Police* (1927), and even moved on to sound films, replacing the dialogue in *Isle of Lost Ships* (1929) with his trademark peppy narration. [41]

Table 1 shows that in 1958, after a thorough search, Warners could only locate 35 mm material on 57 of 477 pre-1929 features that the company owned. It is not clear if the destruction was intentional, but it was certainly comprehensive, as most of Warners' 1928–30 early sound pictures were completely missing also.[42]

Table 1: *Feature films produced by Warner Bros. and predecessor companies known to be surviving in 1958*

Year	Surviving	Lost
1918	1	0
1919	1	2
1920	2	17
1921	6	46
1922	2	29
1923	2	30
1924	4	41
1925	11	65
1926	7	58
1927	10	7
1928	11	56

No sense of history

In retrospect, it seems remarkable that the executives of the companies that produced and still owned silent films did not invest in their survival. Many of the industry leaders during the silent era remained in charge of their companies well into the 1950s, with Harry Warner and Jack L. Warner at Warner Bros., Jack Cohn and Harry Cohn at Columbia, Adolph Zukor and Barney Balaban at Paramount and Nicholas Schenck at Loew's.

Owners showed minimal concern for the survival of older films. This active disinterest was reflected in 1928 in the authorised biography of Paramount Pictures Chairman Adolph Zukor:

> 'My single chance for immortality', said Sarah Bernhardt when she consented to act for the film. Alas, all that remains to America of *Queen Elizabeth* [1912] is one disintegrating print in the storehouse of the Paramount laboratories. Frank Meyer, now laboratory superintendent, ran it off for [biographer Will Irwin] in 1927 – not for years before that had anyone unwound it from its metal reel. Many of the other early Zukor–Lasky successes have rotted or disappeared.[43]

By-and-large, these men focused on the future. The loss of so much of the silent cinema was not all that significant to their producers, as the film industry has almost always held an unsentimental view of its history. The industry's focus is short term, with new pictures always better than the old ones. Since films had a limited commercial life, and were rapidly written down as corporate assets, any expense toward better storage or preservation would reduce current profits with no future return. One industry insider noted that the studios 'were in the razor business, and the films were the blades'.[44]

The Museum of Modern Art's Iris Barry recognised on her initial film-gathering trip to Hollywood that 'no one cared a button about "old" films, not even his own last-but-one, but was solely concerned with his new film'. These very successful businessmen did not look to the past or base their business decisions on sentiment if they gave the silent films any thought at all. While the silent films might have been 'their films', it was also 'their money'. They did not want to watch the films, let alone preserve them. In an industry built on youth, these executives may have resented the films that reminded them and others how long they had been around.[45]

In 1947 and 1948, the Academy of Motion Picture Arts and Sciences held twentieth anniversary screenings of films from the initial Academy Awards ceremonies, given to the best films produced by the industry. With the co-operation of every company, the Academy could locate prints for only ten of fifteen titles from the first year's awards. This series offered probably the last public screenings of Lewis Milestone's comedy *Two Arabian Nights* (UA, 1927) and two dramas starring Emil Jannings, Victor Fleming's *The Way of All Flesh* (Paramount, 1927) and Ernst Lubitsch's *The Patriot* (Paramount, 1928). When the Museum of Modern Art inquired about *The Patriot* in 1955, that print had decomposed.[46]

Why was this allowed to occur?

Industry organisations might have accomplished what individual companies would not. The Academy of Motion Picture Arts and Sciences, for example, might have ensured that each company safeguarded a few films each year. However, motion picture industry charity has always supported health care, not the arts, and nostalgia for old films would have been contrary to the focus on new pictures. During the slump in business that began in the late 1940s, and accelerated with the widespread advent of television, the industry advertised that 'Movies Are Better Than Ever'. If an old film was any good, it would be remade. When James Card requested *Down to the Sea in Ships* (Hodkinson, 1922) for the film collection at George Eastman House, Twentieth Century-Fox sent the 1949 remake with Richard Widmark. When Card called to explain the mix-up, the studio suggested that if he wanted a silent film, he should have the projectionist turn down the sound.[47]

Studio politics probably played a role. There had been many fires, so no one expected all old films to be available. There were few requests for studio screenings of ancient titles, so their loss was not noticeable. Film storage was a cost centre, not a profit centre, and the dramatic benefit of cool and dry storage to the long-term stability of nitrate film was not widely recognised. After all, who in the company would want to admit that it was their fault that the old films were rotting? In 1959, during a research visit to the Paramount lot in Hollywood, William K. Everson found that many Paramount silent films he hoped to see were 'not available'. Yet in 1967, Hazel Marshall, Paramount's film librarian since 1924, seemed sincere when she told historian Robert S. Birchard: 'We have everything we ever made.'[48]

Any preservation effort in the thirties or forties would have copied films to nitrate stock, merely prolonging their existence, not ensuring their survival. More stable triacetate film was introduced in 1952, when the industry was in a slump and profits were down. Companies that are focused on adapting to a rapidly changing market seldom look to the past. Three-dimensional effects and CinemaScope promised to make all previous sound films obsolete. Silent films had become obsolete 25 years earlier.[49]

If there was no significant market for silent films, that was a self-fulfilling prophesy. Properly handled, a small market might have developed. None of the companies tried, and admittedly, even if they had, such a sideline could never have been very profitable. It would have been inexpensive and straightforward to make either a 16 mm negative or a single 35 mm safety print for each film, especially as most companies had some in-house film laboratory facilities. The cost could even have been buried in the budgets of pictures in production. After all, since the old films were gradually disappearing, *not* copying the pictures was an irreversible decision. But without an emotional, historical or business justification, the owners let decomposition take its course.

Producer-stars did take some active measures. Mary Pickford, Gloria Swanson, William S. Hart,

Fig. 3. *The Legion of the Condemned* (Paramount, 1927). William Wellman's air epic, starring Fay Wray and Gary Cooper, was scrapped by Paramount. [Courtesy of Frank T. Thompson.]

Harold Lloyd and Douglas Fairbanks donated prints and negatives to the Museum of Modern Art and George Eastman House and Pickford was one of the few to provide any financial support. Archives offered to save the important films for posterity, at no cost to the industry. As the Museum of Modern Art's Richard Griffith noted in 1955, 'Hollywood feels – and with some logic, it seems to me – that the preservation work should be carried on by some publicly supported institution'. The activities of the archives may have, hypocritically, relieved the companies of any sense of obligation. Eastman House's James Card noted, 'in nearly all quarters everyone felt that every film of any conceivable importance was preserved at the Museum of Modern Art'.[50]

Stock footage companies and documentary

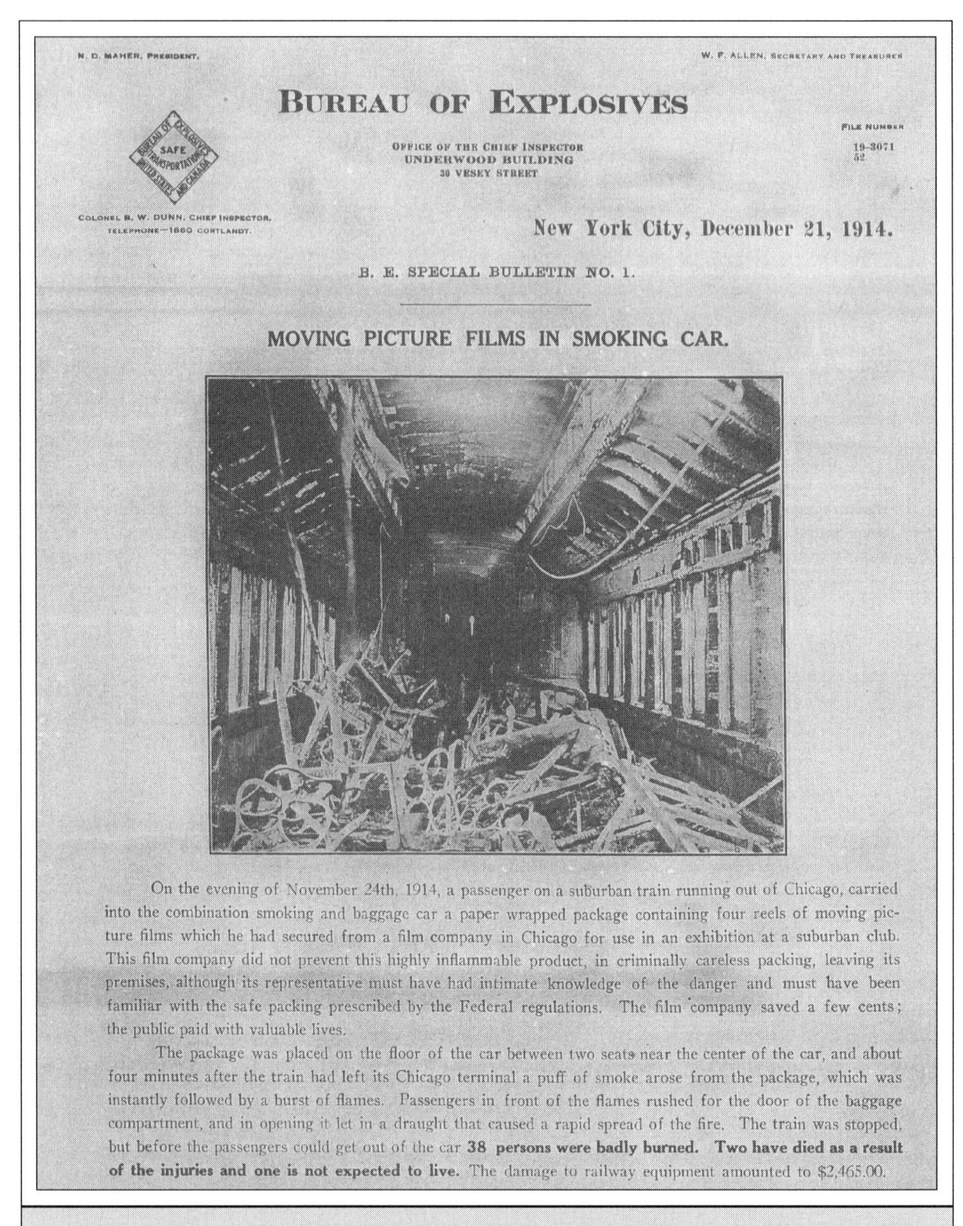

N. D. MAHER, PRESIDENT.

W. F. ALLEN, SECRETARY AND TREASURER

BUREAU OF EXPLOSIVES

OFFICE OF THE CHIEF INSPECTOR
UNDERWOOD BUILDING
30 VESEY STREET

FILE NUMBER
19-3071
52

COLONEL B. W. DUNN, CHIEF INSPECTOR,
TELEPHONE—1860 CORTLANDT.

New York City, December 21, 1914.

B. E. SPECIAL BULLETIN NO. 1.

MOVING PICTURE FILMS IN SMOKING CAR.

On the evening of November 24th, 1914, a passenger on a suburban train running out of Chicago, carried into the combination smoking and baggage car a paper wrapped package containing four reels of moving picture films which he had secured from a film company in Chicago for use in an exhibition at a suburban club. This film company did not prevent this highly inflammable product, in criminally careless packing, leaving its premises, although its representative must have had intimate knowledge of the danger and must have been familiar with the safe packing prescribed by the Federal regulations. The film company saved a few cents; the public paid with valuable lives.

The package was placed on the floor of the car between two seats near the center of the car, and about four minutes after the train had left its Chicago terminal a puff of smoke arose from the package, which was instantly followed by a burst of flames. Passengers in front of the flames rushed for the door of the baggage compartment, and in opening it let in a draught that caused a rapid spread of the fire. The train was stopped, but before the passengers could get out of the car **38 persons were badly burned. Two have died as a result of the injuries and one is not expected to live.** The damage to railway equipment amounted to $2,465.00.

Fig. 4. Bureau of Explosives, *Special Bulletin* No. 1, 21 December 1914. [Richard Koszarski Collection.]

producers saved films, but like their studio counterparts, they were running a business. In many cases original prints or negatives were chopped up for clips and condensations. Preservation was often only a byproduct of delivering a product to a client for a compilation film, documentary or commercial. Nitrate films were a depletable resource, much like an oil well, to be used until they ran out.[51]

Only when silent films were viewed independently of their immediate commercial value would they be saved. The publicly funded archives preserved films because their mission ignored commerce and focused on art and sociological importance. MGM saved many of their silent films due to a value-neutral policy of preserving corporate assets.[52]

In the final analysis, silent films were produced to make a profit, and many of them satisfied that short-term expectation. The economic considerations that caused these films to be made in the first place also led to their demise. Unless they provided ongoing revenue, silent films did not justify their continued existence. Without the timely appearance of the archives to save many films until public interest reemerged and the comprehensive preservation policy in place at MGM, the disappearance of our silent film heritage would likely have been close to complete.

Acknowledgments

This article is dedicated to my wife Shari, who as always has been wonderful and supportive. I extend my appreciation to Bob Birchard, James Bouras, Kevin Brownlow, Philip Carli, Scott Eyman, Scott MacQueen and David Shepard for reviewing drafts of this article, providing insights and making valuable comments. All errors of fact or interpretation remain mine.

For research assistance, I extend my thanks to the research facilities at my home-away-from-home – the Library of Congress. Especially helpful were the staff of the Copyright Office, the Manuscript Division (where Anthony Slide's inventory of the Thomas H. Ince papers was invaluable) and David Parker, Madeline Matz and Rosemary Hanes of the Division of Motion Pictures, Broadcasting and Recorded Sound. Richard Koszarski was very forthcoming with his encyclopedic knowledge of Universal films. Ed Stratman, Philip Carli and Kay MacRae of the George Eastman House were of great assistance. At the University of Southern California Cinema–Television Library Ned Comstock went beyond the call of duty, and Leith Adams at Warner Bros. was extremely helpful with press material on the 1934 Warner Bros. fire.

Finally, I have to thank those who came before me and saved silent films: James Card, Paul Killiam and David Shepard. ♦

Notes

1. The American Film Institute estimated in the early 1970s that only 50 per cent of nitrate-era (pre-1951) films, survive, and less than 25 per cent of silent-era films. The earliest appearance of a version of the AFI numbers is *The American Film Institute Report 1967/1971*, 8, 11. Their veracity is discussed in Anthony Slide, *Nitrate Won't Wait*, (Jefferson, NC: McFarland, 1992): 5. A closer examination of American silent feature films in US and foreign archives appears in *Film Preservation 1993: A Study of the Current State of American Film Preservation*, vol. 1: Report, June 1993; Report of the Librarian of Congress, 3–4. This report claims that the survival rate ranges from 7 to 12 per cent of each year's releases for features of the 1910s, and from 15 to 25 per cent during the 1920s. These numbers would be somewhat higher if studio collections (primarily the silent features preserved by MGM) and private collections were included.

2. 150 prints: Richard W. Saunders, comptroller of Famous Players-Lasky, quoted in Frederick James Smith, 'What Happens to Your Movie Money', *Photoplay* (March 1927): 45. See also: Paul V. Shields, 'The Movie Industry Applies Chain Store Methods', *Forbes* (15 July 1925): 527, which states 'as a general rule, about sixty prints of [each] film are made for foreign use and 100 for domestic use'. According to a 1921 newspaper article, 'the producer makes a limited number of prints for distribution. As a rule, this number is 65; it may be less, it is rarely more'. See: 'When a Film Grows Old', *The New York Times* (28 August 1921).

   In the 1920s, distributors charged the cost of prints to independent producers. In those cases where the distributor was making prints at his own laboratory, a producer could find a significant portion of his potential profits spent on unneeded prints. To protect against this, distribution agreements often had a limit on the number of copies that could be manufactured. Inspiration Pictures' 19 December 1921 distribution agreement with First National allowed up to 100 prints. Three years later, Inspiration agreed to pay for up to 125 prints for domestic distribution. First National was required to have insurance on the negative until 60 prints were manufactured. Inspiration Pictures file, Warner Bros. Collection, University of Southern California Cinema–Television Library.

3. 'Film Exchange Fire Prevention Results', *National Fire Protection Association Quarterly*, (January 1926): 224–229. Henry Anderson, 'Fire Safety in the Motion Picture Industry', *National Fire Protection Association Quarterly* (July 1936): 21. *Show People* and *Our Dancing Daughters*: *The Motion Picture Almanac 1929* (Chicago: Quigley Publishing Company, 1929), 204, 206. Both reports were from the Screenland Theatre, Nevada, Ohio, 'small town patronage'.

4. William R. Donaldson, 'Valuing the Inventories of

Motion-Picture Producers, *The Journal of Accountancy* (March 1927): 171–179. All amounts throughout the article are in US dollars.

5. Albert F. Sulzer, 'The Epoch of Progress in Film Fire Prevention', *Journal of the Society of Motion Picture Engineers* (April 1940): 403. *Suds:* Letter, United Artists Corporation to Mary Pickford Company (11 September 1925), United Artists Collection, State Historical Society of Wisconsin. See also: M. Deschiens, 'Recovery of Constituents of Old Motion Picture Films', *Chemical Age* (May 1921): 93–194.

6. *The Unknown*: Assignment of Copyright, Paramount Famous Lasky Corp. to Universal Pictures Corp. (30 September 1927). Copyright Office Assignment Records, vol. 189, 80–86. Fortunately, that library print of *The Unknown* stayed with Paramount and was among the relatively few Paramount films that survived to be acquired by the American Film Institute. *Little Annie Rooney:* Assignment of Copyright, Mary Pickford Company to Edward Small Productions, Inc. (19 June 1941). Copyright Office Assignment Records, vol. 464, 180–181.

7. The story rights to *Bardelys the Magnificent* were to expire in 1939. MGM memorandum, D.O. Decker to Paul Cohen (9 December 1931), reproduced in Philip J. Riley, *A Blind Bargain* (Atlantic City: Magic Image Filmbooks, 1988), 19.

8. Letter, George D. Swartz of George D. Swartz Pictures, Inc. to Mr. Ingle Carpenter (20 August 1928). Ince Collection, Manuscript Division, Library of Congress.

9. Bill of Sale, Thos. H. Ince Corporation to Warner Bros. Pictures, Inc. (30 January 1930). Ince Collection, Manuscript Division, Library of Congress. The films were *String Beans, The Hired Man* (both 1918), *Greased Lightning, Egg Crate Wallop, Red Hot Dollars, Hay Foot, Straw Foot, Crooked Straight* (all 1919), and *Paris Green* (1920). All of the films starred Charles Ray and were written by Julien Josephson. *Tol'able David*: Agreement, Joseph Hergesheimer and Inspiration Pictures, Inc., in Liquidation to Columbia Pictures Corporation, 16 June 1930. Copyright Office Assignment Records, vol. 250, 42–49. *23½ Hours Leave* and *Civilization*: David Shepard, 'Thomas Ince', in *The American Film Heritage*, (Washington, DC: Acropolis Books Ltd., 1972), 44.

10. Agreement, Albert D. Levin and Triangle Liquidation Corporation to Warner Bros. Pictures, Inc. (5 October 1937). Copyright Office Assignment Records, vol. 392, 92–129.

11. Films sold for $875, purchased for $10,000: Letter from Ralph Lewis, Preston & Files, to R.J. Obringer, Warner Bros., (26 July 1940), Sennett file, Warner Bros. Collection, University of Southern California Cinema–Television Library. Sennett purchased for $75: Order Confirming Sale of Personal Property in the Matter of Mack Sennett, Inc., Bankrupt, No. 21878 C, District Court of the United States, Southern District of California, Central Division (31 March 1936). Copyright Office Assignment Records, vol. 1226, 61–67. Sale to Warner Bros: Ray films: Bill of Sale, Paul J. Guerin to Warner Bros. Pictures, Inc. (30 September 1940). Copyright Office Assignment Records, vol. 1226, 76–84. Attorney: Warner Bros. memo from R.J. Obringer to Morris Ebenstein, (10 July 1940), Sennett file, Warner Bros. Collection, University of Southern California Cinema–Television Library.

12. Inventory of prints and negatives: Bill of Sale, Paul J. Guerin to Warner Bros. Pictures, Inc. (30 September 1940). Copyright Office Assignment Records, vol. 1226, 76–84. The vault inventory, probably dating from the 1936 sale by the bankruptcy court, notes that for Sennett features, there were A and F (American and Foreign) negatives for *The Shreik of Araby* (1923), *Molly O'* (1921), *Suzanna* (1922), *The Crossroads of New York* (1922), and *Down on the Farm* (1920). There were only the F-negatives for *Yankee Doodle in Berlin* (1919) and *The Extra Girl* (1923). The first short released by Warners was *A Small Town Idol* (1939). The subsequent shorts using Sennett footage were two-reelers *Love's Intrigue* (1940), *Happy Faces* (1941), *Wedding Yells* (1942), *Happy Times and Jolly Moments* (1943), *Once Over Lightly* (1944) and *Good Old Corn* (1945). Two one-reelers, *Here We Go Again* and *Hit 'Im Again*, followed in 1953.

13. Storage fees at one facility were 'at the rate of Two Dollars per month or fraction thereof per five reel unit for each of the first five such units, and at the rate of One Dollar per month or any fraction thereof for each five reel unit in addition to the first five'. A seven-reel picture might include a negative and a print. Since owners were likely to have hundreds of reels, my calculation of $35 is based on the one dollar per month storage charge. Memorandum of Agreement, between Lloyds Film Storage and Mr. Ingle Carpenter, Attorney for Thos. H. Ince Corp., (5 April 1930). Thomas H. Ince Collection, Manuscript Division, Library of Congress.

14. Sol Lesser: Sol Lesser conversation with David Shepard during the restoration of Lesser's *Oliver Twist* (1922). David Shepard to author (26 August 1995). Columbia: private source.

15. A 1956 tribute at the Museum of Modern Art showed Goldwyn's *Potash and Perlmutter* (1923) and a fragment, 'all that remains', of Goldwyn's *The Eternal City* (1923). Both are now considered lost. The only other silents included in the series were

Goldwyn's *Stella Dallas* (1925) and *The Winning of Barbara Worth* (1926). Destruction of Goldwyn silents: Robert S. Birchard talked to Mrs. Goldwyn in 1970–71 at a screening of *The Winning of Barbara Worth* (1926) at a tribute to Henry King. Robert S. Birchard to author (29 August 1996).

16. Excellent physical properties: 'Safe Handling, Storage, and Destruction of Nitrate-Based Motion Picture Films', (Rochester: Eastman Kodak Company), *Kodak Publication No. H–182* (September 1995): 1.

17. Storage recommendations: see Storage Standards in the section on Safe and Economical Storage in 'Report of the Committee on the Preservation of Film', *Journal of the Society of Motion Picture Engineers*, vol. 35 (December 1940): 584–606.

18. Private source. The reels were stored in cartons which held ten cans. Storage charges were $6.00 per year per carton.

19. A.H. Nuckolls, 'Cellulose Nitrate and Acetate Film', *National Fire Protection Association Quarterly* (January 1930): 236–242. Kodak Publication No. H–182, 2.

20. Translation of letter from Karl Geyer Filmfabrik to Transocean Film Co., Berlin, (28 October 1926). Microfilm edition, *D.W. Griffith Papers 1897–1954* (Frederick, M.D: University Publications of America, 1982), reel 14, image number 1189. Griffith had the negative returned to New York and inspected by Combined Film Laboratories in New York. They reported that 'the condition of this negative is very poor as it contains water marks, stains, cement marks, fog and blank film throughout the various rolls. It appears as though the negative might have gotten wet, as the emulsion in a good many places is completely peeled off.' Letter, Combined Film Laboratories to D.W. Griffith, Inc. (10 January 1927), reel 14, image number 1972. Thanks to David Shepard for directing my attention to this.

21. Letter, W.D. Kelly, Metro-Goldwyn-Mayer Pictures to James Card, George Eastman House (5 March 1954). MGM file, George Eastman House International Museum of Photography and Film.

22. Destruction: Universal Film Exchanges Inc. memo from F.T. Murray, Mgr. Branch Operations, to Mr. I. Stolzer, Bound Brook, N.J. (27 April 1948). Photocopy of memo courtesy Richard Koszarski. Pathe Laboratory: Letter, John J. O'Connor, Universal Pictures Company, Inc. to Edward P. Curtis, Eastman Kodak Company, (20 February 1950). Universal file, George Eastman House International Museum of Photography and Film. The letter concluded: 'Our oldest films now start with the sound era, which means that the oldest negatives we now have in the vaults do not go back beyond 1929.' It seems likely that Universal simply destroyed everything that did not have a sound track. Several silents with synchronised music scores survived to be donated to the American Film Institute in the late 1960s, suggesting that Pathe's concern over safety was an excuse, as much as a reason, for destroying the films. Cellofilm Corporation: 1927 Annual Report of Universal Pictures Company, Inc. Thanks to Richard Koszarski for directing my attention to Universal's ownership of Cellofilm.

23. Pathe Films: Schedule 'A', 'Negatives at Bound Brook', and 'Positive Prints at Bound Brook', to Indenture between Pathe Exchange, Inc. and Columbia Pictures Corporation (3 July 1935). Copyright Office Assignment Records, vol. 334, 246–282. Triangle Films: Triangle Liquidation Corp., 14–116. The survivors were mostly the higher profile films, including those starring Douglas Fairbanks.

24. Warner Bros. destruction records: private source. *Johanna Enlists* and *Rosita*: Carl Louis Gregory, 'Inventory of Mary Pickford's Film Collection (14 December 1946)'. Mary Pickford folder, Acquisitions, Selection and Distribution, 1940–48, Records Relating to Motion Pictures 1934–54, The Archives of the Library of Congress, Manuscript Division, Library of Congress. Von Stroheim films for Universal: Richard Koszarski, *The Man You Love to Hate: Erich von Stroheim and Hollywood* (New York: Oxford University Press, 1983): 70, 111.

25. He Who Gets Slapped: Letter, W.D. Kelly, Metro-Goldwyn-Mayer Pictures, to James Card, George Eastman House, (30 November 1951). *The Merry Widow:* Letter, William LeVanway, Chief Film Editor, Metro-Goldwyn-Mayer Pictures, to James Card, George Eastman House, (14 November 1950). *The Torrent:* Letter, James Card, George Eastman House, to W.D. Kelly, Metro-Goldwyn-Mayer Pictures (27 July 1953). MGM file, George Eastman House International Museum of Photography and Film. Other titles: private source.

26. David Shepard: Austin Lamont, 'In Search of Lost Films', *Film Comment* (Winter 1971–72): 60. Some of the Paramount films that were 'found at the time of assembly and packing to have disintegrated' included Clarence Badger's *Man Power* (1927) with Richard Dix, Luther Reed's *New York* (1927) with Ricardo Cortez and *The Sawdust Paradise* (1928) with Esther Ralston, Frank Tuttle's *Time to Love* (1927) with Raymond Griffith and William Powell, James Cruze's *We're All Gamblers* (1927) with Thomas Meighan, and several George Melford features: *Crystal Gazer* (1917) with Fannie Ward, *Faith Healer* (1921) with Milton Sills and *Sunset Trail* (1917) with Vivian Martin. Private source.

27. Kevin Brownlow, *Behind the Mask of Innocence* (New York: Alfred A. Knopf, 1990), footnote 235 on 529. Also Kevin Brownlow to author (15 December 1995).

28. Undated Harold Lloyd film inventory, private source.

29. 'Fire Exchange Regulations', *The American Architect* (17 July 1918): 88–94. A similar fire occurred on a Boston subway car in January 1925, when a burlap bag containing scrap nitrate film was placed against an electric heater. No one was killed, but 27 passengers were taken to the hospital with burns. 'Film Fire in Boston Subway', *National Fire Protection Association Quarterly* (January 1925), 183–184. Pittsburgh: 'Film Exchange Fire Prevention Results', *National Fire Protection Association Quarterly* (January 1926): 224–229. Poor vault design was occasionally a contributing factor in these conflagrations, as the exhaust from burning film entered through an adjoining vent to another vault. See: 'Fire Prevention in Film Exchanges', *Safety Engineering* (November 1925): 263–264.

30. Edison: 'Edison Sees His Vast Plant Burn', *The New York Times* (10 December 1914): 1. A more detailed account of the origin of the blaze followed the next day: 'Mrs. Edison Saved Husband's Records', *The New York Times* (11 December 1914): 9. Also see: 'Great Edison Plant Burned: Fire Wrecks Ten Big Factory Buildings at East Orange, NJ – Origin Not in Film Factory', *The Moving Picture World* (19 December 1914): 1662. This article claims that contrary to the New York newspapers, this was not a film fire, but started in the varnishing department of the phonograph building, and that all motion picture negatives were removed before the fire reached the film building.

    Lubin: 'Big Fire at Lubin Plant: Explosion Wrecks Film Storage Vault Causing Damage of Between $500,000 and $1,000,000 – No Interruption in Business', *The Moving Picture World* (27 June 1914): 1803. Lubin's general manager, Ira Lowry, said, 'some of the films which were destroyed had never been put on the market; others cannot be reproduced or duplicated. Our loss on films will be at least $500,000, and on the vault building about $5,000 more'. *The Sea Wolf:* Robert S. Birchard, 'Jack London and the Movies', *Film History*, vol. 1, 32. Famous Players: *The Foundling* was quickly remade with a different director and supporting cast. Peter Bogdanovich, *Allan Dwan: The Last Pioneer*, (New York: Praeger Publishers, 1971): 178.

31. More expensive: In 1921, acetate-positive stock cost 3 cents per foot, while the equivalent nitrate-positive stock was 2.25 cents per foot, so users of acetate stock paid a cost premium of 33 per cent. 'Report of the Committee on Films and Emulsions', *Transactions of Society of Motion Picture Engineers* (May 1922): 166. 'Film Exchange Fire Prevention Results', 224–229. Fire Engineers: 'The Inflammable Picture Film', *National Fire Protection Association Quarterly* (October 1922): 109–110.

32. Nuckolls, 236–242. Sulzer, 405–408.

33. Discussion of W.W. Kincaid, 'Requirements of the Educational and Non-Theatrical Entertainment Field', in *Transactions of Society of Motion Picture Engineers* (May 1924): 111–118.

34. Roger Mayer to author (29 May 1996).

35. Universal: 9 February 1989 letter from Richard Koszarski to author. Warner fire: 'Films Go On Despite Fire', *Los Angeles Times* (6 December 1934): 1. The fire apparently started in a machine shop. An article in the Glendale paper states that the Vitagraph films destroyed were prints. 'Films Valued as Historical Lost: Early Pictures Destroyed When Flames Rage in Library at Studio', *Glendale News-Press* (5 December 1934): 6. The press accounts are uniform in stating that the destruction of sets and support buildings would not disrupt production and the loss was fully covered by insurance. In contrast, photographs of the scene show total devastation. The December 1934 edition of the *Warner Club News* observed 'the boys from the publicity department staying on the job till 2:30 a.m. handling the newspapermen and the cameramen'. It is possible that the studio misrepresented which films were destroyed to indicate that nothing important was lost. Nonetheless, the fire would not have destroyed the Warner Bros. and First National negatives as they were stored on the east coast. Also see: Jack L. Warner, *My First Hundred Years in Hollywood* (New York: Random House, 1965): 240. Thanks to Leith Adams, Warner Bros. Archivist, for providing information on this fire.

36. 'Fox Film Storage Fire,' *National Fire Protection Association Quarterly* (October 1937): 136–142.

37. *The Kid:* David Robinson, *Chaplin: His Life and Art*, (New York: McGraw Hill, 1985), 225. Harold Lloyd: 'Harold Lloyd Saved From Fire by Wife', *The New York Times* (6 August 1943): 17. See also Adam Reilly, *Harold Lloyd: The King of Daredevil Comedy*, (New York: Macmillan, 1977), 7.

38. MGM eyewitness: Rudy Behlmer to author (30 August 1996). Specific films lost: Philip J. Riley, *London After Midnight* (1985). (New York: Cornwall Books), 18. Cause of explosion: Roger Mayer to author (29 May 1996).

39. There are persistent rumours that Warners junked their silent material during World War II, but I was

unable to verify that story. On 4 March 1996, I interviewed Rudi Fehr, who began at the studio in the mid-1930s as an editor, and became the head of Warners' film editorial department. He had no knowledge of the fate of the company's silent films. My own check of the index to the Warner Bros. Collection at the USC Cinema–Television Library and Princeton University, and a subsequent review by USC archivist Ned Comstock found no files of interest.

The Jack L. Warner Collection at the USC Cinema–Television Library holds the surviving telegrams sent between the Burbank and New York offices. I reviewed the telegrams from 1941 through 1946, and there was no indication of destruction of any old material other than trailers. During 1944 and 1946, Jack L. Warner told the east coast lab in Brooklyn to send prints of *My Four Years in Germany* (1918) and *The Divine Lady* (1929) to the west coast. A 1944 telegram requesting a print of *Top Speed* (a 1930 sound picture) read: 'If you have negative yet on *Top Speed* have lab make up black and white print whenever they not busy out of positive short ends if you have enough and send same to me via straight express. Advise.' In 1958, Warners could only locate material on 49 of 76 films from 1930, so the existence of *Top Speed* could not be assumed.

In 1950, James Card at the George Eastman House ordered a print of *The Sea Beast* (1926) with John Barrymore, and it was made from the shrunken, but complete, original negative. Warner Bros. file, George Eastman House International Museum of Photography and Film. In 1952 Jack L. Warner ordered a print of *Noah's Ark* (1929) to review for possible reissue, and the original negative, while deteriorating, was still in existence. Scott MacQueen, 'Noah's Ark: Making and Restoring an Early Vitaphone Spectacle', *The Perfect Vision*, vol. 3, no. 12 (Winter 1991–92): 35–45.

These actions indicate that Warner Bros. held onto its films, and could order copies on demand, while the fact that so few films survive (see footnote 42 below) suggests that at some point there was a complete housecleaning of Warners' early films. The fate of the Warner Bros. silent and early sound material is an area for further research.

40. William K. Everson to author (16 November 1984).

41. Don Juan (1926) became *Some of the Greatest* (1955), while *Old San Francisco* (1927) emerged as *Thrills From the Past* (1953). Other Youngson shorts include *An Adventure to Remember* (1955), adapted from *Isle of Lost Ships* (1929); *A Bit of the Best* (1955), from *Tracked by the Police* (1927); and *Magic Movie Moments* (1953) from *Noah's Ark* (1929).

42. A few additional titles were later discovered in Burbank in Jack L. Warner's personal vault, along with a separate cache of silent feature and short comedies. Negatives to about 50 silent features which Warners' predecessor First National had distributed, but did not own, were deposited with George Eastman House in 1958.

Survival of Warner Films: Copyright Assignment from Warner Bros. Pictures, Inc. to PRM Inc., 23 July 1958, supplementing the original agreement dated 26 July 1956. Copyright Office Assignment Records, vol. 1015, 168–187. This document consists of two schedules, each listing four groups of titles marked with identification numbers preceded by A, B, C or D. I matched the titles listed in each group with the films (both original negatives and projection prints) subsequently shipped by United Artists Television, Inc. (successor to PRM) to the Library of Congress in 1970.

The 'A' list prove to be silent titles that do not survive. 'B' are early sound titles that do not survive. 'C' are silent titles with film material, and 'D' are early sound films surviving, but lacking a soundtrack. The second 'A' schedule includes four titles (including the 1924 Johnny Hines comedy *Conductor 1492*) footnoted as 'Film Property'. I have corrected the numbers in the table for these, and also deleted a few Chaplin films originally released by First National that were mistakenly included in the original assignment. The survival numbers are even more distressing when examined in detail, as 1925s eleven surviving titles include seven Lariat program Westerns released by Vitagraph. The films on these lists were originally released by First National, Associated Producers, Associated First National, Vitagraph and Warner Bros. There was one surviving title from Kalem, *From the Manger to the Cross* (1912), which I did not include on the chart.

While a 13 per cent survival rate might be understandable for such a large nitrate library in 1970, almost every title that was inventoried in 1958 was still in existence in 1970. It appears that the pictures were the victim of intentional destruction, or given the loss of so many of Warners' early sound films, there may have been some disastrous, but undocumented, fires.

43. Will Irwin, *The House That Shadows Built*, (New York: Doubleday, Doran & Company, 1928): 224–225.

44. Razor business: Roddy McDowell to author (28 August 1995).

45. Iris Barry, 'The Film Library and How It Grew', *Film Quarterly* (Summer 1969): 22.

46. Academy screenings: Held in the fall of 1947, the complete series consisted of *Wings, Seventh Heaven, Laugh Clown Laugh, The Fair Coed, Two Arabian Nights, Street Angel, Underworld, The Jazz Singer, The Way of All Flesh* and *Telling the World*. The films that were listed as unavailable were *The Last Command, Sunrise, The Dove, Tempest* and *The Circus*. Of these five films, all survive in 35 mm. *The Patriot* was an Oscar winner at the second ceremonies, and was shown in the continuation of the series in January 1948. 'Calendar of Screenings, Academy of Motion Picture Arts and Sciences, 1947–48', author's collection. Museum of Modern Art inquiry: Richard W. Nason, 'Emergency Operation: Campaign to Save Desiccating Movie Classics Begun by Film Library', *The New York Times* (9 October 1955).

47. James Card to author (7 November 1987).

48. Everson was researching films for potential use in *The Love Goddesses*, which was not released until 1965. William K. Everson to author (16 November 1984). Hazel Marshall: Robert S. Birchard to author (29 August 1996).

49. 'Changes in TV (Colour) and Films (Size) Up Film Interest in Video Rentals', *Variety* (21 October 1954).

50. Richard Griffith: Nason, op cit. James Card: Herbert Reynolds, '"What Can You Do for Us, Barney?" Four Decades of Film Collecting: An Interview with James Card', *Image*, vol. 20, no. 2, (June 1977): 19.

51. As one example, silent film distributor Paul Killiam purchased Rupert Julian's *The Yankee Clipper* (1927), a Cecil B. DeMille production starring William Boyd. In the 1960s, Killiam edited the original negative from eight reels to five for use as a pilot for his television series *Hour of Silents*. Killiam kept the trims, and donated all of his material on the film to the American Film Institute in 1981. Paul Killiam to author.

52. MGM: Roger Mayer to author (29 May 1996).

Film History, Volume 9, pp. 23–48, 1997. Copyright © John Libbey & Company
ISSN: 0892-2160. Printed in Australia

Still in the dark – silent film audiences

Gregg Bachman

Almost from its inception as an acceptable part of the college curriculum back in the sixties, film scholarship was dominated by its literary traditions of thematic interpretation of individual films and the mounting of 'large-scale' theories of how cinema creates meaning. The conventional wisdom was to isolate the film in some sort of aesthetic vacuum and attend only vaguely to the social context while essentially ignoring the audience appeal.[1]

In the mid-seventies, there was a major shift in film scholarship. So-called 'revisionist' film historians began to turn from speculation of meaning towards how films functioned as a business.[2] As Charlotte Herzog explained: '(A)n understanding of the total process of commercial film production is incomplete without taking into account the fact that films are made in order to be ... exhibited.'[3]

Unfortunately, this preoccupation with economics over the past twenty or so years has created a curious result. As Richard Koszarski observed in 1990, '... we (now) have better information on the location of the theatres ... (and the) makeup of the theatre programs than on the audiences who patronised them'.[4]

Bruce Austin noted the published regret at not having recorded the name of the first kinetoscope patron, let alone his reaction, on 6 April 1894. He writes:

> (This) ought to have served as an impetus for related research ... (but) such was not to be the case ... we have a sharp picture of the industrial and technological development and growth of the medium while, comparatively, the development and growth of the medium's audience is, at best, fuzzy ...[5]

There certainly were attempts at bringing this fuzzy picture of silent movie audiences into better focus. Most recently, Miriam Hansen in her *Babel and Babylon: Spectatorship in American Silent Film,* suggests that to '... focus on the cinema's function for a particular social group at a particular social juncture must remain *speculative* since it is difficult to know how ... any group received the films they saw and what significance movie going had in relation to their lives'. Instead, she proposes '... to reconstruct the configurations of experience that shaped their horizon of reception, and ask how the cinema as an institution, as a social and aesthetic experience, might have interacted with that horizon'.[6] Quoting David Bordwell, the early cinema spectators become merely *hypothetical* entities.[7]

Within the last few years I have found myself resisting this emphasis on stones over bones and reliance on speculation and hypothetical constructs. As Gordon Allport said more than fifty years ago, if you want to know something about people's activities, *the best way of finding out is to simply ask them.*[8] So four years ago I began an oral history project, interviewing people who could recall going to silent motion pictures.

Oral history, unfortunately, is treated in most academic circles as the poor relation, the unwanted guest at the dinner party, the non-traditional 'specter that haunts the halls of the academy'.[9] It is almost as if it has become an academic tradition in itself to marginalise oral history, keeping it out of journals, not even mentioning it in research method texts.[10]

Gregg Bachman teaches at the University of Tampa, Florida, and is currently editing a book on marginalised figures in silent film history. Correspondence c/o PO Box 931, Crystal Beach, Florida 34681, USA.

So why is oral history made to appear more venal than venerated? Perhaps a key lies in the direction of the on-going methodological battle between quantifiable and qualitative research.

Barbara Mostyn sums up the differences between the two succinctly: '(Q)uantitative (methodology) seeks to answer the questions what, where, when and how many ... qualitative ... seeks ... why.'[11] Quantitative has become the default methodology, the 'traditional' paradigm, concerned with what is 'objective' and what is 'measurable', testing pre-conceived hypotheses through a limited number of controlled variables. Qualitative methodology, such as oral history, is inductive, it '... uses a multiplicity of variables and their relationships are considered not in isolation but as being interconnected in the life context'.[12]

Workers trained in quantitative methods view the manufacturing of evidence as the worst offense, yet, in a sense, as Valerie Yow points out, '... this is what (qualitative) oral history does, it's a research method based on direct intervention ... (which is the) major sin in the realm of traditional methodology'.[13] Thus, although audiences were acknowledged as an integral part of social and economic theories in mass-communication as early as the 1960s, the collection of introspective data supplied by audience members was never considered applicable to *serious* historical study.[14]

The traditional methodologies have maintained a dominant position in the discipline of history in particular,[15] where written documents have achieved a sort of 'holiness' as Alessandro Portelli wryly notes.[16] Paul Thompson in *Voices of the Past* explains that documents achieved the status of 'reality' during the nineteenth century as the new discipline of the professional historian came into being.[17] An accepted hierarchy of sources emerged, with legal depositions, parliamentary records and letters occupying the heights and oral reports located near or at the bottom.[18] 'We have a sense if something is written down it is immutable, can withstand the onslaught of time ... (that) it is fixed, (forever) frozen ...'[19]

Conventional film history was not immune to these prejudices. 'Film historians' concepts of the nature and function of film determine(d) ... the kinds of materials they chose for analysis, the kinds of events they (saw) as significant ...'[20] Thus, as mentioned above, the revisionist film historians of the 1970s turned '... to the vast archives of primary material generated by the film (industry) ... (and) focused on film as a business, or a function of economic principles'.[21] These business histories struggled to fill a void[22] but were constrained by their reliance on the document-based, traditional methodology. And even though there was an acknowledged void in audience studies,[23] turning to the people themselves would be considered 'unscientific' or subjectively biased,[24] with film scholars preferring to rely on Bordwell's 'hypothetical audience'.[25] This 'preference' is often dictated by prevailing currents, with articles based on methods other than the traditional paradigms often suffering the penalty of publication rejection, which would put the opportunity for tenure and advancement in jeopardy.[26]

By focusing on what traditional methodologies would deem acceptable, then, we miss the opportunity to address the fundamental question that Garth Jowett presciently asked back in 1974: '... who was this (first) audience ... and *why* were they attracted to this new entertainment ...?' He continued:

> (I)t is becoming ... obvious (the movies) answered a deep social and cultural need of the American people ... the work in this area has just begun, and only by continuing such research can we hope to recontruct the dimensions of the social impact of the motion picture in American society in the last seventy years.[27]

The irony is that when Jowett first posed this question in 1974, those who most readily had the answer, the actual people who attended the first motion pictures, were still available. Tragically, this is no longer the case. With the possible exception of some *Guinness Book of World Records* centenarians, those who could recall for us the mid-1890s are all long gone.

I would like to suggest here that perhaps there is something also a bit more cynical, but no less revealing, than the old quantitative versus qualitative battle in the resistance to oral history in the academy. Paul Thompson put it best:

> ... the problem of the oral historian and the academy is that we must sit at the feet of the

Fig. 1. The first audiences encountered their films within a wide variety of social settings. The Gem Theatre at Portland, Maine, served the resort community of Peak's Island. [Richard Koszarski Collection.]

> common person, admit they have something to teach us ... (and) perhaps (that) they 'know more about something'.[28]

Few of us are willing to dispute the charge of elitism levelled against the academy which has often been accused of keeping the non-academic at bay through the haze of dense language, through the intimidation of imposing texts. Portelli nails it on the head: '(The) intellectual community is (simply) always suspicious of "news from outside" ...'[29]

Oral history is also considered dangerous in some quarters, assailing cherished, closely held beliefs, and has 'often ... been associated with political activists, uncovering suppressed memories ... and disarrang(ing) many accepted truths ...'[30] It is typically done with older or powerless people who historically lack access to publication.[31] Communication is power and oral methodologies to a certain extent open the portals of power to the marginalised, to those who traditionally do not have voices.

Whatever the motivations for resistance, I personally think there is something intrinsically 'common-sensible' about oral history. I have conducted 65 interviews with silent movie spectators to date that have enriched both my teaching and writing (see Appendix for complete listing of narrators). Others (lead primarily by feminist scholars) have turned to oral history as a method integral to their work, and they are finding themselves gradually being accepted into, at least, the 'margins of the mainstream'.

Perhaps this grudging acceptance has been predicated on the richness of information revealed through oral histories, information, as Duchet writes, that '... highlights the complexity, the ambiguities and even the contradictions of the relations between the subject and the world ... (while) providing access to a body of information that is more detailed, more discerning, but also far more complex to analyze than that collected through other approaches ...'[32]

More than likely, however, oral history's reputation has grown with the well-documented reversal of fortune of the whole concept of 'objectivity' upon which quantitative methods as well as the paper-based historical documentary school rests.

Most of us know the arguments. The idea of an individual being a *Tabula Rasa* has been seriously called into question in many quarters, undermining the more traditional models of research methodology. Once a question is posed, or a hypothesis formulated, argues Myra Jehlern, '... one already circumscribes an answer ... (making) analytical neutrality ... a phantom'.[33] Your very expectations are coloured by your beliefs, subtlety influencing the design of your experiment and the questions you've selected for your survey. Simply '... applying mathematics to ... data does not ensure rigor', argues Barbara Mostyn: '... [Q]uantitative procedures such as counting do not guarantee objectivity ... since the determination of all categories (in quantitative procedures) involves qualitative judgments in their first instance ...'[34]

With this in mind, serious questions must be raised about the previously sanctified written record in traditional historical research. What we once saw as incontrovertible fact now becames what was important to that particular record keeper at that particular time.[35] As Paul Thompson indicates, now '(e)ven the most basic social statistic must be called into account'.[36] He serves up a veritable cornucopia of possibly corrupt data: there's census information (who fills it out and what may they be trying to hide?); marriage records (are the ages of the individuals true, or could the dates be fudged to cover a pregnancy?); food consumption statistics (there's a need to market a new kind of fish so data are skewed) or how many rooms a dwelling has (what you count as a 'room' is open to question, depending how you want to argue the case of overcrowding). Thompson also illustrates his point by discussing one revealing question of whether one has a 'skilled' job; the census data (of course filled out by the workers) show skilled jobs were rising at the exact same time that employers' surveys showed them falling off.[37] Will future historians be making assumptions about us based on our income tax forms, I wonder?

Data concerning movie-audience-related issues must inevitably fall hard under this line of questioning. Here we are confronted with, in the words of Bruce Austin, '... a veritable forest of verbiage, little of which seems to be theoretically and methodologically systematic, coherent, or valid'.[38] Jarvie suggests the reason so little work was done on the film audience was that the movie business was such a seller's market that there was little incentive to explore that market.[39] Austin agrees, but pushes further. 'Hollywood ha(d) almost a phobic reaction to the study of audiences ...', he explains, '... since it (didn't) sell advertising, it (didn't) have to account to anyone for the size of its audience ...'[40] Audience research was proprietary information and jealously guarded by the studio heads and covertly manipulated by minions trying to make a point. 'Industry leaders mistrusted and feared (outside) researchers ... some saw it ... not an instrument for their use, but a [potential indictment of] executive acumen ... [even as late as the 1980s] motion picture research [can be] best summarised [as] ... growing from humble beginnings to more grandiose beginnings ...'[41]

When social scientists started to take a hard look at silent movies they could barely hide their own biases. Young children, for instance, were hooked up to the latest scientific equipment to measure galvanic skin response. The results revealed that movies created emotional responses, and that younger children were more susceptible to scenes of danger. This lead researchers to warn of possible damaging psychological effects.[42] Just taking a look at the journals in which social scientists were publishing their movie data (*Journal of Delinquency* or *School Review*) reveals motivations. Even the Payne Studies, often pointed to as the most thorough and comprehensive available on the effects of motion pictures on youth, were initiated and shaped by a vocal opponent of the medium.[43] For example, the sampling of films that one group of researchers selected '... were films dealing chiefly with romantic love, sex and crime ...' leading them to the inevitable conclusion that '... films ... give a cock-eyed picture of the world ...'.[44] Indeed, studies which proved otherwise or were inconclusive on movies' effects, were often ignored and rarely followed up.[45]

So where does all of this lead us?

Well, for one thing, once we accept the idea that subjectivity works its way into even the most supposedly 'objective' design, we then can gain a level of comfort with more 'qualitative' work that overtly acknowledges the possibility of bias. We can also be more open to methods which allow us the opportunity to check and recheck this subjective reporting, and use these methods in orchestration with more quantitative forms.

One such avowed subjective method is oral history. We can return once again to Paul Thompson to put it best:

> ... [I]f the study of history teaches us that *all* historical sources are suffused with subjectivity right from the start, the *living* presence of those subjective voices from the past ... obliges us to test them against the opinions of those who will always ... know more than ourselves ... (w)e are dealing with living sources, unlike inscribed stones or sheaves of paper, and we can have a two-way conversation ...[46]

In an essay entitled 'History and Community', Thompson suggests that oral history then '... implies for most kinds of history a shift in focus. Thus the educational historian becomes concerned with the experiences of children and students as well as the problems of teachers. The military and naval historian can look beyond command level strategy and equipment to the conditions, recreations and morale of other ranks and lower deck ... '.[47] And the film historian can now reconsider what Robert Allen derisively called 'introspective data' which he and many others once unfortunately dismissed as invalid or 'not applicable' for historical film study.[48]

The life experience of common, every day people can now be used as history's 'raw material'.[49] With this raw material, Thompson writes, '... a new dimension is given to history ... oral historians can think of themselves as publishers: imagine what evidence is needed, seek it out and capture it'.[50] Or, perhaps, in this context, we can see ourselves as directors. Movie history traditionally has been focused upon the producers or the stars. With the oral history method we can now, for the first time, turn the camera, as it were, 180 degrees and train it on the watchers, focusing in on the viewers instead of the viewed.

For example, in 1991 Miriam Hansen asked, '... what happens to the viewer as a member of a plural, social audience?'.[51] My narrators can offer a glimpse:

> You felt part of it; you became part of the picture with what was taking place. We were part of the picture.[52]

> In our theatre it was nothing for the women to sob right out loud. And that of course would make it a particularly entertaining evening because you know how sadness and tragedy, if you can express it, you feel cleansed afterwards. You've had a very satisfying movie. The men of course, in those days, were not manly if they showed it, so they would have to keep it in. But nobody thought it unusual for the women to cry. I remember this Polish girl – the tears would be streaming down her face and she gave a real good picture of the meaning of movies in the lives of people that had no entertainment whatsoever.

> Talk about escapism and its highest degree, this was it. You could see it anyway, they expressed themselves in their actions. Like praying when the hero was in trouble and tense and alert and cheering. It was real to them. It was real. You couldn't explain to them that people weren't right there. If you were to tell them that no, the people were thousands of miles away doing whatever they wanted to be doing, they couldn't comprehend that. This was how real it was.

> Well, the movies taken as a whole, were everything in entertainment. It's just inexpressible, the pleasure that people got out of movies, as compared to the way they spent their time, which as I have mentioned, was pretty much their own life. There wasn't any media or entertainment at that time. They just could not wait until the movie started. It meant everything to them to be going to the movies. Believe me. If you picture the vacuum of entertainment available, you can understand and appreciate that. It was an entirely new existence to them, to be relished every little minute of it. That you could extract as much from it as you possibly could.[53]

> We thought silent movies were just an absolute thrill and something new. People didn't think that it could possibly exist that you could sit in your seat and see something on the screen being projected. So, I think, a lot of the begin-

Fig. 2. Neighbourhood theatres directly addressed their role as anchors of their local commercial districts. In 1921, Chicago's Pantheon, a 1587-seat house on Sheridan Road, incorporated a gallery of shops within the theatre's streetside facade.

> ning was ... ahh ... you looked at it and you saw the plot and you saw the actors. I think the audience became much more involved than they do now, unless it's a horror movie. *Perils of Pauline* – we'd see something like that where Pauline would be tied to the railroad tracks and a train would be coming ... continued 'til next week. I don't think people now would accept it but at that time ... ahh ... you couldn't wait to go back 'til next week.[54]

The movies became the highlight of the week:

> I was just tickled to death. Every Saturday or Saturday night, because it was darker, I would see the show. My dad said we were going to see the show. I couldn't wait till Saturday came. It was usually a weekend or a Sunday night. Once a week we were going to get to go.[55]

It was unthinkable to live without them:

> We always looked forward to going there and all the kids in the neighborhood and at school, that's what we would talk about. All week. Especially on *The Perils of Pauline*. Oh, is she going to get out, or is she going to fall off of the cliff, or will the train hit her, you know. She was so real. She was part of us. It was ... I don't know, movie stars nowadays are away from it, they're up there some place. These people were right down here where they were just everyday people like we were. I don't know what we would have done without the Saturday movie. And of course any punishment that was needed ... the worst they could give to us was when you can't go to the movie on Saturday. Anything but that, we'd promise anything just as long as we got to go to that movie. Very

seldom did we get that punishment, I'm glad to say that.

We looked forward to Saturday, that was the highlight of the whole week. Everybody wanted to go down to the picture show. So we had to walk to the picture show – it was a small town, that was no big deal at all. So, we'd go to the movie, we'd get there early and of course we'd always go down in the front row.

It was one of the fondest memories of my childhood. Going to the movies, earning the money and then talking about it. We talked about it all next week. And, of course, we children, and I think older people are the same way, nobody ever sees the same thing in a movie. Some are interested in this, some are interested in that. Like a Western, the boys are interested in the guy with the gun shooting and we're interested in the heroine what she's going to do and how she's going to get out of it. It just made something to talk about for a whole week.

I don't know, there was a difference about it, you lived through the movies in those days. There wasn't just something you were looking at that was a way off, it was real to you. That's as near as I can describe it.[56]

That was the highlight of our life. We were six, seven and eight years old. That was a highlight of the childrens' amusement. That's really all I can think of. Looking back, it was interesting. I'm glad I didn't miss it. It was a phase that will never come back. You'd have to live a long time to start remembering back that far ... you'd have to be born a long time ago.[57]

Going to the movies might have respresented a special occasion:

My uncle dressed us up, I have the two sisters, and the three of us – he used to like to dress us alike with the little white lacy dresses and blue sashes and big ribbons and your hair in braids and all that and dress you up as if you were going to a party and your uncle was going to take you to the movies. He used to take us for a walk around the capital which was pretty then and we've been back and it's nothing like what it used to be. Then going home from the movies everybody stopped at the Palace Sugary, which was an ice-cream parlour. And everybody had to have that ice-cream before they went home because, being early in teens (and the parents were strict then) and at that age, you couldn't go out nights so you went in the afternoons. So the town used to be buzzing with children you know, teenagers especially.[58]

I went with my sister. It was a night out. Going to the movie was extra special. I thought it a luxury to see a silent movie.[59]

For others, going to the movies became part of, as Jarvie suggests, a well-established routine:[60]

We'd go every time they would change the film, which was probably twice a week. Regularly on Saturday afternoons and probably once during the week. My father was quite enthused about the movies. He always enjoyed them. He used to take me to the movies.[61]

We'd go down on a Saturday evening. We'd do our grocery shopping and then [go] to the movies. I usually didn't unless my parents went to the show, which was in the evening. We'd go then and see that. My mother liked the movies better than my dad. We used to, I know we did many times, we'd go into town, we didn't have an automobile, and we went into town on what they call the interurban. It's like a streetcar. The interurban kind of went out in the country a little bit. There was a regular street-car that came from Detroit right up into Royal Oak; but the interurban, it went out into the more rural areas. Anyway, they would go in there and go to the grocery store. Then we would go to the movie, park our groceries on the side. The guy at the place had a place where you could put the groceries. Then we'd go in and then pick up the groceries, get on the interurban and go home.[62]

They didn't care much about it if the movie was bad. They were welcome to their money back if they didn't care to see the film being shown – most people stayed. It became a habit.[63]

Some children found it particularly difficult to catch this 'habit' of motion pictures. Certain interest groups, finding movies '... without a redeeming feature to warrant their existence ... ministering to the lowest passions of childhood', ... wanted children entirely banned from attending motion pictures[64] and many local governments, under the pretense of safety, restricted access to children over sixteen unless accompanied by an adult. But a New York law, which specifically targeted children between the ages of six and sixteen, limiting their access during the day, indicates that they were trying more to keep the children in school than keep them from the movies.[65] Perhaps it is not surprising these regulations were more often than not evaded:[66]

> I can remember going to the city. At that time, my folks went shopping and I wanted to go to the movies. I'd have to go up and ask someone to buy my ticket for me because they would not sell tickets to anyone, at that time, under 16 years of age. Well, I would just go up to them and ask them if they would mind buying a ticket for me. They would buy the ticket for me and I'd go on in. We just walked with the crowd.[67]

> They would not permit you to go by yourself and the movies were a nickel. Our mothers and fathers certainly didn't have time to take us to the movies so we would hang around the movies and we would see somebody that looked as if they were going in and we would tell them that we needed somebody to take us and we had the money and would they take us and they did. Then, of course, when we got into the movie, we didn't sit with them or anything, ya know.[68]

Then there were pressures at home:

> It took my mother and father quite a while before they were convinced that movies weren't sinful. I had an uncle, who used to call up and ask if he could borrow me. He'd take me out to see things. I was the first member of the family who saw a movie. There was nothing as sinful as today.[69]

> No, I think the reason I didn't go, my family – typical of that generation – felt that it was improper for me to go to a movie where the leading lady and leading man might kiss. Nowadays we'd call it prudish that they protected my tender sensibilities and over zealous concern. So the movies I got to see would be documentaries or historical movies.[70]

> That's it, the cartoons. That's all we used to go for. And we used to get a whipping from our father because we used to go see them twice. I guess we were about ten or twelve years old.[71]

> No, you weren't allowed to go, mother was strict and we weren't allowed out at night. We had all the freedom we wanted during the day but we had to be in for meals and at night.[72]

As it is today, there was a great deal of agitation over the control and censorship of motion pictures. At the forefront were religious organisations, such as the Methodists:[73]

> My parents were raised conservative Methodists, with very conservative views. They were against dancing, card playing, smoking, drinking and anything that would excite young people's sex lives. So in our earliest days their very disapproval of those kind of things – well the movies, of course, did have all of these aspects in them, the smoking, the drinking, and certainly wouldn't be compared to what goes on today – but in those days dancing in the movies, kissing and the love scenes were something that were sort of frowned on by the more conservative people. My parents got over a lot of that before they finished their life. So it was rare that we went to the movies until I got to my, maybe, middle teens and maybe I would see a movie as much as three or four times a year, that's about it.[74]

As is the case in these movements, the clergy would lead by example:

> My father was a minister. We weren't allowed to go to the movies; in those days, the pastor's kids weren't really allowed to go but I never found out why. I was just informed. These rules were just something we had to live with ...

And, as many of us have seen, sometimes the clergy's children would choose to go their own directions:

> ... but once in a while we would sneak out and

> cover for each other. We would say, like, 'I'm gonna meet Helen!'. I really never would say where we would go so it really wasn't a lie but it wasn't the truth either. I might say I was going to go to somebody's house or my sister would say that. I would say that for her too. We would alternate times. I would probably go every other Saturday and she would go on the opposite Saturdays. Sometimes we would both go if it was something we really wanted to see. We had to figure that one out on how we were gonna do it. I don't really remember what we did but we both had to get together so that we both said the same thing.
>
> We walked. It wasn't too far. Maybe six blocks or four blocks. We wanted to be like the other kids. We wanted to talk about various movies. On Saturdays, they'd have special movies. They were usually a nickel. I honestly don't remember where I got it. I know I didn't steal it. I hate the word 'lie', but that's what we did until we were teenagers and by that time we had dates and went to movies. I was probably seventeen. Somehow, he really never asked where we were going. We had to be in by eleven or something like that.[75]

The movies would cast an imposing shadow over many of the children's lives in the games they played and in the looks they affected. The Westerns, of course, proved to be popular:

> The only movies I remember where there were more children were when they had a cowboy movie. Something like that and of course that carried over when my brother and I would be at home playing in the yard we would get the clothesline poles and ride them around like we were riding horses. Yes, Tom Mix and some of those guys. It was a play act of what we had seen in the movies I guess you'd call it.[76]

But certainly other genres made their way into their play acting:

> Oh I can recall movies of the Salome dancers in these long, diaphanous-looking gowns. I used to imitate them. When mother had company sometimes then she would want me to show off and show her how the Salome dancers were dancing.[77]
>
> What I remember seeing there was a series of *Robin Hoods* and that was in the silent era, too. I don't remember the actors' names but I still remember the incident when they were going across the log ... little John ... and somebody would fall in. But, that was a weekly series. So, every week we went and saw *Robin Hood* and us kids would go around with bows and arrows. We absorbed what was going on at the time. During the week, we would probably reenact some of the things we saw. It's wonderful what they did at that time. It started our imaginations.[78]

But sometimes the play almost went too far:

> We'd organise it you know and, of course, the boys always went in for the Western part of it and I'd be the girl. I'd get tied up to the tree – almost got hung once (laughter). But I didn't: the rope slipped and got up around my neck, my hands were tied and I'm making all kinds of noises. My brother said 'what's the matter with you, you're supposed to hold still' – still gagging and finally he said 'oh, wait just a minute' so he came and loosened the rope around my neck. So I tried to stay out of that situation if I could. Always the *Perils of Pauline*. I was always the one who got tied and laid on the streetcar track and all that stuff. That was kind of dangerous, I think. We'd use the real tracks. And one'd be the hero and one would be the villain and I always got rescued in time.
>
> The movies had quite an influence on our lives. My brother, he's 85 now. We reminisce about those things every now and then – what we used to do and how we would do it. And how wonderful it was. We enjoyed seeing it and now enjoy thinking about it.[79]

Some studies, however, suggest that as few as 10 per cent of the patrons came solely for the feature movie, with 68 per cent coming mostly for the 'event'.[80] Part of this event certainly wasn't officially allotted space on the program: a time for people to gather together in one place at one time and get caught up with one another.

Fig. 3. Although seating 2817 people, the Loew's Pitkin was essentially a Brooklyn satellite of the much larger Capitol Theatre in Manhattan. Its marquee boasted 'Shows From The Capitol NY', including 'Venetian Carnival', which accompanied the run of *New York Nights* in 1930.

> That was part of the event, now that you mention it, of going to a movie would be to go in, to sit down, older people would gossip and talk and everything.[81]

> The whole family would go. We did everything as a family. In the country, that's what everyone did at that time. And, of course, you'd mingle with the neighbours.[82]

> You saw the same people, if you were from Scotland you would cling together with them.[83]

> But it was a meeting place. It was something good for everybody, more or less community life. I don't know, work towards one project after working all week for that nickel to go to that theatre was number one priority in our lives. It wasn't good grades at school.[84]

> If somebody was going to have an event, if they were going to have something special, why they would have someone get up and announce it before the movie.[85]

Vaudeville and live acts

It was not uncommon for theatre managers to speed up a feature by increasing the projection speed to fit in everything else.[86] Taking up a large part of the evening's program were the live acts, usually vaudeville bits with musical accompaniment.

> Some of them showed vaudeville too you know in them days so naturally when I got big I went to the theatre that showed you vaudeville.

> They would show you the movie first. Then at the intermission then they would show you the

vaudeville. They had generally five acts of vaudeville. When they got through there would be intermission again so some of the people left, others come in and then they would show you the movie again. It was continuous from the earliest I guess was from 9 o'clock until 9 o'clock at night or 10 o'clock at night.[87]

We then had the vaudeville house and usually there would be a vaudeville show and a movie, also. They'd have singers or animal shows, mainly. And we would go in the balcony – cause it was cheaper there. But later on, as a teenager, in New York, we had some beautiful theatres. They used to have the Loew Theaters. They had vaudevilles and movies.[88]

In many of the larger theatres there would be a travelling company of actors, with their own equipment and established routines. These were often times advertised more heavily than the movie itself.[89]

We used to go to vaudeville for a quarter. We'd see all the acts and go through the same routine, Pathe news, a comedy and a big picture. All the live acts on the stage, like jugglers, or they'd have companies come out and do a scene where they'd go through something bad like the *Perils of Pauline*.[90]

We'd have a movie and a vaudeville, it was part of the program. Going to the vaudeville, that was a revelation to me, unheard of. Of course, we had seen the road shows that came and put on plays and things like that. I loved them, but I loved that vaudeville. I remember Joe Penner coming out there with his little ducks falling and saying 'Want to buy a duck? Want to buy a duck?' That must have been 1923–24. I didn't know I could remember that far back. Things that are really comical really stick in your mind.[91]

Sometimes the theatres would even bring in a headliner with a national profile:

And then we had another theatre up the street, about three or four blocks later, and that was a larger theatre. And they had loads of vaudeville acts. They always had six acts, the last of which was, generally, a review of some kind. And, the first acts were, generally, comedians. Then, the hook would come on. Then, I remember seeing Tom Mix and his horse on stage with his lasso ... galloping around on stage doing things.[92]

And farther down, a few blocks away was quite a few movie houses. That was where I lived. A few blocks away there was a place called the Astoria. Most of these places had a vaudeville show along with it. That was where we saw George M. Cohan. Some musicals were put on and that was along with the movies. A lot of vaudeville. Later on when we moved to Jackson Heights we had another movie house which also had vaudeville. I saw Blanche Yurka, a famous actress at the time, in a play.[93]

Yes, you had vaudeville, you know. I remember seeing Al Jolson on one of – he came out of vaudeville, you know, in addition to the movies.[94]

Smaller theatres had to rely on local talent for their live acts, and experienced, as you can well imagine, varying success:

Then they had a stage where they had entertainment. Sometimes they had people come up there and sing and dance, especially we had amateur nights once a week where everybody would go up and do their stint or whatever they wanted, usually before the movie and during the intermission. I never went up; you had to be bold to go up. The audience, they applauded and they liked them. It was something for nothing. In them days you were getting something for nothing because you only came to see the movies.[95]

There was some attempts to have an amateur night. It usually failed dismally. Two or three shots. We had to wait for Major Bowes to make that a form of the art.[96]

The audience might show their appreciation for the quality of this entertainment in a unique way:

In the movie houses, if they had an act on the stage, they'd take pennies and throw them

> down on the stage. They'd scale them right there on the stage.[97]

Music in the theatres

As the popularity of the vaudeville might suggest, one of the major attractions in any theatre, no matter what the size, was the music. At times it seemed as if the music itself took precedence over everything else.

> The theatre we used to go to in Batavia had a marvelous organ and a pretty darn good player. You never saw the thing until the music started and up came the organ and would sit in a corner off from the screen. That man could play that thing. He had a nickname, something like Organ Andy, but everyone loved to hear him play. In fact, I heard the people comment, 'why don't they do away with that comedy and let the man play the organ'.[98]

Music was always perceived to be a significant part of the experience of motion pictures. Edison initially became interested in the idea of synchronising pictures with music as a way of selling more phonographs. Then, at the turn of the century, filmmakers such as James White approached movies almost as illustrated songs, with scenes carefully chosen to fit the words and music sung by a trained vocalist.[99]

> My friend's sister was Clare Todd. She is the one who went to the McPhale School of Music. She would sing during the silent movies where they would have music in the background in the early days.[100]

Used primarily as a way of drawing attention on the sidewalk in front of arcades[101], music soon found a place within the theatres. Whether a single piano player, an organist or an orchestra, the musician and musical accompaniment soon became a staple of the typical theatrical program.

In 1922, a Motion Picture News survey revealed that 30 per cent of the theatres surveyed had an orchestra of some sort:

> Then most of the little better theatres had an orchestra, a three or four piece orchestra but most of them only had piano players. They played the piano and that was it during the movie.[102]

> We had an orchestra, which was down in the pit. The conductor was underneath the stage in a little box conducting the orchestra. That was in the better houses. I think we paid fifty or seventy-five cents in the Roxy and the Music Hall in those days, the Capital.[103]

Forty-five per cent relied on an organ:

> I know on one side they had an organ and during the movie that organ would play. Now if a guy was riding a horse or something, it would play real fast and when cowboys and Indians came they'd hit that 'bang, bang, bang'.[104]

Twenty-five per cent still maintained the solitary piano:[105]

> The floor was on a raised portion and they had a stage at the front and also a place for an orchestra below, but we never had an orchestra. We had a piano player who usually gave the sound effects with the type of program that we had.[106]

While some theatres would be able to afford an orchestra on some occasions and rely on solitary players for others:

> There were about five theatres in Buffalo in those days. They had orchestras then. One theatre had a man that played the organ and we called him 'B Sharp Minor'. I don't know what his real name was and he played beautifully. I know they had an orchestra, too, that would rise from the pit and would play and then the picture started.[107]

> The front of the theatre was a box which had a pianist and sometimes they had a small orchestra.[108]

Others, whether in more out of the way places or with managers too cheap to lay out cash, rarely had an accompanist:

> We didn't get to go to the theatre where they had music in North Dakota, so I don't know about it. There was no piano or organ. Just the film and Pathe news.[109]

Well what they had was some kind of music box. But usually they would try, if it were a special attraction, to have a piano there for it to go along with the movie. Otherwise we just had a machine there to have music, to have noise, I think that's all. The music would be playing, not loud, but sort of background music. No we didn't have anyone playing music ... we didn't get musicians until quite a bit later.[110]

So when you were going to the movies, this was early 1920s now, there was no music at the Caldwell and none at the Park. So it was a completely silent experience. Absolutely silent until the sound came on.[111]

Most revealing, however, are two studies done in the mid to late twenties which indicated audiences rated music higher than anything, including the movie itself, when considering the overall appeal of a theatre.[112]

I got a kick out of the piano player. He'd come up with the heavy music when the bad guy was up, then they'd go boom, boom, boom. He made the sound according to the picture. He'd use light music if it was a love scene. He was great.[113]

I enjoyed the movies because it seemed that the piano player was very good; whatever came on he played something to go with it. The music would match the picture. The piano was the background of the picture. We didn't miss the talking. He played by ear, he was a wonderful player, razzmatazz and everything with the silent movies.[114]

And of course the entry of the piano player was the huge event. Finally, when they would see the girl who played the piano over in the corner coming down, they would sit up. She would get an ovation, I believe. They would clap and jump up and down and stomp on the floor. And then, she would play some kind of an overture for the movie and they'd start up a clamour again. It didn't take much.[115]

Music was not considered something tangential to the movie; many in the audience recognised its pre-eminent place in the overall experience:

It would have been a pretty dull show if we didn't have music to go with it – with the motion of the show.[116]

But she was a marvelous pianist. Oh, they would holler at her sometimes. They didn't think she played fast enough. She'd have to play the Midnight Fire and get that going. I think as a whole they'd miss it when she wasn't there, however. That music was a part of it.[117]

But, until you saw it without any music in the background, when you did see it with music, it augmented the action. It was really fascinating. Music played such an important part in the movies because you'd see the sound effects on the screen.[118]

Music would be used as the emotional underpinning to a scene, serving as the driving force behind a chase or a way of adding poignancy to a quiet moment:

It was exciting. They would have 'The Perils of Pauline', ya know. Oh heavens, she'd be tied to the railroad tracks and a train would be coming and then she would be rescued just in time. They would have a music player and she would play music according to what the movie was like. Boy it was exciting music ... that sort of thing.[119]

When the scenes got rough and wild on the screen then the music from the piano would run to a person, or something like that. And if it was a sad scene, the music would be sad.[120]

It could be very sentimental music or you know horses galloping – the music was real hepped up.[121]

There wasn't anything that he couldn't play. If there was a horse race, he'd play some classical piece that had a horse sound like horses hooves.[122]

I can remember the silent movies very well because they had the piano player down in the front and if they had the cowboys and it was

Fig. 4. The orchestra pit of the Ambassador Theater in St. Louis, Missouri could accomodate some twenty pieces, including a piano, pipe organ and harp. The 3000-seat theatre, designed by the firm of Rapp & Rapp, opened at the end of the silent era in 1928.

exciting then she would play fast music and if everything was serene then she would go back to a waltz or something like that.[123]

Well, I happened to be a very good friend to my friend Marge and she was a terrific pianist. They had asked her to play the piano. This was new to her but she could just play anything. And, to sit beside her and look at the screen … here come the horses … if a storm came through … a love scene would go real slow and graceful. And, then, you realised that this sound was coming from her if you sat way in the back. Someone was really setting the mood by what you were watching by innovating. Someone, within seconds, would dub in the music.[124]

We all would get excited, especially when the piano would lend itself to the situation.[125]

Beginning in the 1890s, there was a strong trend of sing-alongs in cabarets, vaudeville houses and theatres, supported by elaborate, hand-coloured slides, projected by a 'magic lantern'.[126]

In movie theatres around the country, this tradition would continue at intermissions:

It was in a little theatre in town they had a piano player. In the palaces they would usually have – I don't know whether it was a piano player – you know they would have the screen with the dots going up and down on the screen in rhythm with the music and the songs and the words of the songs so that they could get the people involved in the audience singing and going along with them.[127]

Gale Lancaster was the pianist or the organist and he would perform before and during if there were any intermissions. He was an attraction – I think maybe it was his movie – I don't know – he always worked there. He played before and when we would have a sing-along, in the intermission – you know.[128]

But, I must say, when you got to hear the organ, it was very nice. Sometimes, they would have two shows and an intermission in between. And, in between, they would either have an organ player or an entertainer on stage.[129]

Sure. Intermission, that's where our little lady down in front of the movie screen came into her own because they would flash the sheet, the lyrics and the bouncing ball and she would play along and everybody would sing and they thought it was wonderful.[130]

Or even during one of the unfortunately frequent interruptions caused by projection problems:

They'd just wait until it got fixed. Then the piano would play and maybe sometime they'd sing while they were waiting on it to get back together.[131]

We can imagine, then, that an audience even slightly schooled in music would be able to evaluate and appreciate the musicianship of the accompanist:

Whoever played the piano and organ must have been a genius to have mood music that fit into the situation.[132]

The theatre was very small. This was pictures only. There was a woman that played a piano. She played the piano through the whole thing. If they had something exciting, she would embellish that. They had the piano player for quite a few years. I don't remember what year they stopped. The audience loved her. Oh yeah. They would clap for her.[133]

Although how the accompanists managed to come up with the appropriate music was a matter of amazement for some, it was not entirely up to individual choice.

She had to know what was going on to play like she did.[134]

This narrator's suspicions are confirmed by Richard Koszarski:

Formal musical accompaniment of silent films was a specialised craft that developed and disappeared within a decade and a half ... its creative centre was the (individual) theatre ... while the largest theatres maintained huge in-house libraries and their own conductors–arrangers (who needed to perform at a moment's notice) small-town piano players had access to volumes such as Erno Rapee's *Motion Picture Moods*. This work was so indexed that the performer could quickly flash from 'mother-love' to 'fire-fighting' as the occasion arose. Such volumes could help if the musician had to face his or her subject cold, but generally accompanists could count on at least some guidance from the distributor.[135]

They'd send a score with the picture. And the piano player would try to dub in music to fit the picture.[136]

> Music came with the movies and there was a cue sheet, telling you what to play and how long to play it and when.[137]

> There used to be a little lady sitting down in front of the screen, watching the screen, playing what they called dramatic tension music. She had sheets for cowboys and Indians, wars and love scenes and you name it.[138]

Koszarski, however, recognises that this 'original music for silent motion pictures' can only document the wishes of the producers or distributors, not the actual performance in theatres. Films were rarely previewed, cues rarely used and the pianist had to be an 'instant composer': [139]

> I wasn't very old the first time I played for the movies. Yes, just sitting there in that – you know how you all see them – da ra da ra da ra – I'm watching. Yeah I was. But it was up to me to play whatever I wanted. You see my mother had loads of music in the attic. That was what I loved to do on rainy days, was go up to the attic and spread the music out and I memorised it. It gets in my head and stays there. And Mother would take me to Pittsburgh and I could pick out whatever sheet music I wanted. And I would play whatever came to mind, whatever was appropriate.[140]

> My step-mother had to play ... she had no format, she had to improvise as she went along. I remember one time, I think it was one of Lillian Gish's movies, where the mother had died and it was very sad and they were standing there at the graveyard and she was playing 'The End of a Perfect Day'. We never let her forget that (laughter). It was marvelous, though, how she could cope. You know that picture changes and she had to change her brain just as fast as that picture. But she was marvelous. I don't know if she got a dollar or two. She didn't get very much a week for playing it but at that time a dollar or two meant a lot. I can remember her at those movies that we would go to, switch from one to the other, there would be a very sad scene and then over here would be the fire wagon. Maybe that piano would have to turn from this scene to that and the music would have to go along with and follow that. I don't know how she did it, even to this day. She had so much of it in her mind. I'll never forget the 'Midnight Fire Alarm' because whenever there was a chase, you know Mack Sennett Cops or anything like that, she'd always play and I happened to know it. Of course, she played all this music at home, too. But I'll never forget that sad thing at the funeral she was playing 'At The End Of A Perfect Day'. I still think that was funny.[141]

With the exception of the larger theatres which could afford professional musicians, most neighbourhood theatres relied upon what local talent they could hire.

> One of the high school teachers for two dollars would come and thump that piano all during that show. We showed it one time. No point in doing anything else because everyone was there to begin with and they all left and there was no reason for running a second show. She was very faithful and did a good job on it. I gave her all of $2. Couldn't do much more than that.[142]

> Well, it started out ... a man started out and I don't know what happened to him. Then, girls we knew started to play. They got paid for it, you know. I don't know, they'd play an hour, an hour and a half. Not much more. That girl couldn't play too long. When one would get done, she'd get married and go somewhere and someone would take her place.[143]

> The woman wasn't a star, she was really a dressmaker and she played the piano in the evenings there.[144]

> The pipe organ ... I used to enjoy watching that. The girl would play the organ and when her shift was over, another one would come in and she would sit on the bench beside the other one, and she would, automatically, pick up the music as she was going off the other side. So, there was no break in the music.[145]

All of this leads me to wonder if, perhaps, the term 'silent pictures' is, if not a misnomer, then misleading, in the very least.

> That's where the silent movies came in. It wasn't

> really silent, there was a roll of film and there was a lady who played the music according to whether it was sad or happy.[146]

Snacks

One of the things we take for granted when we arrive at the theatre is the choice of what to eat. Today, it is not uncommon to be able to eat your dinner, from main course through to dessert, at a multiplex establishment. There was a time when this was simply unheard of.

> No, there was no food and we didn't bring any. People would laugh at you at that time. Everybody ate three meals a day at home and if they did anything else after that they didn't have to go eat anywhere. There was not even a coffee shop in town. There was only about 1200–1300 people in it.[147]

> We didn't have food in those days. They didn't have popcorn in the theatre. We just went and saw the picture and went home.[148]

However, the ever resourceful audience soon began bringing their own refreshments and snacks:

> I think the children used to buy candy and things and take it from the grocery store and go to the movies. They didn't have any refreshment booth there at the movie.[149]

> I made fudge and stuff in the bakery and we sold that and all the kids would come up and buy the candy. They didn't have popcorn, that much, or cokes. It just didn't exist up there. I'm sure in the cities is where they had many movies.[150]

> There was always a Saturday matinee for ten cents for the children and we all took our own popcorn. They didn't serve popcorn in the theatre. We'd all take our own popcorn, pop a big sack full before we left home and take it to the movies.[151]

> No, they wouldn't have snacks at the theatre, but you could buy candies at the grocer and take it with you.[152]

> I don't remember if they had popcorn like today. I think people took stuff to munch on.[153] You might take something to the movies, you know, so that you wouldn't starve in between.[154]

No doubt some clever theatre managers realised another source of revenue was at hand and began offering food of their own for purchase and prohibiting folks from bringing their own:

> Another thing you could never bring candy or popcorn or anything like that in the movies. I remember that. I remember getting the popcorn. On certain days they had popcorn. They gave you too much.[155]

Although the prohibition against bringing your own food didn't have an effect on some with a particularly acute sweet tooth:

> At the entrance on this side was a bakery. Just to the right of the entrance. The bakery was on the outside but you could still go to the door there and this big entrance way to the theatre and then they had the big glass windows with all the baked goods. So my sister and I were usually the ones that went together. So what would we buy? Cream puffs. Can you imagine eating cream puffs in a dark theatre? They didn't know it. We'd put it in the bag and go in. Ah yes, we were hasty to become educated to cream puffs. I can imagine what we looked like when we came out of the theatre (Laughter).[156]

The trick was where and how to make the food available to the patrons. Some took it right to the audience, conjuring up a ballpark experience:

> It was in the afternoon, we'd go to a matinee. And that was all right. They'd used to come around throwing samples of candy and then come up and sell it They would throw samples of candy up and down the aisle, then they would come around with their little sacks and try to sell candy.[157]

Others resorted to a convenient, albeit primitive vending machine apparatus:

> There was a Hershey chocolate machine on the back of every chair in front of you. This was a mark of theatres in my mind for years and years. You would put in a coin and you'd get

> a big Hershey bar, although I never saw one of them that worked or anybody that used it. That always intrigued me as to where did these come from and why they were there.[158]
>
> Also, on the back of the seats in the vaudeville houses they had change machines. You'd put money in and get candy. They worked. If some of them didn't work, your money would come back.[159]

Other managers set up little concession stands within the theatre auditorium proper:

> This was way back – I guess in the 1920s. Right inside the theatre, separated from the seats, there with like a railing, they had a little bar there where you could buy ice-cream or candy or tonic in paper cups and they charged you a nickel apiece for the ice-cream cones and a nickel for the tonic. Generally, you'd go up before or after the movie. If it wasn't interesting then you would go up during the movie.[160]
>
> No. There was generally someplace that sold popcorn. Not much more than that. It would be at the back end of the theatre – a concession. They would be in the back away from disturbing the film. Toward the back of the theatre and it wasn't noisy. On Saturdays, it would be ten cents to see a movie and if you got popcorn it would be five cents.[161]
>
> The drink was in the back. You had to go back and get it. You could drink it at the bar. It was only a nickel. You used to roll the bottles on the floor.[162]

Sometimes, having the refreshments within the theatre would inspire some shenanigans:

> The floor was pitched this way to the screen. They'd take the empty bottle and throw it down on the floor and let it roll, it would be hitting on the edges of the benches. I don't want to say this out loud but some of them would pee in the bottle and throw it down that way.[163]

And perhaps because of this type of high jinx, the food concession was moved out into the lobby. Although it has been suggested that this type of concession was a result of the Depression, my narrators' reports indicate this was a widespread practice in the silent movies:

> Oh, yes they sold candy and the one was taffy. Almost all the theatres sold taffy. You would get a good size block of taffy for a nickel. Can you imagine? I know we used to get a bag of candy and that would be maybe 2 cents or 3 cents. We'd have a little extra to go to the movies with.[164]
>
> They had popcorn and sometimes cookies.[165]
>
> And I believe they had a popcorn machine there, on which was put an ungodly amount of butter because if you didn't get that you wouldn't want it. So it would be about '24-'25-'26, serving popcorn.[166]
>
> It would be in the lobby. A machine there, and then I think, the popcorn thing was on this side, on the right side, and the water fountain was on this side. They didn't have cold drinks. Nothing but popcorn. That's all they had there. Yeah, for a nickel you used to get a big bag of popcorn. And they frowned on us taking candy and stuff like that in because the kids would sneak in peanuts in the shells every now and then and a lot of times you'd go in there and crunch, crunch, crunch on the floor they'd be the peanut hulls.[167]

Outdoor theatres

Oral history relies on what Reinharz calls 'semi-structured' interviewing which includes free interaction between the researcher and the interviewee.[168] Oral historians are essentially tolerant of ambiguity,[169] and herein lies the beauty of the method. Unlike a rigid question/answer format, which '... tends to confirm the (researcher's) previous frame of reference ...',[170] we work from an outline that simply supplies a framework from which to work, a plan that allows for flexibility.[171] We enter into a dialogue, or an 'inter/view', as Portelli has observed, '... literally a mutual sighting ...'[172] We hope to discover new directions to go, new questions to ask, and we need the '... freedom to follow what people choose to tell us'[173] and this cannot be accomplished if we accept the outline as inviolate.

One of the directions in which my narrators led

Fig. 5. The open-air urban theatre, or 'air dome', had strong appeal to city residents, especially in summer months. But by the 1930s it was almost extinct, with suburban drive-ins usurping its market niche. [Courtesy of Q. David Bowers.]

me was the discovery of how prevalent outdoor movies were in the silent days. At some locales the movies would be free, sponsored by civic groups or local governments. Consider the following 1916 ordinance from St. Louis, MO: '(The) Commissioner of Parks and Recreation (is authorised) to provide motion pictures in public parks and playgrounds ... before 1 July each year (he will) invite bids ... to furnish first class moving picture machines, furnish an operator therefor (sic) and provide the necessary films ... of such character as the Commissioner ... may designate ...'.[174] By 1920 local governments were still being urged to pursue this idea as an appropriate means for organised, summertime entertainment.[175]

> ... (B)ut then later on they started having outdoor movies in all the parks every summer. We had a park about four miles from where I lived – Crompton Park – that was the name. It was named after Crompton Knowles Company, the President – it was a big, big company. They made looms for weaving you see. Well anybody could go – it was right inside the park but just about a hundred yards away from the road and it was generally in a gully like, with hills and little mounts surrounding it and the truck would go in there and they had a screen set up and they would start showing the movie see. No admission charge at all. It was just free anybody could go. Yes the town did it. Oh yes, the town did it. They took good care of the people there. You would sit on the grass. You would bring a blanket with you or a towel and put it on the grass, sit there and watch the movie. There was a big, big screen and everybody was close. You only get about a couple of hundred people would be the most that could watch it. Just the neighborhood would watch it because every neighborhood had their own.[176]

I came from a town that had a population of 200. In the summer, if it wasn't raining, they had the movies outdoors every Saturday night. It would start about the first of June. It wasn't too cool to sit outside. It would run 'til about when school started in September. It was free.

> Probably the merchants there at Nodaway would put it on. It was outdoors behind an oil station, where people would get gas.
>
> It just had a big screen out in front. It was up high, we'd have to look up, it seemed like you had to look up in the air. They had those bridge planks. They had 'em on cement blocks in rows. Some of 'em would sit in their cars if they didn't want to sit on those planks. They had music and a piano player. They'd bring it on a truck and a woman played the piano. You never knew what movie was playing 'til you went. You just knew if it was rainy, they wouldn't have it.
>
> Oh my, we just looked forward to it every week. Never spent a dime while I was there. There'd be oh, about 100 people, or so. In the afternoon, I'd lay out what dress I was going to wear. I'd get supper early. I'd get mom around, set in her wheelchair. Then, we would take off. I usually ran. My sister used to say that she wasn't running, so I'd run and she'd walk. Before it got dark, us girls would walk up one sidewalk and down the other. There was just seven streets and we thought it was so wonderful to see the cars and buggies lined up in the street and when it got dark and they turned the lights off, we would run and get our seats. Some of them with money would run into the store and buy a bottle of pop, a coke for five cents. A penny meant more to me than a dollar means to kids now. Everyone came, adults and kids. It got real quiet. Then, when it was over, they'd stand around talking. They liked that as good as the Saturday night before. So we stuck around until it was all over. We knew we had to get home, and it would be over around ten or something like that. I hated to see the movies be over in the fall. Another thing that was nice was that a couple of girls would get up and sing, it was kinda a treat. They'd sing between the intermissions; then they would buy some popcorn or something.[177]

Other outdoor movies were money-making alternatives during the hot months of summer:

> This was an open-air movie, right around the corner from where we lived. The man who owned it and the other movie, which was in the same neighborhood, was Mr. Reilly. In the summer my mother and my father and I would go to the open-air movie. It was not what they have now, where they smooch. There were seats and I remember this big apartment house in back of where the movie was and they would sit at their window and looked down on the movie for free. It was a very nice way to spend a summer evening. For a short period of time it was hot and we had no air-conditioning. People would spend an evening at the movie and then go home. These were popular but there weren't big crowds. It was a small area I lived in and it was neighborhood people who went. And farther down, (a few blocks away) was quite a few movie houses.[178]

Some proprietors would set up their outdoor movies in places where there was less of a chance that neighbouring residents would get a free peek:

> This one was set up next to a cemetery. The movies would come on at dusk. We were like animals chasing the bugs, of course. But we enjoyed it. That was in Queens. In those days they didn't have too many in Manhattan, but they had more outdoor movies in Queens. It was more rural in those days. It was fun. Of course, it was silent and they had a piano player. They had benches set up.[179]

Another direction in which my narrators led me was to begin to consider how the weather played an important role in their movie-going patterns. Winter appears to have been a bad time for some:

> Well, if the weather was nice we were allowed to go. We would get together on the street where we lived and would walk over there. If the weather wasn't nice, well, then we wouldn't go I suppose.[180]
>
> The winters were terrible. No, we'd never go in the winter.[181]
>
> We wouldn't go when it was bad weather, it was too difficult to walk. We didn't have transportation in National Park unless you were lucky to have a car. We were used to it. No

> sense moaning about it. We were lucky when we could go.[182]
>
> Yes, we'd go in the summer. I wouldn't go in the winter. We didn't have any car at that time.[183]
>
> We lived way out. There was only one other family that lived next door to us. It was like a rural community. We went once in about four months because we just couldn't get there. On Saturday afternoon we went. It would take about a half hour maybe to walk from where we lived. We didn't go in the cold weather because it was too much walking in the cold. It was more like in the fall or the early spring. We had no favourite movies because anything that was good we liked.[184]

For others, ironically, winter had quite the opposite effect:

> Well, weather had a lot to do with it. In the winter time, things were pretty dull. We would go skating. In the flat land of Massachusetts, skiing wasn't too popular, anyway. The best they would have was skis that were made out of barrel staves. If you had your fun going down the hill, you'd take a spill, but it was all laughable. So we would go to the movies.[185]
>
> In those days I had a boyfriend that used to take me to the shows maybe two or three times a week, in the wintertime especially. In the summertime we'd go for rides down to the Falls and places like that. We went to the theatre more in the winter than in the summer.[18]

Final words

When I first began this project three years ago, my initial impulse was not unlike '... much of the most worthwhile work in oral history: the search for "more reality", for direct experience, and for first-person "testimony"'.[187] Now I am faced with wondering what exactly it is that I have accomplished.

Beyond methodological issues, William Moss presents us with an important and difficult question when faced with the final interpretation of any historical project: '... is the information provided really needed ... (does it) contribute richness of detail and description, or perhaps a richness of affective response and commentary that aids insight'?[188] Well, as Portelli writes, 'ever since the Federal Writers' Project interviews with former slaves, oral history has been about the fact that there's more to history than presidents and generals and there's more to culture than the literary canon'.[189] So often 'history' is about dates and events and major 'movers and shakers'. Without the benefit of oral histories we lack a crucial social context; '(o)ral history reveals the daily stuff of daily life which is rarely written into the public record ... (they) reveal dimensions of life (and) values ...'.[190] The personal testimonies I've gathered in my oral history project will enable us to glimpse the meaning behind not only the cultural artifacts that we know as the movies, but the whole phenomenon of movie-going in the first part of this century.

This project can take its place next to others in fields as diverse as labour and economic history, rural and urban social histories, or even the history of religions – anywhere, quite honestly, where there is inadequate documentation or vast gray areas of local beliefs, rituals or just plain poor bookkeeping.[191]

The worth of oral histories can be measured against our own belief in the importance of a record of not only what people did, '... but what they wanted to do, what they believed they were doing and what they now think they did'.[192] The historical value of the remembered past rests, in part, on the strength that it '... conveys the individual and collective consciousness which is part and parcel of (the) past ... (and that) ... (i)t is precisely this historical perspective which allows us to assess long term meaning in history ...'.[193]

A common complaint about oral history is the fallibility of memory. Recent research has proven, however, that what many of us have been suspecting all along is actually true: older people have more memories from their deep past than for the most recent years.[194] Further tests have shown that initial memory loss during the first years is as great as that during the subsequent 34 years.[195] Other evidence indicates that '... strong feelings and memory are very consistent'[196] and that '(a)ccurate memory is ... much more likely when it meets a social interest and need'.[197] Thus, it could be argued, that one of the more popular pursuits of my narrators' youth (the silent motion pictures) would tend to lend itself to long-term recall.

Another major criticism of oral history is that oral sources are not objective and thus unreliable, making any data invalid.[198] However, as Louis Starr explained: '(E)valuation and corroboration are not really any different from using any other source ... check for internal consistency and cross check with documents or other narrators.'[199] In other words, an '... historical interpretation or account becomes credible when the pattern of evidence is consistent and is drawn from more than one viewpoint'.[200] This 'consistency across other histories' can be achieved through a comprehensive content analysis [201] as well as by consulting other sources and comparing accounts.[202]

Some have called my work anecdotal at best, or perhaps even apocryphal. In the final analysis, however, as we argue over the validity of oral history, opportunities to record them slip through our fingers like the sands of time. As one of my narrators sighed at the end of our interview:

> You never miss the water until the well runs dry – that's an old saying – that you never realise what you had until it is gone.[203]

I, for one, urge all of us to drink more deeply from this well of memories *before* it's gone. Who knows what kind of questions we may want to ask this audience. I have, in effect (to once again borrow Paul Thompson's words) collected '... information for scholars (I) don't know in order to provide information for research topics ...' that I can't begin to anticipate.[204] But now, at least, the audience's voices can be heard, people's words recorded and down on tape and transcribed to paper, as a part of the mosaic of history♦

Appendix: Alphabetical list of narrators

	Sex	DOB	Location of Birth
Adriance	F	1911	Harleston, NC
Anderson	F	1995	Anderson, SC
Barden	M	1907	Suffouk, VA
Bender	F	1911	Paduka, KY
Berko	F	1907	London, KY
Bertrand	M	1901	Sheridan, IN
Bertrand	F	1902	Loogooter, IN
Borowski	M	1909	Worcester, MA
Brown	F	1920	Colorado Springs, CO
Carpenter	M	1911	Newark, NJ
Carrol	F	1908	New York City, NY
Cole	M	1904	Princeton, MN
Cole	F	1905	Princeton, MN
Davisson	F	1907	Ridgeville, IN
Deyo	F	1907	Buffalo, NY
Duarte	F	1914	Tampa, FL
Duncan	F	1910	Texline, TX
Eckdahl	F	1921	Berlin, PA
Erving	M	1921	Brockton, MA
Farrar	F	1911	Clear Creek Township, IN
Fischer	M	1913	Columbiaville, NY
Folley	F	1907	New York City, NY
Friz	M	1911	Grand Rapids, MI
Glover	M	1912	Farmington, MS
Harwood	F	1903	Grafton, MA
Heilbert	F	1997	Warren, PA
Heywood	M	1998	Media, PA
Huffman	F	1904	Wheaton, MN
Judge	M	1915	New York City, NY
Kay	M	1921	Cleveland, OH
King	F	1906	Amherst, OH
Langford	F	1909	Detroit, MI
Lambert	F	1909	River Rough, MI
Lee	F	1906	Marion, IN
Lindsey	F	1907	Amherst, OH
Lowe	F	1905	Stone Church, PA
Massure	F	1908	New York City, NY
Mathieu	F	1910	Chicago, IL
Mattke	F	1907	New York City, NY
McFarland	F	1918	National Park, NJ
Miller	M	1915	Corning, IA
Miller	F	1916	Carbon, IA
Muir	F	1910	Newton, PA
Nunez	F	1906	Tampa, FL
Olson	M	1906	Sweden
Orihuela	M	1912	Tampa, FL
Peterson	M	1909	Brooklyn, NY
Peterson	F	1908	Wierton, W.VA
Pla	F	1915	Tampa, FL
Randall	F	1907	Minneapolis, MN
Roth	M	1905	New York City, NY
Sims	M	1910	New York City, NY
Smiley	M	1915	Springfield, MA
Smith	F	1908	W.VA
Stevens	M	1904	Minneapolis, MN
Stevens	F	1906	St. Paul, MN
Sucher	M	1916	Butler, IN
Sukup	F	1921	Courtdale, PA
Sykes	M	1912	Chicago, IL
Sypher	M	1904	Belair, MD
Testa	F	1913	Harrisburg, PA
Tippett	F	1998	Luckey, OH
Van Dyke	F	1907	New York City, NY
Wagner	M	1904	Irvington, NJ
Wood	M	1905	Birch, NY
Total: 65			

Notes

1. Eric Rentschler, 'Expanding Film Historical Discourse: Reception Theory's Use Value for Cinema Studies'. *Cine-Tracts* 4.1 (1981): 59–60.

2. Douglas Gomery, *Shared Pleasures* (Madison: The University of Wisconsin Press, 1992), ix–x.

3. Charlotte Kopac Herzog, *The Motion Picture Theater and Film Exhibition: 1896–1932,* (Unpublished Dissertation, Northwestern University, 1980), I.

4. Richard Koszarski, *An Evening's Entertainment: The Age of the Silent Feature Picture 1915–1928* (NY: Charles Scribner's Sons, 1990), 25.

5. Bruce Austin, *The Film Audience: An International Bibliography of Research* (NJ: The Scarecrow Press, 1983), xvii–xix.

6. Miriam Hansen, *Babel and Babylon: Spectatorship in American Silent Film* (Cambridge: Harvard University Press, 1991), 101.

7. Hansen, 3.

8. Michael Brenner, Jennifer Brown and David Canter, (Eds.) *The Research Interview: Uses and Approaches* (London: Academic Press, 1985), 2.

9. Alessandro Portelli, *The Death of Luigi Trastulli and Other Stories: Form and Meaning in Oral History* (Albany: SUNY Press, 1991), 46.

10. Shulamit Reinharz, *Feminist Methods in Social Research* (NY: Oxford University Press, 1992), 132.

11. Barbara Mostyn,'The Content Analysis of Qualitative Research Data: A Dynamic Approach'. *The Research Interview,* eds., Michael Brenner *et al.* (London: Academic Press, 1985), 116.

12. Valerie Yow, *Recording Oral History* (Thousand Oaks: Sage Publications, 1994), 6.

13. Yow, 5.

14. Robert Allen, *Vaudeville and Film* (NY: Arno Press, 1980), 14–15.

15. David Samuels, 'The Call of Stories'. *Lingua Franca* 5.4 (May/June 1995): 35.

16. Portelli, 53.

17. Paul Thompson, *The Voice of the Past: Oral History* (New York: Oxford University Press, 1988), 48.

18. Thompson, *Voice,* 101–102.

19. Portelli, 60.

20. Rentschler, 59.

21. Gomery, ix–x.

22. Timothy James Lyons, *The Silent Partner: The History of the American Film Manufacturing Company, 1910–1921* (NY: Arno Press, 1974), 14.

23. Austin, xvii.

24. Allen, 15.

25. Hansen, 3.

26. Toby Epstein Jayaratne and Abigail Stewart, 'Qauntitative and Qualitative Methods in the Social Sciences. In Mary Margaret Fonow and Judith Cook (Eds.), *Beyond Methodology* (Bloomington: Indiana University Press, 1991), 90.

27. Garth Jowett, 'The First Motion Picture Audience', *Journal of Popular Film 3* (Winter 1974): 39.

28. Thompson, *Voice,* 45.

29. Portelli, 46.

30. Portelli, viii.

31. Reinharz, 141–142.

32. Marie-Francoise Chanfrault-Duchet, 'Narrative and Socio-Symbolic Analysis', *Women's Words: The Feminist Practice of Oral History.* . Sherna Berger Gluck and Daphne Patai (Eds.) (New York: Routledge, 1991), 89.

33. Myra Jehlern, 'Archimedes and the Paradox of Feminist Criticism', *Feminism: An Anthology of Literary Theory and Criticism.* Ed. Robyn Warhol and Diane Price Herndle (New Brunswick: Rutgers University Press, 1991), 80.

34. Mostyn, 120–121.

35. Yow, 12.

36. Thompson, *Voice,* 104.

37. Thompson, *Voice,* 104–105.

38. Austin, xviii.

39. Jarvie, 94.

40. Austin, xxiii.
41. Austin, xvii–xviii.
42. Alice Keliher, 'Children and Movies: A Critical Summary of the Scientific Literature', *Films* 1 (Summer 1940): 43.
43. Austin, xxvi.
44. Arthur Kellog, 'Minds Made By the Movies', *Survey Graphic* 22 (May 1933): 245.
45. Garth Jowett, *Film: The Democratic Art* (Boston: Little, Brown and Co., 1976), 219.
46. Thompson, *Voice,* 149.
47. Paul Thompson, 'History and the Community', *Oral History.* (Eds.), David Dunaway and Willa Baum (Nashville: American Association for State and Local History, 1984), 41.
48. Allen, 15.
49. Portelli, 2.
50. Thompson, *Voice,* 40.
51. Hansen, 2.
52. Willard Sims. Audio Tape. Recorded 7 October 1994. Private Collection.
53. Harry Fischer. Audio Tape. Recorded 13 February 1993. Private Collection.
54. Dorothy Peterson and John Peterson. Audio Tape. Recorded 28 October 1994. Private Collection.
55. R.M. Kay. Audio Tape. Recorded 2 October 1994. Private Collection.
56. Jessie Lee. Audio Tape. Recorded 5 July 1994. Private Collection.
57. Ernestine Bender. Audio Tape. Recorded 3 February 1994. Private Collection.
58. Antoinett Test. Audio Tape. Recorded 20 August 1993. Private Collection.
59. Freda McFarland. Audio Tape. Recorded 14 July 1994. Private Collection.
60. Jarvie, 94.
61. Henry Heywood. Audio Tape. Recorded 29 June 1994. Private Collection.
62. Lewis Sucher. Audio Tape. Recorded 27 February 1993. Private Collection.
63. Heywood.
64. Lewis Jacobs, *The Rise of the American Film* (NY: Teachers College, Columbia University, 1968), 473.
65. Lucius Cannon, *Motion Pictures: Laws, Ordinances and Regulations* (St. Louis: St. Louis Public Library, 1920), 132.
66. Boyd Fisher, 'The Regulation of Motion Picture Theatres', *American City* (December 1912): 520.
67. Sims.
68. Ann Mosher. Audio Tape. Recorded 21 February 1994. Private Collection.
69. Edwin Stevens. Audio Tape. Recorded 6 July 1994. Private Collection.
70. Ched Smiley. Audio Tape. Recorded 1 June 1993. Private Collection.
71. Minerva Pla. Audio Tape. Recorded 10 May 1994. Private Collection.
72. Agnes King. Audio Tape. Recorded 8 December 1993. Private Collection.
73. Garth Jowett, *Film: The Democratic Art* (Boston: Little, Bron and Co., 1976) 154.
74. Hugh Glover. Audio Tape. Recorded 25 September 1993. Private Collection.
75. Marge Mathieu. Audio Tape. Recorded 5 July 1994. Private Collection.
76. Mary Eckdahl. Audio Tape. Recorded 13 August 1993. Private Collection.
77. Eckdahl.
78. Dorothy Peterson and John Peterson.
79. Lee.
80. Koszarski, 10.
81. Harry Fisher.
82. Maude Duncan. Audio Tape. Recorded 20 November 1993. Private Collection.
83. King.
84. Lee.
85. Libby Muir. Audio Tape. Recorded 27 July 1993. Private Collection.
86. Hansen, 99.
87. Peter Borowski, Audio Tape, recorded 29 July 1993. Private Collection.
88. Mosher.

89. Vernon E. Augustin, 'Moving Picture Preferences', *Journal of Delinquency* 11 (1927): 209.
90. John Roth, Audio Tape, recorded 28 June 1994. Private Collection.
91. Lee.
92. Dorothy Peterson and John Peterson, Audio Tape. Recorded 28 October 1994. Private Collection.
93. Edith Matke. Audio Tape. Recorded 1 November 1993. Private Collection.
94. Glover.
95. Borowksi.
96. Smiley.
97. Roth.
98. Ira Wood. Audio Tape. Recorded 28 January 1994. Private Collection.
99. Charles Musser, *Before the Nickelodeon* (Berkeley: University of California Press, 1991), 150.
100. Glover.
101. John F. Barry and Epes Sargent, *Building Theatre Patronage* (NY: Chalmers Publishing Company, 1927), 383.
102. Borowski.
103. Roth.
104. Sucher.
105. Koszarski, 41.
106. William Friz. Audio Tape. Recorded 12 January 1993. Private Collection.
107. Violet Heilbert. Audio Tape. Recorded 29 June 1994. Private Collection.
108. Byron Erving. Audio Tape. Recorded 17 January 1993. Private Collection.
109. Glover.
110. Lee.
111. Smiley.
112. Koszarski, 31.
113. Roth.
114. McFarland.
115. Fisher.
116. Garnett Davisson. Audio Tape. Recorded 13 July 1994. Private Collection.
117. Lee.
118. Dorothy Peterson and John Peterson.
119. Mosher.
120. Bender.
121. Mary Carrol. Audio Tape. Recorded 28 August 1993. Private Collection.
122. Warren Carpenter. Audio Tape. Recorded 2 October 1993. Private Collection.
123. Eckdahl.
124. Dorothy Peterson.
125. Elizabeth Lindsay. Audio Tape. Recorded 8 December 1993. Private Collection.
126. John W. Ripley, 'Song-Slides: Helper to Unify US Communities and Sell Sheet Music', *Films in Review* (March 1971): 147.
127. Glover.
128. Romanelle Farrar. Audio Tape. Recorded 28 February 1993. Private Collection.
129. Elizabeth Anderson. Audio Tape. Recorded 21 February 1994. Private Collection.
130. Smiley.
131. Lee.
132. E. Stevens.
133. Matke.
134. Farrar.
135. Koszarski, 41.
136. Sims.
137. Wood.
138. Smiley.
139. Koszarski, 44.
140. Muir.
141. Lee.
142. Wood.
143. Ralph Cole. Audio Tape. Recorded 3 October 1994. Private Collection.
144. Heilbert.
145. Sims.
146. Davisson.
147. Wood.

148. Heilbert.
149. Eckdahl.
150. Glover.
151. Ruth Huffman. Audio Tape. Recorded 4 April 1994. Private Collection.
152. Lindsey.
153. Kay.
154. Mosher.
155. Anna Folley. Audio Tape. Recorded 6 May 1993. Private Collection.
156. Lee.
157. Roth.
158. Fischer.
159. Roth.
160. Borowski.
161. Ervin.
162. Roth.
163. Roth.
164. Puria Lowe. Audio Tape. Recorded 28 March 1993. Private Collection.
165. McFarland.
166. Fischer.
167. Lee.
168. Reinharz, 18.
169. Mostyn, 121.
170. Portelli, 54.
171. Yow, 36.
172. Portelli, 31.
173. Portelli, 54.
174. Cannon,156.
175. Cannon, 119.
176. Borowski.
177. Imogine Miller. Audio Tape. Recorded 14 January 1994. Private Collection.
178. Matke.
179. Roth.
180. George Wagner. Audio Tape. Recorded 2 August 1993. Private Collection.
181. Bernice Bertrand. Audio Tape. Recorded 6 July 1994. Private Collection.
182. McFarland.
183. Glenn Miller. Audio Tape. Recorded 14 January 1994. Private Collection.
184. Mabel Sukup. Audio Tape. Recorded 18 August 1993. Private Collection.
185. Erving.
186. Heilbert.
187. Portelli, vii.
188. William Moss. 'Oral History: An Appreciation'. *Oral History.* Eds. David Dunaway and Willa Baum (Nashville: American Assoication For State and Local History, 1984), 98.
189. Portelli, viii.
190. Yow, 13–14.
191. Thompson, *Voice,* 73.
192. Portelli, 50.
193. Thompson, *Voice,* 149.
194. Yow, 19.
195. Thompson, *Voice,* 112–113.
196. Yow, 21.
197. Thompson, *Voice,* 112–113.
198. Portelli, 53.
199. Louis Starr, 'Oral History', *Oral History.* (Eds.) David Dunaway and Willa Baum (Nashville: American Association for State and Local History, 1984), 5.
200. Thompson, *Voice,* 248.
201. Alice Hoffman, 'Reliability and Validity in Oral History', *Oral History.* Eds., David Dunaway and Willa Baum (Nashville: American Association for State and Local History, 1984), 70.
202. Yow, 21.
203. Muir.
204. Thompson, *History*, 38.

Film History, Volume 9, pp. 49–70, 1997. Copyright © John Libbey & Company
ISSN: 0892-2160. Printed in Australia

Screen images of the 'other' in Wilhelmine Germany & the United States, 1890–1918

Daniel J. Leab

> The cinema is the mirror of our epoch
> in which everything must be reflected ...
> *G. W. Pabst, 1933.*
>
> Was ist aus den Durschnitts-Produktionen ...
> zu entnehmen über *ihre* Zeit?
> *Rainer Rother, 1991.*

Art is influenced by history. Film is art, but it is also commerce – and much more. For the past few decades, the influences on art, on history and on film have been the subject of vigorous, sometimes foolish debate, much of it unfortunately centred on marginalia at the edges of important substantive areas. Thus, even a film with limited distribution becomes a touchstone, but it cannot and should not serve as the basis for a theoretical framework designed to displace a *Casablanca* with its extremely popular World War II view of the German, or a widely distributed *Verlorene Sohn* and its 1934 depiction of the Depression in New York City. A great many arguments have been postulated about the differences between the 'personal' and the 'political', between the 'political' and 'art'. The oft-cited Jurgen Habermas, in a somewhat different context, strenuously discussed the urgent need to 'force a reconciliation between 'art' and 'life'.[1] It seems to me, however, that his 'take' on life narrows it, especially in terms of movies. Whatever restrictions on censorship may have existed, the bulk of the movies produced in the United States and Germany never lost their ability to perceive external reality (probably they helped to create and refine it). Whatever ambivalent images they project now or did at the time of their initial release, the movies made in these two countries, because they had a solid sense of self, did not alienate their viewers.

What is 'self'? The word has had different meanings over the years. A generation ago, according to Webster's, 'self' as an adjective meant 'Having its own or a single nature or character, as in colour, composition, etc.; as self-coloured' – and as a noun, 'self', among other things, was defined as 'an individual considered as an identical person; ... a being in relation to its own identity'.[2] More recently, 'self' as a concept has become more fluid,

Daniel J. Leab, author of numerous books and articles on film and history, is Professor of History at Seton Hall University. He delivered an earlier version of this paper in July 1995 at the German Historical Institute in Washington, D.C. Correspondence c/o PO Box 1216, Washington, CT 06793, USA.

especially as post-structuralist thought has developed, influenced by such theorists as the French psychoanalyst, Jacques Lacan. Its promised insights are based, of course, not only on Lacanian psychoanalysis but also on the equally fascinating but sometimes contradictory theories derived from Derridean deconstruction, feminist discourse, Althusserian Marxism, reception studies and Foucauldian historiography. They have all played a significant role in the changing perceptual shifts that mark recent scholarship and academic discourse in fields such as literature and history, as well as the study of film and its impact.

In the latter area one manifestation of what Bill Nichols termed 'the self-as-subject' means that its determination becomes (in his words) 'an ideological question' best treated by looking at 'roles, conventions, attitudes, language', which through the 'constancies of repetition' result in a particular view of the self – a broad view.[3] Thus the self is represented by, and represents, a series of images, spiralling through reiteration. These images, even though periodically inconsistent and occasionally contradictory, form at one important level a national cinema. This cinema grapples with the present, the past, and occasionally even the future. The French historian Pierre Sorlin has astutely declared that film 'is a mere framework, serving as a basis or counterpoint ...'[4] There is, then, what the Germanist Richard McCormack has termed a 'Politics of the Self'.[5] Thus, each national self as defined by a particular cinema differs dramatically. And, therefore, the movies produced for much of this century in the United States and Germany (before and during partition, and after reunification) highlight various concepts of nationhood and individual destiny for men and women.

One valid, interesting approach to studying the images of self that a film-making process attuned to such concepts generates is to examine various movies at different points in time. I am limiting myself to those years when movies were becoming the mass medium in Germany and the United States (a time span from the 1890s to the end of World War I) and to some of the early cultural influences which helped to shape the medium in those countries. The German view of the American self during those years serves as a useful vehicle for comparison. The American film image of Germany during that same time frame may be even more important because of the global cultural hegemony that came to be exercised by movies produced in the United States. By 1919, the movies, to use critic Gilbert Seldes' phrase, 'came from America'.[6]

World War I made that hegemony possible. After war's outbreak in 1914, European film activity declined precipitously. As a recent history points out, the continental film-makers 'increasingly felt the effect of lost personnel, lost resources, lost markets', while their United States counterparts took 'advantage of their competitors' distractions'.[7] The statistics speak for themselves: film exports from the United States, which did not enter the war until 1917, rose from 36,000,000 feet in 1915 to over 158,000,000 feet in 1916. By war's end in 1918, according to Robert Sklar, the United States 'was said to produce some 85 per cent of the films shown throughout the world'.[8]

Such films, because of the American movie industry's frenzied commitment to the war effort, portrayed Germans viciously; as part of an overheated propaganda campaign, their self and their society were given no redeeming qualities and many reprehensible ones. But even before the war, American movies did not portray Germans attractively. Even in the decade before the war, when, as a group, German men and women (and German-Americans who could be viewed as their surrogates) elicited much admiration for their thrift, honesty, industriousness and perseverance, they did not fare well in the popular culture. It made no difference, for example, that in 1908, as historian John Higham reports, 'a group of professional people, in rating the traits of various immigrant nationalities ranked the Germans above the English and in some respects superior to native whites'.[9]

Nor did it really matter that Wilhelmine Germany received praise from many Americans for its scientific, industrial and cultural achievements, for its university system (at the time, as historian Frederick Luebke notes, American 'leaders in higher education ... repeatedly expressed their indebtedness to the German example') and for its value system (Theodore Roosevelt among others extolled its 'genius for order and efficiency').[10] Indeed, in 1913, in his best-selling autobiography former President Roosevelt, whose mind World War I poisoned against Germany, declared it 'impossible' to

Fig. 1. The Katzenjammer Kids' by Rudolph Dirks. A 1901 panel from the Hearst press.

feel that 'Germans were really foreigners'.[11] Yet, for all that, Americans did not cotton to Germany, its ruler Kaiser Wilhelm, or its people. Many in the United States deemed Wilhelmine Germany's domestic politics and foreign policy as arrogant and capricious, and scholars have pointed out that Americans often found ominous a 'militaristic ... Imperial Germany that followed Bismarck's "blood and iron" policy' which was seen as 'the subordination of civilian to military considerations in the conduct of government'.[12] Americans might have respected, admired, at times emulated, and occasionally feared Germany and the Germans; but, in the context of American popular culture, the country and its citizens were not well liked.

That lack of affection can best be gleaned and understood by quickly reviewing the German-American image prevalent in American popular culture for a generation before World War I. Ethnic stereotyping, unfortunately, remains a useful measurement of popular culture in a free society such as the United States The response to the German in America provides an interesting and useful yardstick. An inward-looking United States, concerned with many social problems, had relatively little concern about 'the old country', but much interest in an immigrant group, which in 1910 numbered among the largest ethnic blocs in the United States In an era when racial libels abounded (consider the treatment of Jews, Blacks and Italians), the stereotyping of Germans did not deteriorate into nastiness, but was unkind, condescending, disparaging, ridiculous and all too often mean-spirited – what the journalist Mark Sullivan described subsequently as 'a mocking note ... a little touched by jeering'.[13] One of the many popular pre-World War I songs dealing with

Germans in America, 'Dot Leedle German Band', typifies many of these attitudes:

> Dot leedle German band, dot leedle German band;
> De beoble cry and say 'oh my!' as we march drough de land
> Ve go around de screeds almost every day
> Und sit de beoble vild mit de music dot ve blay;
> 'Goodbye Sourheart', und 'Heime Sweet Heime', we blay so fine,
> But ve always do our best ven ve blay 'De Wacht am Rhein.[14]

Making fun of an ethnic group denies it positive qualities. The image of the male German, either in the United States or in his homeland, emphasised beer drinking and a lack of imagination. The stage, burlesque and vaudeville, abounded with pig-headed, comically bellicose Germans, all of whom – according to one show-business history – had 'padded stomachs, wore chin whiskers, blond wigs, small brown derbies, checkered trousers, big shoes, fancy vests with heavy watchchains, and murdered the English language'.[15]

From its debut in 1897, *The Katzenjammer Kids* – one of the earliest and most successful of the newly developing newspaper comic strips – highlighted such fracturing of the language. An unabashed ripoff of the German cartoonist Wilhelm Busch's popular *Max und Moritz* (the illustrated adventures of two devilish young boys), *The Katzenjammer Kids* depicts, as comic enthusiast Maurice Horn puts it, 'the guerilla war ... conducted by Hans and Fritz ... against any form of authority... indeed against society itself'.[16] The strip's creator, Rudolph Dirks, made very effective use of crazy-quilt English–German pidgen. For the boys, 'society isst nix', but they were likeable and not really threatening, perhaps because of the attention proferred them by 'die Mama' (a rotund, middle-aged, stereotypical hausfrau), 'der Captain' (their adoptive father, a shipwrecked sailor rescued by die Mama), 'der Inspector' (a white-bearded truant officer patterned on the lower-echelon German civil service). Occasional characters included die Mama's somewhat dimwitted brother, not so subtly called 'Heinie'.

Commercial production and exhibition of motion pictures (in one form or another) began in the United States during the mid-1890s. Charles Musser convincingly argues that 'commercial motion pictures in fact began in 1894 with Edison's peephole kinetoscope'.[17] Well into the first years of the twentieth century, the movie industry produced only short films, most of them running only a few minutes. Exhibitors strung them together to make up a program. Emphasis on a film which told a story did not come until 1907–08. The already prevalent stereotypes of the German self found their way easily into all types of films. As I have pointed out elsewhere, a good example of such stereotyping is *A Bucket of Cream Ale, a* 1904 Biograph film that ran less than 360 seconds and was meant to be funny; it showed a black serving woman, after considerable provocation 'dumping a bucket of beer on the head of a stereotypical German burgher'.[18]

More than just occasionally a positive note does creep in. The 1909 Biograph drama, *The Voice of the Violin* represents this side of the coin, but one with relatively few imitators. In this short film Herr von Schmitt, an immigrant who makes his living as a violin teacher, falls in love with the daughter of what the Biograph plot synopsis describes as 'a wealthy capitalist'. The violinist saves the lives of father and daughter in a stirring climax: a bomb has been planted in the basement of the family mansion; 'bound hand and foot von Schmitt crawls towards the bomb', and as the company publicity blurb declares, 'with his teeth bites the fuse in two as its is within a few inches of igniting the terror bomb'.[19]

Such unambiguous representation found little duplication in the longer feature films that became the bulk of the American industry's output in the years immediately preceding and following the outbreak of World War I in August 1914. What Eileen Bowser has characterised as 'feature fever' transformed United States film production.[20] The traditional stereotypes of the German self found their way into these features. To cite just a few examples: Cecil B. DeMille's 1915 drama *Kindling* (based on a 1911 Broadway play) centred on 'Honest' Heinie Schultz and his family, who escaped from the snares of New York City slum life; the actor Lew Fields transferred from the stage to the movies his characterisation of 'an old-fashioned ... German' who finds his way in America;[21] in November 1915 Triangle films, then an important studio, successfully released *Old Heidelberg,* with the rising star Wallace Reid as the lead, which dealt with the heir to a Central European throne who temporarily finds happiness while enrolled at a German university (any similarity to *The Student Prince* is not coincidental).

These representations of the German self gave way to other, much more antagonistic images as the war strongly and adversely affected United States popular culture even before America became a belligerent in April 1917. The country's road to war was a winding one upon which the United States trod gingerly and slowly. In 1914 when the war began, President Woodrow Wilson urged citizens of the neutral United States to be 'impartial in thought as well as action', neutral 'in fact as well as name'. He even urged that movie audiences (in his biographer's words) 'refrain from demonstrating in any way in favor of either side'.[22] The general response was relief that the Atlantic separated the United States from the belligerents and the battlefields. But in time, anti-German sentiment became the order of the day. In part this attitudinal change resulted from a skillful British propaganda campaign, and in part the change was due to ill-conceived German actions such as the invasion of Belgium (and the dismissal by the Kaiser's government of the treaty guaranteeing Belgian neutrality as just 'a scrap of paper'), the implementation of unrestricted submarine warfare (which periodically resulted in the sinking of passenger vessels and the deaths of noncombatants, most notably in 1915 with the torpedoing of the *Luisitania*), and the occasionally destructive but ultimately ineffectual attempts by German agents to sabotage American industries producing war material. While there was also a push among some Americans for 'preparedness', for increasing military strength, it had relatively little support. Wilson successfully ran for reelection in 1916 as a 'peace candidate' ('War in the East! Peace in the West! Thank God for Wilson! ... He Kept Us Out of the War!!')[24]

Americans may have voted for peace, but at the movies they opted for war. Film historian Timothy Lyons has said that themes of war 'figured importantly in providing the type of escapist entertainment demanded by audiences'.[25] Between 1914 and 1917 some features dealt with hostilities abroad, some favoured preparedness, some endorsed neutrality, and some dealt with supposed invasions of the United States Invariably the Germans came off badly. One of the greatest box-office triumphs of 1916 was Thomas Ince's *Civilization,* a mammoth spectacle that ended with Christ successfully preaching his gospel of peace to a mythical, aggressive war-making king; but as *Variety* pointed out at the time, 'while the 'foreword' ... announces the spectacle as pure allegory, the mythical kingdom, the king ... and the soldiers ... were unmistakably Teutonic types ...'.[26]

Such anti-German sentiment pervaded more propagandistic films. *The Battle Cry of Peace* (1915), another box-office hit made a shrill cry for 'preparedness' in which New York City is shelled into submission by an invading fleet. Captured American civilians are machine-gunned, and a mother kills her two daughters to spare them 'a fate worse than death'. The film avoided identifying the enemy, but as he AFI catalogue points out, 'the beer drinking parties and the Kaiser Wilhelm moustaches of the invading soldiers typified prevailing German stereotypes'. Certainly the film's creator counted on this response: J. Stuart Blackton thought that 'America's ... interests were closely identified with the Allies'.[27]

Thomas Dixon's *The Fall of a Nation* (1916) did not hesitate to identify Germans as the enemy. In this controversial but commercially unsuccessful sequel to his racist *The Birth of a Nation* (1915), Dixon put together a tale of invasion, rape, and what *Variety* described as 'spirited, night-riding' conspirators backed by German finances, arms and troops who seize control of the United States before finally being routed.[28]

This kind of 'political fiction' (to make use of a term utilised by two Swedish critics in dealing with this kind of film) found its counterpart in other sorts of films which also presented a negative view of the German self.[29] In *Arms and the Woman* (1916), a somewhat overwrought drama centred on a Hungarian immigrant who becomes a successful opera singer in America, German spies blow up a munitions factory. Towards the end of *The Ivory Snuff Box,* an indifferent 1915 mystery, the German head of a Brussels sanitarium tortures an American detective in front of his new wife. *The Ordeal,* a 1914 film set in part during the Franco–Prussian War, includes a scene in which a German general strongly resembling Kaiser Wilhelm fails to extract

Fig. 2. In *The Flying Torpedo* (Fine Arts, 1916), a futuristic tale of enemy agents preparing the invasion of America, the presence of Erich von Stroheim was a strong clue to the ethnicity of the conspirators. [Richard Koszarski Collection.]

information from a French officer, and so shoots the officer's mother, sister and sweetheart before his eyes. (This film was so biased that during the height of the anti-German hate campaign of 1918 it was re-released as *The Mother of Liberty*.)[30]

Social scientists and others concerned with the impact of the movies on public opinion have long been sharply divided as to whether films influence an audience or mirror its ideas and feelings. However one views that influence, it is clear that during the three war years that the United States was officially neutral, Germans on-screen (as in many other areas of American popular culture) fared badly. All positive aspects of the German self had dribbled away. Social historian Garth Jowett correctly points out that 'the American cinema was mobilised against Germany well before Wilson led the nation into war'.[31]

That bias notwithstanding, American movie audiences before United States entry into the war did have some opportunity to see a different view of the Germans, in so-called 'factual films' akin to feature-length newsreels and dealing more with life on the home front than with combat at the trenches. According to one study, such movies as the 1916 *Germany on the Firing Line* were 'highly successful ... and widely shown'.[32] A cynical *Variety* reviewer commenting in 1915 on the newly released *The German Side of the War* described it as 'a direct appeal to the German-American' and concluded that 'somebody ... is taking advantage of the hyphenated'.[33] And did so with considerable success. The film journalist Terry Ramsaye in 1926, recalling 'four-block-long lines', wrote 'no attraction before or since has the record of such a sensation in so short a time'.[34] But ultimately such films had little impact and could not offset the increasingly negative movie image of the German.

Whatever chance there might have been of improving the image of the German collapsed on American entry into the war in 1917. The Wilson administration maintained that the enemy was the autocratic Kaiser and his undemocratic regime, not the German people, towards whom the president expressed 'sympathy and friendship' in his speech asking Congress for a declaration of war. But the administration's frenzied rousing of support for the war resulted in an anti-German hysteria sweeping the United States.[35]

For the next years, every possible manifestation of German influence came under attack. Operas, symphonic music, even hymns of German origin were boycotted. The syndicators of *The Katzenjammer Kids* found it expedient to rename the comic strip *The Shenanigan Kids.* Renaming became a popular pastime: sauerkraut became 'liberty cabbage', hamburgers became 'liberty sandwiches' and daschunds became 'liberty pups'; the Germanic Bank of Milwaukee became the National Bank of Commerce, and the Germania Life Insurance of St. Paul became the Guardian Life; the well-known actor Gustav von Seyfferittz changed his name to G. Butler Clonbaugh, explaining that he had 'a perfect right' to this new name as it 'belonged to his mother'; after the war he reverted to the original.[36]

Anything of German origin became suspect. An auxiliary of the Federal government's Bureau of Investigation justified its extra-legal monitoring of German-Americans by charging that Wilhelmine Germany counted upon them 'to help her win the war'. A Brooklyn Congregational minister described the Lutheran Church as 'not the bride of Christ but the paramour of Kaiserism'.[37] German-Americans were accused of subversions, sabotage and worse (e.g. they were accused of putting ground glass in bandages and food sent to soldiers). The German-American Karl Struss, a noted innovative photographer in pre-World War I New York City, suffered grieviously for his ethnic heritage and indiscreet attitudes,and after war's end went West to become a celebrated cinematographer (but although realising he was not the only person who had been treated unfairly as a result of the country's overheated patriotic fervour. He remained 'bitter' as well as concerned, and later 'fabricated' and stuck to a story that would obcure his detention). Significantly contributing to this chorus of hate was a propaganda-oriented American film industry which participated with a vengeance, so much so that, as film historian Kevin Brownlow quite rightly points out, the industry 'must take a large part of the responsibility for the campaign launched ... in the United States during World War I'.[38]

That campaign, although directed at German-Americans, contributed significantly to the extremely negative view of the German self. As a group, the German-Americans received just as rough treatment on-screen as did the citizens of 'the Fatherland'. Many an American movie in 1917 and 1918 expressed concern about the loyalty of German-Americans and stigmatised them. As historian Jack Spears put it, German-Americans were 'condemned ... as a people disloyal'.[39]

Ad infinitum, ad nauseam, features showed German-Americans planning to destroy United States munitions plants, to undermine the war effort by spreading pro-German propaganda, to pass vital secret information to the enemy. German-Americans, acting as agents for the enemy, operated on every level of society in the United States according to the movies. *Draft 258* laid bare, according to the *Motion Picture News,* 'the workings of German intrigue ... to enlist the ... pacifist as a tool ... against the United States'.[40] In a 1918 William S. Hart vehicle, *The Border Wireless,* a German-American mine owner supervises a gang of spies transmitting to Berlin intelligence that they had gathered. *On the Jump,* a 1918 action film, has a dashing reporter expose his newspaper's owner as 'custodian of a German fund to establish anti-Allied newspapers in the United States' and as a spy.[41]

In 1900 Kaiser Wilhelm II, while inspecting German troops being sent to participate in the international response to the Boxer Rebellion in China, with his usual exuberant thoughtlessness exhorted the troops to 'Give no quarter! Take no prisoners! Kill the foe ... Even as a thousand years ago, the Huns under ... Attila ...'.[42] His speech received a great deal of publicity both inside and outside Germany. When World War I broke out, a highly effective British propaganda campaign made 'Hun' a common derogatory synonym for German, and upon American entry into the war the United States movie industry became a very active part of the 'Hate-the-Hun' campaign.

The Hun behaved with unbelievable brutality on screen. In the 1917 melodrama *For France* the Huns humble a French mother. The 1918 Cecil B. DeMille production *Till I Come Back to You* included scenes of Belgian children working in German war

Fig. 3. Lithographic poster for *Hearts of the World* (Griffith, 1918). [Foundation for Modern Art.]

industries as whipped and starved slave labour. Master filmmaker D. W. Griffith's *Hearts of the World* (1918), much of which is set in a French village, depicted what the *New York Times* critic described as 'the horrors of German occupation'.[43] In *A Maid of Belgium* (1917), whose Belgian scenes one critic described as 'a typical account of that country's distress', a young woman as the result of a devastating German shelling of her village suffers amnesia and dreadful hardships before being brought to the United States.[44] The Hun did not even scruple to unleash the 'yellow peril'; one of the advertising tag lines of Samuel Goldwyn's *For the Freedom of the East* (1918) was 'Berlin's sinister sneering agent advanced to raise the floodgate and drown the world under the flood of China's 400 million people'.[45]

Two of the most sensational and commercially successful atrocity films were *The Little American,* a 1917 feature film starring 'America's Sweetheart', Mary Pickford and *My Four Years in Germany,* a 1918 effort loosely based on the memoirs of James Gerard, a wealthy Democrat politician who served as the American ambassador in Berlin from 1913 to 1917.

In Pickford's film, as the result of what can be described as an extraordinary series of circumstances, she, the eponymous heroine, witnesses the drowning of women and children in the aftermath of a U-boat attack, the burning of priceless antiques from a French chateau by indifferent German soldiers in need of firewood, the execution of innocent civilian hostages by heartless Hun officers. The film's characters also include Karl, a German immigrant to America who loves 'the little American'. In 1914 he goes back to Germany for military service. So brutalised does he become that on a dark night our heroine is assaulted by Karl, 'who in his lust and the dark does not recognise her until it is almost too late', as one historian gently puts it.[46] She becomes a French spy as a result of her experiences, is found out and sentenced to death. A repentant Karl denounces the Kaiser and joins her before the firing squad, but at the last moment they escape death and, as one reviewer put it, 'they live happily ever afterward'.

My Four Years in Germany, an ambitious film dealing with Gerard's tenure, included scenes set in German prisoner-of-war camps. People are shown being beaten, set on by vicious guard dogs, scrambling for scraps of bread. British soldiers are thrown in with Russians suffering from typhus; a German officer who is asked why the Russians are not quarantined responds that 'they're Allies. Let them get acquainted.' A trade journal summed up this film when it admiringly declared that 'there is no stone left unturned to arouse the audience to a sense that the German manner of conducting war is synonymous with barbarism ...'.[47] Kevin Brownlow has found 'the simplemindedness of the film ... beyond belief', but points out that audience reaction 'everywhere was ecstatic ... enthusiastic'.[48]

My Four Years in Germany vilified the Kaiser so broadly that he was burlesqued. A recent viewer of the film found that it still had impact, but that the Kaiser as a character 'calls up memories of Groucho Marx'.[49] But in many a film, the Kaiser became the focal point for anti-German propaganda. He served the same purpose as Goldstein (Big Brother's arch-rival) in Orwell's *1984*; the Kaiser was an object of 'HATE ...'. He fit perfectly the stereotype of the 'hated Hun', with his arrogant stare, upturned mustache and arched eyebrows. Winsor McCay's animated one-reeler *The Sinking of the Luisitania* (1918) ends with the title: 'The man who fired the shot was decorated for it by the Kaiser! – and yet they tell us not to hate the Hun.'[50] And in movie after movie the Hun in the form of the Kaiser was vilified and so were the actions of his people. The American movie industry produced a series of 'Get-the-Kaiser' films incorporating the usual atrocity clichés. The most notorious of these films, *The Kaiser – The Beast of Berlin* (1918), was advertised as 'giving insight into the man guiding the most horrible outrages'.[51]

Other ethnic groups in the United States have been treated harshly and depicted viciously. Racism, bigotry and prejudice are unfortunately also part of the often splendid American heritage. The German self therefore was not unique in the treatment it received from the American movie industry before and during World War I. Ethnic stereotyping, as with the movie depiction of Afro-Americans, lasted for generations. Unfortunately, because of subsequent circumstances, Germans (who certainly were not unique in being perceived negatively) never really overcame on-screen the image that damned them. The view of the German self arrived at during World War I, although ultimately modified, remained, in one critic's words 'like a bad stain in a washed garment ...'.[52]

The image of the United States never suffered such maltreatment on-screen (or off) in Wilhelmine Germany, not even after American entry into World War I in 1917. Indeed, from the outset of hostilities in 1914, Germany's war propaganda was marred by inadequacy and was poorly organised and co-ordinated; as media specialist Philip Taylor has convincingly demonstrated, Germany's civilian and military leaders 'appreciated too late that modern warfare required as much attention to the munitions of the mind as to the planning of battles'.[53] The Germans had never been of one mind about the United States between the mid-1890s and the end of World War I in 1918. During these years, the emphasis of what a German critic has termed 'cliché ideas' about the United States and its inhabitants obviously were influenced not only by events on the world stage but also by class attitudes.[54] These ideas found little middle ground. As the German-born American historian Hans Gatzke has remarked, they 'tended towards extremes of admiration or condescension'.[55]

The latter included a view of Americans as unceasingly violent and crassly materialistic. Even years later a German journalist, looking back, despaired at the interest in a 'fast buck'.[56] German elites especially considered the United States a 'nation without culture' ('*ein Land ohne Kultur*'), given to excesses of democracy. Even so friendly and thoughtful an observer as Count von Bernstorff, Wilhelmine Germany's ambassador to the United States in the years preceding World War I, wrote home to a friend that Congress 'might just as well adjourn, as its debates were not likely to be effective' ('*Nach unseren Erfahrungen ware es jedenfalls an besten wenn die Leute bald wieder nach Hause gingen, denn bei dem Herum doktorieren ... kommt doch night viel heraus ...*').[57] One German professor at the time maintained that 'as a result of ... the immodest striving after success ... Americans have had their nerves overstrained and ... become an unhealthy nation'.[58]

Andrew Dickson White, American ambassador to Germany between 1897 and 1902, was 'especially concerned' about the 'strong anti-American disposition among the highly educated'.[59] And it existed on both sides of the political fence. The radical Socialist Karl Liebknecht during his 1910 tour of the United States expressed deep concern at 'the effort to secure the almighty dollar' and the 'worship of the god Mammon'.[60] Columbia University historian Fritz Stern, in looking back on this era, reports that 'conservative writers in Imperial Germany' feared that its 'soul would be destroyed by "Americanisation", that is by mammonism, materialism, mechanisation and the mass society'.[61]

Many other Germans, however, saw America

in a very different, more positive light. They drew their inspiration from the judgment expressed decades earlier by Goethe:

> Amerika, du hast es besser
> Als unser Kontinent, das alte ...
> (America, thy happy lot
> Above old Europe's I exault ...)[62]

They believed that the United States was a 'golden country' ('ein Goldenes Land'), ripe with opportunity, the prototypical democratic society where everybody had a chance to make good. What one historian has characterised as 'open minded Germans trying to modernise their country' looked to the United States as a model for political and economic systems.[63] For them, Americanisation was not a blight but a guidepost to a better future.

That belief in America had led tens of thousands of German to emigrate to the United States (Kathleen Neils Cozzens estimates that 'between 1850 and 1900 Germans were never less than a quarter of all the foreign born' in the United States and that between 1880 and 1920 they were the 'largest single element among first-generation immigrants'; Walter Nugent in his study of 'the great Atlantic migrations' in the half-century before World War I notes that 'German migrants overwhelmingly opted for the United States'.)[64] Many of these emigrants wrote home about the wondrous opportunities available in America; and often accompanied these letters with remittances, or in due course returned home for a visit (such visits by a 'rich uncle from America' became a recurrent motif in Wilhelmine Germany's popular culture, including the movies).

An admiration for America and things American manifested itself in a variety of ways and for a number of reasons. Notwithstanding the condescension of the elites, the Kaiser, in pursuit of an admittedly ambiguous foreign policy, both confronted (especially in Latin America and the Far East) and courted, the United States. Attempts, for example, to woo America and President Theodore Roosevelt between 1901 and 1909 included the establishment of 'Roosevelt Professorships' in American subjects at leading German universities, the donation of a valuable collection to a Harvard University museum, the Kaiser's commissioning of a United States boatyard to build a yacht later launched by President Roosevelt's daughter Alice, a 'good will' tour of the United States in 1902 by the Kaiser's brother, and the gift of a bronze statue of Frederick the Great to the American people for their friendly reception of the prince. Unfortunately, Germany mishandled many of these actions and, as Hans Jürgen Schröeder points out, they proved 'counterproductive'.[65] Yet interest in America remained strong. Between 1903 and 1906 at least 17 German travel books on America were published, and by 1913 over 250 translations of Mark Twain and Bret Harte had appeared. Germany's capital, Berlin, was characterised by an English observer as among 'the most American of European cities'.[66] Situated along the Spree river, this bustling, dynamic city was often referred to by many Germans as 'Spreechicago' in those years.[67] A logo of crossed German and American flags was on top of the proscenium framing the screen in the city's first large movie theatre (opened in 1909 and seating over 600) as well as in the ads announcing the films being shown.[68] But while interest in America remained strong, 'analysis of the German image of America during the years 1890–1918' (as Ragnhild Fiebig argued presciently a few years ago) 'suggest that a transformation process was underway that did not strengthen a good German-American understanding'.[69]

Until recently the early years of the German cinema have been a neglected field of study, in large measure because of the late Siegfried Kracauer's 1947 book *From Caligari To Hitler,* which has been correctly summed up as an 'ingenious fusion of mass psychology, popularisation of the philosophy of negativity and historiographical simplification of barbarism ...'; for many years Kracauer 'laid down the law governing any treatment of silent cinema in Germany'.[70] A refugee from the Nazis, he wrote the book in New York City in the early 1940s, drew on his memory and experiences as well as the limited materials available to him, and produced a seminal work on 'Weimar cinema', which maintained that 'it was only after the first World War that the German cinema really came into being. Its history up to that time ... was insignificant.'[71] Those challenging Kracauer's judgment are fortunate to have many more resources (including films) at their command. A dynamic new gener-

Fig. 4. German troops attend a screening at a front-movie theatre. [Courtesy Wolfgang Mühl-Benninghaus.]

ation of scholars (mostly but not exclusively German, many of them women) have provided new insights as well as having revised older arguments, although continuing, as a recent historiography avers, 'to be mediated to one extent or another by ... Kracauer's work'.[72]

The film industry in Germany began as in the United States during the mid-1890s, but developed more slowly than its American counterpart. Production, distribution and exhibition evolved at a less frenetic pace. And only because of the war was the German screen able to break free from foreign (especially French) domination and establish what Corinna Müller, one of the best practitioners of the new film history, has termed an 'indigenous Kinokultur'; she found that in 1914 at war's outbreak 'only about 15 per cent of the German demand for film could be covered by domestic production'.[73] Germany was inundated with productions from France, Italy, Scandinavia and the United States. The war and censorship had by 1917 ended most imports.

The cutoff from the international film market stimulated the German film industry in various ways. In 1913 there were eleven production companies, in 1918 over 130; in 1913 there were 19 distributors, by 1918 over 50; between 1914 and 1919 nearly 700 movie theatres opened. The populace clamoured for diversion from the increasingly bitter, all-consuming war, and as a German journalist recalled, 'cinemas grew up like mushrooms in the cities and large towns'.[74] Initially, after war's outbreak, the industry produced what one history aptly described as *feldgrau Filmkitsch*, films such as 'How Max Got the Iron Cross' (*Wie Max des Eiserine Kreuz erwarb*).[75] But movie goers wanted escapism, not celluloid excesses of patriotism.

Germany's ruling classes recognised the importance of the movies as a force to raise morale at home and counter Allied propaganda abroad (especially among European neutrals such as the Dutch). In early 1917, at the initiative of General Erich Ludendorff, the all-powerful virtual dictator of wartime Wilhelmine Germany (the Kaiser had become almost a figurehead), the army set up the Photograph and Film Office (Bild und Film Amt) to create and distribute cultural propaganda. Anxious to enhance BUFA's mission, Ludendorff, who believed that 'the war has demonstrated the superiority of ... film as a means of information and persuasion', asserted that 'it is of the utmost importance for a successful conclusion to the war that films should be made to work with the greatest possible effect'.[76] His urgings led to the formation in December 1917 of the Universum Film AG, which incorporated most of Germany's leading film companies. The government supplied one-third of the capital of 25 million Marks. Despite the government's one-third ownership of UFA (which did assume various of BUFA's responsibilities), it did not live up to Ludendorff's expectations. The exigencies of the war kept UFA, which later became a giant, in 'diapers' (to use Erich Angermann's term).[77] Moreover, UFA's leadership, in decisions which reportedly 'enraged' Ludendorff, emphasised entertainment at the expense of propaganda.[78]

The general presided over a country increasingly weary of war. The troops had marched off in 1914 certain of victory and a quick return home. Instead they stumbled into a deadly war of attrition in the trenches on the Western front. Meanwhile, on the homefront, for many Germans the standard of living steadily deteriorated as there were shortages of almost everything. Given the ongoing massive casualties, few families escaped unscathed. Real life was very different from the censored war on the nation's screens. Yet the country escaped the ecstasy of hate that had spread so rapidly across America in 1917 after the United States declared war and the Wilson administration mobilised the country. Still, the German patriotic zeal of 1914 had an effect on the country's public life: UFA established its offices on Berlin's Potsdamer Platz in a building called 'Haus Vaterland' (which until the war had been called 'Picadilly'); elsewhere in Berlin the 'Picadilly Cafe' became the 'Deutsches Cafe'. Max Winterfeld, a composer who before 1914 had adopted the French pseudonym Jean Gilbert, found it expedient to drop the first name and pronunciation 'a la Francais' for the duration of the war; later, reports Michael Hanisch, 'he again remembered that first name' (*Spater, nach dem Krieg, sollte er sich wieder seines Vornames eninern*).[79]

Fig. 5. Lithographic poster by Josef Fenneker for Fern Andra's *Genuine* (Decla-Bioscop, 1920). [Deutsches Filmmuseum.]

Even after United States' entry into the war, America remained less of a propaganda target than Britain or France. The United States was, as

Frank Trommler has argued, 'only a thin silhouette on the western horizon behind' them.[80] Fern Andra, who specialised in what have been called 'Demi-Mondaine' roles, had been born in Illinois in the early 1890s.[81] As Fern Andrews she had worked her way to Europe as a dancer. She made her first German film in 1913. She quickly became a leading player, Germany's first 'vamp'. Sexy, charming, talented, she reportedly wore only enough clothes on-screen to make clear what she would have looked like naked. Extremely ambitious, she produced and wrote her films. Expert at public relations, she was described by a German journalist as a 'Genie der Reklame' (a genius at advertising). In 1917 she overcame hostile feelings towards her as an American, including absurd charges of espionage, in part by marrying a Prussian baron.[82] He was killed in action, but the Fern Andra Film Co. and its principal carried on successfully through the war.

In the main, World War I had little impact on how the German cinema portrayed the American self. That image had been established visually by the American films imported from the United States. Although the war ultimately ended their exhibition, the national image of America remained. That image drew on others prevalent in the popular culture of pre-war Wilhelmine Germany. Thus the American Westerns imported by the score built on the fanciful writings of Karl May, novels that Kracauer, among many others, described as 'set in an imaginary Far West and full of fabulous events involving Indian tribes, covered wagons, traders, hunters, tramps and adventurers'.[83] What was described as 'amerikanischen Knock-about-Farce', with comedians like John Bunny and Fatty Arbuckle (because of the war Charlie Chaplin films did not get distribution until after 1918), achieved great acceptance; the artist George Grosz remembered with pleasure laughing at Bunny and his jokes ('Schnünen').[84] But overall, unlike the United States where almost no German films achieved exhibition, in Germany until the war, movies from America (even if imported in numbers far fewer than their French or Italian counterparts) substantially contributed to the establishment of particular images.

These images played a pivotal, fascinating role during the debate in Wilhelmine Germany on what movies should be. American movies were very popular in Germany. But with their emphasis on slapstick and action, they were judged to have a touch of 'brutality'.[85] Thus even many of the popular Bronco Billy westerns were *verboten* by the censor for children or would have scenes such as a lynching cut from the released prints. Moreover, the very qualities which made American films popular were part of what the better elements (who emphasised the quality of German *kultur*) denigrated and denounced as trash (*Schundfilme*). Interestingly, the Kaiser, contemporaries agreed, 'had a personal interest in movies'.[86] He was a fan of movies, both as entertainment and as propaganda; he had a secret private-screening room, and he gave film-makers what now would be called photo-opportunities for all kinds of functions such as state visits or military manoeuvres with the resulting 'Akualitätten' promoted as undertaken at the command of the Kaiser ('Allerhöchster Befehl') or with the Kaiser's approval ('Allerhöchster Genehmigung'). The industry characterised him as a 'friend of cinema' ('Freunde des Kinos').[87] The criticisms of what was shown in the main did not stem from him.

In order to meet such criticisms, the nascent German film industry just as it was turning to feature production in 1912–13 began producing films based on plays and novels of recognised value or on scripts by established literary figures. One result was movies that did not move. Another was audience dissatisfaction. An irritated German writer of the time, who did not think much of American movies (which he judged as 'ein ganz Kleines Kaliber'), ultimately, in exasperation at the unattractiveness of much of the domestic film product, declared that it should be possible to go to the movies without running into 'Hamlet, Dostoyevsky, Ibsen, Maeterlinck, Stefan George, Nietzsche, Freud and Schopenhauer', or adaptations of sonnets, psychological novels and 'theories of relativity'.[88] The Germanist Anton Kaes has usefully summed up the situation: 'The literarisation of the German cinema between 1910 and 1920 did not win many friends either among the working class public who went to the movies for ... entertainment ... or among intellectuals who ... deplored the debasement of 'high art ... into the unrefined language of film ...'.[89]

Certain themes mark the appearance of America and Americans in German films between the 1890s and 1918, and these themes help to define the self presented. These movies depict cities like New York and Chicago as bustling, attractive metropolises, fascinating if perhaps occasionally dangerous urban centres. Take the following as examples of how the United States city is treated. In the 1915 movie of Bernhard Kellerman's futuristic novel, *Der Tunnel*, New York is the harbour city chosen as the North American terminus for a trans-Atlantic tunnel. Even though marred by 'very poor cinematography' ('sehr schlechten Photographie') according to one critic, the film did emphasise American technological progress. And New York's Flatiron Building, then among the best known of the city's skyscrapers, shown flying the American flag, figured prominently in the film's advertisements. New York remained a desirable goal whatever the machinations of the city's financiers, who opposed the project. The city also remains a place to go to in the Danish filming of a novel by the then well-known German author Gerhart Hauptmann. The production company found his script for *Atlantis* 'totally unusable' ('vollkommen unbrauchbar'), but the subsequent writers on the project hewed closely to the novel because it came out shortly before the *Titanic* disaster in 1912 and Hauptmann's effort had included such a disaster.[90] New York also featured prominently if briefly in the 1913 adventure film *Die Jagd nach der Hundertpfundnote* or *Die Reise um de Welt* ('The Hunt for the Hundred Pound Note' or 'The Trip Around the World'); this film also included scenes placing its protagonists in 'the Wild West'.

The West certainly was quintessentially American, as was the genre it featured – especially on screen. Westerns flourished in Wilhelmine Germany (as elsewhere in the world). The Kaiser was a fan; his interest went back to childhood days when he had happily played 'Cowboys and Indians' with the son of an American diplomat.[91] Cinema scholar, Deniz Göktürk, in reviewing the Western's impact on Wilhelmine Germany, maintains that the genre had an 'enormous power of fascination' ('eine ungeheure Faszinationskraft').[92] American cowboy stars such as Broncho Billy Anderson and Tom Mix quickly captured the affection of German audiences. The self they projected was strong, brave, the 'good bad man' with a tough exterior and a sentimental core. They were men of action, willing to take a chance, ready to fight Indians or villains without fear or hesitation.

Even before the American Western hit its stride in Europe, some production companies there made a stab at the genre. In 1908 the Danish Great Northern Company filmed in Copenhagen the short film *Texas Tex,* utilising 'genuine Indians' recruited from a touring Wild West show; in 1909 Pathe filmed *A Western Hero* in Paris. Both these attempts foundered and were 'caustically dismissed as a strange assemblage of customs, costumes and surroundings, and derided for not being authentic or American ...'.[93] The French firm Eclair, one of the powerhouses in early film production, did succeed during the first decade of the twentieth century with about a dozen 'Arizona Bill' films (about 2–3 reels long), featuring Joë Hamman, who was promoted as the 'National Cowboy'.[94]

The Germans also tried their hand at Westerns, which projected an American self, like that found in the home-grown product. They did so in 1911 films such as *Der Pferdedief* (The Horse Thief) and *Wild-West-Romantik*. The German film industry also produced a significant number of films that included Western sequences with the usual stalwart characters (as well as some others) that projected a positive image of the American self. Typical are three 1913 adventure films. Gold mines and the prairie are part of *Evinrude: Die Geschichte Eines Abenteuers* (Evinrude: The Story of an Adventure). Part II of *Menschen und Maske* continued the adventures of detective Kelly Brown, whose efforts also took him out West. The family melodrama *Heimat und Fremde* (Home and Strangers) began in a European metropolis, but included, as advertised, scenes 'in wilden Westen' that one critic found 'handsome' ('hübsch').[95]

Notwithstanding the war, censorship and the patriotic mien of the industry, Western films that set forth a positive view of the American self continued to be made. The estimable director and producer Richard Oswald in the early stages of his career wrote the screenplay for the 1915 *Die Goldfelder von Jacksonville* (The Goldfields of Jacksonville), described as a 'Drama aus dem Amerikanischen West' (a drama from out of the American West).[96] In 1916 there appeared the film *Cowboy-Liebe* (Cowboy Love), a shorter film with Eddie Seefeld and Ria Jende. Shortly before the end of the war

Fig. 6. Eddie Seefeld and Ria Jende in *Cowboy-Liebe* (1916).

Eric Pommer, subsequently a major force in the pre-Hitler German film industry, produced *Der Cowboy*, whose final reel took place at a castle 'somewhere in Europe' ('eingenwo in Europa').[97]

Westerns were not the only film genre during the war in which Americans featured prominently and not unfavourably. Another example is the Anglo-American detective film, which already had been popular in serial form and became even more so in feature films. British and American detectives became a staple and a cliché. Detectives like Sherlock Holmes, Stuart Webb, Joe Deebs and an American counterpart such as Tom Shark continued their adventures during World War I, unravelling mysteries and aiding folks in distress. In 1915, for example, Stuart Webb in *Der Gestreifte Domino* (The Striped Domino) in his usual 'English gentleman' fashion, helps distraught American millionaires by clearing their son of false criminal charges. An interesting aside to this film and others like it is that they adopt American racial attitudes towards people of colour. Often the villain's helpers are non-whites who threaten a leading lady. There are Oriental white slavers, Chinese opium denizens, black sub-thugs (an important villain is never black). The 'ubermensch' of detectives (according to a German trade journal in December 1917) was Tom Shark, advertised as 'the best snooper in America'.[98] The talented Alwin Neuss directed and starred in a number of Shark films during World War I. Shark in these films seems to have been positive and typical of the 'can-do' spirit that typified the American self in other genres.

Two early Emil Jannings films also, despite the war, demonstrate a positive American self. In the long, complex, emotion-charged 1918 two-parter *Keimendes Leben* (The Germ Life's End), Jannings plays two roles, one of them being that of an American engineer involved in a romantic triangle that is resolved by a tunnel cave-in. That same year Jannings also played an American in *Der Mann der Tat* (The Man of the Deed), who seems initially a bit silly ('ein wenig lächerlich') but ultimately proves capable both in love and business.[99] The production

Fig. 7. Lithographic poster by Robert L. Leonard for Ernst Lubitsch's *Die Austern Prinzessin* (PAGU, 1919). [*Das Plakat*, October 1920.]

of such movies, despite what has been described as 'the militarisation of the film industry' ('die Militarisieung des Kinos'), is what led to General Ludendorff's rage about UFA's failure as a propaganda vehicle.[100]

Still another approach to the American self was reflected in the depiction of 'the rich uncle' who returns to Germany from the United States after many years. In 1913 the 29-year-old Max Brod, subsequently a well-known critic and Franz Kafka's literary executor, contributed to a plot outline which centred on 'Der Dollaronkel' (the Dollar Uncle) to a work edited by Kurt Pinthus.[101] A 27-year-old Leipzig journalist, Pinthus in *Das Kinobuch* (The Movie Book) brought together 17 writers (mostly young Expressionists) whose suggested film scenarios underscored Pinthus's sharp rejection of the 'elitist attitudes of German intellectual and expressed his longing for a cinema true to its own means of expression'.[102] In Brod's effort, a young student's uncle returns for a visit. This uncle, though extremely well-off and generous in the student's daydreams, in which he appears wearing a high hat with the stars of the union on it and with money flowing endlessly out of his pant's pockets, on first appearance seems old and shabby. After a series of fantastic events that mix daydreams and reality, he turns out to be a generous millionaire.

Variations on this theme were to be found in a significant number of films. Even Germany's first great star, the Dane Asta Nielsen, the 'Duse of the movies' (Die Duse der Films), made a film centering on a rich uncle.[103] Nielsen, who after her 1911 breakthrough in Denmark-spent the next two decades filming in Germany, in 1913 starred in *Engelein* (Little Angel). The 32-year-old Nielsen convincingly played a 17-year-old who impersonated a 12-year- old in order to stop a rich uncle from America from letting his fortune leave the family. As exemplified by the returning uncle, the American self in these films was presented as energetic, determined and hard working, even if (as in the Nielsen film) a bit comic.

The American self in German films comprised a series of often contradictory images. Cowboys did not seek wealth; the primitivism of the 'wild West' was a far cry from urban technological progress; energy and determination failed to compensate for the much-heralded lack of culture; money-grubbing overshadowed sentiment and emotion. Moreover, most of the images were male. The madcap American heiress (although found elsewhere in Wilhelmine culture) really made her way on-screen after World War I, as in Ernst Lubitsch's

Die Austernprinzessin (The Oyster Princess). The director's second feature, this 1919 film starring the very popular Ossi Oswalda, known as 'the Mary Pickford of Germany', was based on a 1909 operetta *Die Dollarprinzessin.*[104] In both the operetta and the film the father was presented as a loving but culturally embarrassing nouveau riche money-grubber who wants the best for his daughter. Obviously, the father and his determined, if scatter-brained, daughter on stage and on screen, at best are not very favourable images of American men or women, but for all the drawbacks found in the presentation of the American self by German filmmakers, they never demonised it, as was the case with the American wartime Hate-the-Hun campaign.

Indeed, over the next half-century during which movies dominated the mass media, the German cinema, as the program notes to a recent exhibition at the Deutsches Historisches Museum point out, came to develop fully an image of the 'blessed land over the sea' only hesitatingly ('Nur zoegerlich vesucht des deutsche Kino, eigene Bilder von geloebten Land jenseits des Ozeans zu entwerfen'). And the only truly venomous depictions of Americans on a broad scale came after World War II in East German films such as the 1963 thriller *For Eyes Only.* In it American secretaries are promiscuous and wear falsies, GI's sell and use narcotics, the United States tries to subvert and blackmail citizens of the German Democratic Republic (GDR), and only its vigilant, aggressive counterintelligence enables Western operatives to be successfully countered. Such movies carefully and convincingly present what has been called a 'Feindbild' (picture of the enemy).[105] No Hitler-period film attacked the American self as venomously, as diligently, as concretely as did some GDR films. During the Nazi era (1933–45) hate films were made, excoriating Jews, Communists, the Soviets and the British. Americans, as in the 1942 business epic, *Diesel,* came under attack, but there was another side to the story, as in the 1936 UFA hit, *Glückskinder* (Lucky Children). An imitation 'screwball comedy' set in New York City, which, for inspiration ('Motiven') drew on the very successful 1934 American film *It Happened One Night,* it deals with the comic adventures of a newspaperman and a young woman.[106]

Conversely, United States' moviemakers during World War II did not produce *en masse* German-bashing movies in World War I style. After 1918, the German self with a few notable exceptions disappeared from American films. Even American antipathy to the Nazis became ever stronger after 1933; the United States film industry – hesitant about losing the German market (which grew with the 1938 annexation of Austria, the 1939 occupation of Czechoslovakia and Poland and the 1940 conquest of much of Western Europe) – overall avoided explicit anti-German or anti-Nazi films until 1941. And during World War II, although Hollywood turned out its fair share of 'nasty Nazi' propaganda, it avoided the excesses of the earlier Hate-the-Hun films, and followed the guidelines of the Office of War Information (co-ordinating American propaganda), which urged 'don't make blanket condemnations of all Germans ... as this country does not regard the German people as our enemies, only their leaders'.[107]

Not all filmmakers followed this advice, and Germans often were presented virulently, but even the staunchest anti-Nazi films could contain what later came to be called 'Good Germans'. Over a generation after the war's end, a West German critic noted with some awe and astonishment that 'even during the height of the war, films were released in which "good Germans" were presented sentimentally and respectfully, as if Hitler and the war did not exist'. (*Selbst auf dem Hohepunkt des Krieges, kamen doch Filme heraus, in denen die 'guten Deutschen' sentimental und respectwoll vorgefuert weiden als habe es Hitler und den Krieg nie gegaben*).[108] After war's end, Communism replaced Nazism as the chief threat to the American way of life; the 'nasty Nazi' gave way to the 'rotten Red'. The exculpation of Germany (or at least anti-Communist West Germany) meant that United States movies increasingly drew a very clear distinction between 'the good German who fought for his country and the Nazi fanatical beasts'.[109] As the movies (and other media) refurbished German society, it became a victim rather than an accessory to the Nazis.[110] While Nazis did not disappear from American film, they became distinct from Germans.

But the years since 1918 are another story, which must be dealt with in more detail. As it is, for the years prior to 1918, a comprehensive analysis of the self in films remains difficult. The interpretation of the intertext in films dealing with the self during these years, whether produced in Germany or the United States, poses various questions. In an attempt to catch up with the scholarship available and continuing about early American film, those on both sides of the Atlantic interested in German cinema prior to 1918 have undertaken yeoman, broad-based, and in the main, successful efforts. Typical is Heide Schlüpmann's work in which, through a close reading of selected films, she has set forth intelligent ideas about the relationship between cinematography and women's emancipation in Wilhelmine society (*Komplizenschaft zwischen Kinematographie und Frauenemanzipation in der Wilhelminische Gesellschaft*).[111] She surveys broadly, but must do so on the basis of reading relatively few films, since not that many of the movies produced during those early years have survived (albeit substantially more from the United States than Germany). The very well-versed scholar Thomas Elsaesser, in one of his recent challenges to Kracauer, has succinctly summed up the situation: 'We know too few films, and we possess too little information about the ones we do have ...'.[112]

Yet, even the limited number of films available are valuable because of how a movie is created. Filmmaking is a team effort, the auteur theory notwithstanding. Even a short film of the early 1900s can be assumed to have been the product of collaboration. Such joint effort explains in part why movies have a closer relationship to the group processes in society than individual efforts like a painting or a short story. It may well be that early movies were what Kracauer in 1930 called a 'flight from reality' (Wirklichkeitsflucht) or these films may have been what in 1933 was described as 'longed-for pictures' (Wunschbilder).[112] However these early movies are categorised, placing them in historical context makes it possible to avoid just a nostalgic recycling of images and allows, even given the shortcomings I have outlined, to do more than merely report on the self presented to German and American movie audiences.

To come to definite conclusions about the dialectical process which determined the definitions of self may be premature, but certain implications are clear. Before 1918, film as a medium, depending on the perspective from which viewing took place, took on different characteristics. This holds true for both German and American cinema. Moreover, film (like any other discourse) is never really neutral. Movies, even at their most primitive in the latter 1890s and early 1900s, were connected and influenced in complex, not always comprehensible or rational, ways. The factors involved (and often overlooked until relatively recently) included class, gender, race, ethnicity and sexual preference, as well as audience response, production history and the impact of technique in conjunction with technological developments.

Film developed its own language with explicit and implicit prejudices. In both Germany and the United States the movies, even during these nascent years, contributed mightily towards the rapid transformation of the public sphere. As the late Jay Leyda – still among the most prescient of commentators on early film – asserted years ago, 'each film historian ... is struck by the speed with which the peculiar expressiveness of the medium was developed'.[114] We know more about the self in older German and American films than we did a generation ago, even more than we did just five years ago. As scholarship progresses on both sides of the Atlantic, as more resources are discovered, we shall be able increasingly to move from tentative theorising to assertive conclusions. ♦

Notes

1. Jürgen Habermas, 'Modernity – An Incomplete Project', in Hal Foster, ed., *The Anti-Aesthetic* (Port Townsend, WA: Bay Press, 1983), 11.
2. *Webster's New Collegiate Dictionary* (Springfield: G. & C. Merriam, 1951), 767.
3. Bill Nichols, *Ideology and the Image* (Bloomington: Indiana University Press, 1981), 30.
4. Pierre Sorlin, *The Film as History* (Totowa, Oxford, UK: Blackwell, 1980), 208.
5. Richard W. McCormick, *Politics of the Self: Feminism and the Postmodern in West German Literature and Film* (Princeton: Princeton University Press, 1991).
6. Gilbert Seldes, *The Movies Come From America* (New York: Scribner,1937).
7. Robert Sklar, *Film: An Illustrated History of the Medium* (New York: H.N. Abrams, 1993), 75.

8. Robert Sklar, *Movie-Made America,* rev. and updated edition, (New York: Random House, 1994), 47.

9. John Higham, *Strangers in the Land: Patterns of American Nativism* (New York: Antheneum, 1963), 196.

10. Frederick C. Luebke, *Bonds of Loyalty: German Americans and World War I* (DeKalb: Northern Illinois University Press, 1974), 58; William Henry Harbaugh, *Power and Responsibility: The Life and Times of Theodore Roosevelt* (New York: Farrar, Straus & Cudahy, 1961), 288.

11. Theodore Roosevelt, *An Autobiography* (New York: Macmillan, 1913), 26.

12. Allen L. Woll and Randall M. Miller, *Ethnic and Racial Images in American Film and Television* (New York: Garland, 1987), 221; Geoff Eley, *From Unification to Nazism* (Boston: G. Allen £ Unwin, 1930), 390.

13. Mark Sullivan, *Pre-War America* (New York: Charles Scribner's Sons, 1930), 390.

14. Quoted in Maldwyn Jones, *Destination America* (London: Weidenfeld and Nicolson, 1976), 139.

15. Abel Green and Joe Laurie, Jr., *Show Biz: Variety from Vaude to Video* (New York: Holt, 1951), 7.

16. Maurice Horn, ed., *The World Encyclopedia of Comics* (New York: Chelsea House, 1976), 421.

17. Charles Musser, *The Emergence of Cinema: the American Screen to 1907* (New York: Scribner, 1990), 1.

18. Daniel Leab, 'The Gamut From A to B: the Image of the Black in Pre-1915 Movies,' *Political Science Quarterly*, 88 (1973): 61.

19. *Biograph Bulletins,* 1908–12 (New York: Octagon Books, 1973), 73.

20. Eileen Bowser, *The Transformation of Cinema 1907–15,* (New York, NY: Scribner, 1990), 224.

21. *Motion Picture News* (4 November 1916): 2863.

22. Wilson, quoted in Richard Morris, ed., *Encyclopedia of American History* (New York: Harper & Row, 1976), 358; Arthur S. Link, *Woodrow Wilson and the Progressive Era* (New York: Harper & Row, 1954), 148n.

23. John Whiteclay Chambers II, *The Tyranny of Change: America in the Progressive Era, 1890–1920,* 2nd ed. (New York: St. Martin's Press, 1992), 217.

24. Thomas Bailey, *Voices of America* (New York: Free Press, 1976), 331.

25. Timothy J. Lyons, 'Hollywood and World War I', *Journal of Popular Film I* (1972): 17.

26. *Variety* (9 June 1916): 23.

27. Patricia King Hanson, *et al.*, eds., *The American Film Institute Catalog of Motion Pictures Produced in the United States: Feature Films, 1911–20* (Berkeley and Los Angeles, CA, London, UK: University of California Press, 1988), 48; David H. Mould, *American Newsfilm: 1914–19 – The Underexposed War* (New York: Garland, 1983), 162.

28. *Variety, American Newsfilm: 1914–18 – The Underexposed War* (9 June 1916): 23.

29. Leif Furhammar and Folke Isaksson, *Politics and Film* (New York: Praeger, 1971), 9.

30. *Variety* (23 October 1914): 22.

31. Garth Jowett, *Film: The Democratic Art* (Boston: Little, Brown & Co. for the American Film Institute, 1976), 66.

32. Kevin Brownlow, *The War, The West, and the Wilderness* (New York: Knopf, 1979), 79.

33. *Variety* (8 October 1915): 21.

34. Terry Ramsaye, *A Million and One Nights* (New York: Simon & Schuster, 1926), 686.

35. 'Woodrow Wilson: War Message (1917)', in James Andrews and David Zarefsky, eds., *American Voices* (New York and London: Longman, 1989), 410.

36. Lewis Jacobs, *The Rise of American Film* (New York: Harcourt, Brace and Co., 1939), 259.

37. Emerson Hough, *The Web: A Revelation of Patriotism,* (Chicago: 1919), 23, quoted in Barbara McCandless, 'A Commitment to Beauty', in McCandless, *et al.*, *New York to Hollywood: The Photography of Karl Struss* (Albuquerque: University of New Mexico Press, 1995), 32; Mark Sullivan, *Over Here 1914–18* (New York: Charles Scribner's Sons, 1933), 471; McCandless, 41, 48, 50.

38. Brownlow,134.

39. Jack Spears, *Hollywood: the Golden Era* (South Brunswick: A.S. Barnes, 1971), 29.

40. *Motion Picture News* (1 December 1917): 3857.

41. Ibid., (3 October 1918): 2594.

42. Quoted in Virginia Cowles, *The Kaiser* (London: Collins, 1963), 177.

43. Quoted in Spears, 33.

44. *The New York Times* (5 April 1918): 13.

45. *Moving Picture World* (19 October 1918): 448.

46. Richard A. Oehling, 'Germans in Hollywood Films', *Film and History,* 3 (May 1973): 1.

47. *Motion Picture News* (23 March 1918): 1768.

48. Brownlow,136.

49. Brownlow, 137.

50. Jacobs, 257.

51. Id.

52. Richard Oehling, 'The German-Americans, Germany and the American Media', in Randall M. Miller, ed., *Ethnic Images in American Film and Television* (Philadelphia: The Balch Institute, 1978), 51.

53. Philip M. Taylor, *Munitions of the Mind* (Northamptonshire, UK: Stephens, 1990), 174.

54. Alfred Gong, ed., *Interview mit Amerika* (Munich: Nymphenburger Verlagshandlung, 1962), 11.

55. Hans W. Gatzke, *Germany and the United States* (Cambridge: Harvard University Press, 1980), 48.

56. Peter von Zahn, 'Germany', in F. M. Joseph, ed., *As Others See Us* (Princeton: Princeton University Press, 1959), 96.

57. Graf J. H. Bernstorff, *Errinerungen und Briefe* (Zurich: Polygraphischer Verlag, 1936), 80.

58. Eduard Mayer, quoted in W. W. Coole and M. F. Potter, eds., *Thus Spake Germany* (London: George Routledge & Sons, 1941), 192.

59. Reinhard Doerries, 'Empire and Republic: German-American Relations Before 1917,' in Frank Trommler and Joseph McVeigh, eds., *America and the Germans,* vol. II, (Philadelphia: University of Pensylvania Press, 1985), 15, n. 14.

60. Philip S. Foner, *Karl Liebknecht and the United States,* (Chicago: Greenleaf Press, 1978), 18.

61. Fritz Stern, *The Politics of Cultural Despair* (Berkeley and Los Angeles: University of California Press, 1961), 131n.

62. Goethe quoted in J. W. Schulte Nordholt, 'Anti-Americanism in European Culture: Its Early Manifestations', in Rob Kroes and Maarten Van Rossem, eds., *Anti-Americanism in Europe* (Amsterdam: Amsterdam University Press, 1986), 12, translation, 18, n. 19.

63. Peter Krüger, 'Traditional Patterns of Ambiguous Misunderstanding in a Period of Transition ...' Unpublished paper presented at a symposium on Recurrent Patterns of Mutual Understanding in German–American Relations, University of North Carolina, Chapel Hill (September 1986), 12.

64. Walter Nugent, *Crossings: The Great Atlantic Migrations,1870–1914* (Bloomington: 1992), 69; Kathleen Neils Cozzens, 'Germans', in Stephan Thernstrom, *et al.*, eds., *Harvard Encyclopedia of American Ethnic Group* (Cambridge: Indiana University Press, 1980), 406.

65. Sigmund Skard, *American Studies in Europe* (Philadelphia: American Philosophical Society, 1957), 238; Hans Jürgen Schröder, *Deutschland und Amerika in der Epoche des Ersten Weltkrieges,1900–24* (Stuttgart: Franz Steiner Verlag, 1993), 23. In 1902 Edison's film company produced a 39-foot actuality shown in Germany and the United States which was a German and American tableau occasioned by the prince's visit. The film begins with a German soldier and an American soldier facing each other, giving way to pictures of the prince and President Roosevelt, and at the other end of the film 'the soldiers turn, step forward, face one another and shake hands ...'. See Kemp Niver, *Early Motion Pictures ...* (Washington, DC: Library of Congress, 1985).

66. W. T. Stead, *The Americanization of the World or the Trend of the Twentieth Century* (New York: Garland, 1972, original ed., 1902), 67.

67. Wolfgang Jacobsen, *et al., Geschichte des Deutschen Films* (Stuttgart: Metzler, 1993), 13.

68. Ad in Michael Hanisch, *Auf den Spuren der Filmgeschichte: Berliner Schauplatze* (Berlin: Henschel, 1991), 209; Hans-Michael Bock and Michael Toteberg, *Das UFA Buch* (Frankfurt am Main: Zwei Tausand Eins, 1992), 60.

69. Ragnhild Fiebeg, 'Clashes over Assumed World Power Status, 1890–1918: Conflicts Created by Extreme National Egoism', paper presented at the symposium on Recurrent Patterns of mutual Understanding in German–American Relations, University of North Carolina, Chapel Hill, Sept. 1986,16.

70. Paolo Cherchi Usai, *et al.*, eds., *Before Caligari: German Cinema, 1895–1920* (Edizoni Beltola Dell' immogine, 1990), 16.

71. Siegfried Kracauer, *From Caligari to Hitler* (Princeton: Princeton University Press, 1947), 15.

72. Bruce A. Murray, 'Introduction', in Murray and Christopher J. Wickham, eds., *Framing the Past: The Historiography of German Cinema and Televi-*

sion (Carbondale: Southern Illinois University Press, 1992), 8.

73. Corinna Müller, *Frühe Deutsche Kinematographie* (Stuttgart: Metzler, 1994), 191; Müller, 'Emergence of the Feature Film in Germany between 1910 and 1911', in Murray and Wickham, ibid., 94. It has been argued that German productions accounted for the majority of dramatic films seen by Germans, but these were a limited number of the films shown. Herbert Birett, *Das Filmangebot in Deutschland,* xvi (Munich: Winterberg, 1991), a systematic study of the films released, confirms Müller's projections.

74. H. H. Wollenberg, *Fifty Years of German Film* (London: Falcon Press, 1948), 12.

75. Friedrich v. Zglinicki, *Der Weg Des Films* (Berlin: Rembrandt, 1956), 389.

76. Quoted in Furhammer and Isaksson, 12: for the full text in German see Bock and Töteberg, 34.

77. Erich Angermann, '1917: Jahr der Entscheidungen', in Schröder, 64.

78. Thomas J. Saunders, 'History in the Making: Weimar Cinema and National Identity', in Murray and Wickham, ibid., 46.

79. Hanisch, 292–3.

80. Frank Trommler, 'The Rise and Fall of Americanism in Germany', in Trommler and McVeigh, 334.

81. Klaus Kreimeier, *Die UFA-Story* (Munich: Hanser, 1992), 181: according to Oskar Kalbus, *Vom Werden deutscher Filmkunst: Der Stumm Film* (Hamburg: Cigaretten Bilderdienst, 1935), 26, she began her German film career as Fern André.

82. Ute Schneider, 'Fern Andra', in Hans-Michael Bock, ed., *Cinegraph*, E2.

83. Kracauer, ibid., 20. Very early on, German moviegoers could see 'Indianer und Cowboys' as part of a group of short films (1905 advertisement for a Berlin theatre in Zglinicki, Friedrich v. Zglinicki, *Der Weg Des Films* (Berlin: 1956), 389, 695).

84. Urban Gad, *Der Film* (1918) in Uta Berg-Ganschow, *Berlin: Aussen und Innen – 53 Filme aus 90 Jahren* (Berlin: Argon, 1984),104; Grosz quoted in Fritz Güttinger, *Der Stummfilm im Zitat der Zeit* (Frankfurt am Main: Deutsches Film Museum, 1984), 62.

85. Sabine Hake, *The Cinema's 3rd Machine: Writing on Film in* Germany, 1907–33 (Lincoln: University of Nebraska Press, 1993), 17.

86. Hanisch, Ad in Michael Hanisch, *Auf den Spuren der Filmgeschichte: Berliner Schauplatze* (Berlin: Hanish, 1991), 209; Hans-Michael Bock and Michael Toteberg, *Das UFA Buch* (Frankfurt am Main: Bock and Totenberg, 1992), 60, 226.

87. *Hätte Ich Das Kino: Die Schriftstellen und der Stummfilm* (Munich: Koesel, 1976), 25; on the occasion of the 25th anniversary of the Kaiser's ascension to the throne a book, *Der Deutsche Kaiser in Film* (Berlin: n.p.,1912) was published; among other things, it was generously illustrated with photos taken from 'actualities' of numerous film companies including Pathé, Union, Decla-Bishop and Vitascope.

88. Hans Siemsen, 'Deutsch-amerikanischer Filmkrieg', in Fritz Güttinger, ed., *Kein Tag ohne Kino* (Frankfurt am Main: Deutsches Filmmuseum, 1984), 435.

89. Anton Kaes, 'Mass Culture and Modernity ...', in Trommler and McVeigh, ibid., 320–21.

90. The Danish newspaper *Politiken* quoted in Zglinicki, 375.

91. Edward Taylor, *The Fate of the Dynasties* (Garden City: Doubleday, 1963), 157.

92. Deniz Göktürk, 'Neckar Western, statt Donau Walzer', *Kintopp, 2* (Frankfurt am Main: 1993), 118.

93. Robert Anderson, 'The Role of the Western Film Genre in Industry Competition, 1907–11', *Journal of the University Film Association 31* (Spring 1979): 24, n53.

94. Göktürk, 125.

95. Hanisch, 147.

96. Helga Belach and Wolfgang Jacobsen, eds., *Richard Oswald: Regisseur und Produzent* (Munich: Edition Text + Kritik, 1990), 140.

97. 'Alwin Neuss', in Hans-Michael Bock, ed., *Cinegraph: D11.*

98. *Der Kinematograph* (12 December 1917), quoted in 'Alwin Neuss', in Hans-Michael Bock, ed., *Cinegraph,* D1.

99. Bock and Toteberg, 44.

100. Kreimeier, 31.

101. Max Brod, 'Ein Tag aus dem leben Kühnbecks, Des Jungen Idealisten', in Kurt Pinthus, ed., *Das Kinobuch* (Zurich: Verlag Der Arche, 1963, original ed., 1913), 71–76.

102. Hake, 71.

103. 'Asta Nielsen', in Bock, ed., *Cinegraph*: B2.

104. Sabine Hake, *Passions and Deceptions: The Early*

Films of Ernst Lubitsch (Princeton: Princeton University Press, 1992), 45.

105. Wolfgang Gersh, 'Film in Der DDR: Die Verlorene Alternative', in Jacobsen, *et al.*, eds., 340.

106. 'Amerika, du hast es besser?' – Deutsche Perspektiven auf ein Gelobtes Land , Program for Zeughaus Kino, Deutches Historisches Museum (October 1996), 2. Rainer Rother, 'Komödie mit Vorbild', in *UFA Magazin*, Nr. 13, 'Glückskinder', one of a series of program notes for the exhibitions and screenings *Der UFA 1917–1945*, (Berlin: Deutsches Historisches Museum, 1992), 5.

107. Hans C. Blumenberg, 'Hollywood und Hakenkreuz', in Alice Goetz, ed., *Hollywood und die Nazis* (Hamburg: Verband der Deutschen Filmklubs, 1977), 9.

108. Bureau of Motion Pictures, OWI, quoted in Richard Lingeman, *Don't You Know There's a War On: The American Home Front 1941–1945* (New York: Putnam, 1970), 186.

109. Oehling, 'The German-Americans', 60.

110. For an overview of American treatment of Germans since 1941, see Daniel J. Leab, 'Good Germans/Bad Nazis: Amerikanische Bilder aus dem Kalten Krieg und ihre Ursprünge', *Deutsches Historisches Museum Magazin 5* (1992): 25–39.

111. Heide Schlüpmann, *Unheimlichkeit des Blicks: Das Drama des* Frühen deutschen Kino (Basel and Frankfurt am Main: Stroemfeld/Roster Sterne, 1990), 8.

112. Thomas Elsaesser, 'National Subjects, International Style ... ', in Usai, 342.

113. Kracauer, quoted in Thomas G. Plummer, 'Introduction', in Plummer, *et al.*, eds., *Film and Politics in the Weimar Republic* (Minneapolis: University of Minnoseta Press, 1982), 7; Hans Traub, *Der Film als politisches Machtmittel* (Munich: Muenchener Druck und Verlagshaus, 1933), 6.

114. Jay Leyda, 'A Note on Progress', *Film Quarterly*, 21 (Summer 1968): 28.

Film History, Volume 9, pp. 71–94, 1997. Copyright © John Libbey & Company
ISSN: 0892-2160. Printed in Australia

German film censorship during World War I

Wolfgang Mühl-Benninghaus

German film censorship is almost as old as the medium itself.[1] Under pressure from the press and the 'monopolistic demands of the intelligentsia of written culture to give significance and meaning to life',[2] fear of the popular and suggestive new medium of film was especially pronounced in the nationalist, militaristic, semi-autocratic German Empire.[3] A series of different guidelines for film censorship arose as a result of discussions about cinema reform in the separate German states. They were linked by the merging of decision-making and administrative powers in the respective film review offices. On 5 May 1906, film censorship was introduced for the first time in the jurisdiction of Berlin, which did not issue its first order until two years later[4] however . As in all the other German states which introduced film censorship, even in the smaller states like the Grand Duchy Saxony-Weimar which only had four cinemas,[5] film censorship was treated the same as the censorship of the press. Since censorship in the Empire had been done away with in the wake of the Press Law of 1874, film-makers filed suit against Berlin's censorship order. According to the judgement passed down by the Prussian Higher Administrative Court, Berlin censorship rulings were legal since they were based on the Theater Censorship of 1850.[6] This court approval of cinema censorship laws was also applied in the other German States in the ensuing years. A prophylactic police censorship went into effect in April of 1909. Stemming initially from the ministerial decree of 1909, Bavaria issued detailed censorship orders in January 1912.[7] Württemberg followed this step in June of 1914 by issuing orders that were particulary severe. On 16 December 1910, by way of order, all governing presidents were held responsible for introducing film censorship. Within the framework of simplification and administrative relief, the decisions of the Berlin cinema censorship became authoritative for the entire governmental jurisdiction.[8] By contrast, Hamburg's senate only authorised a commission of teachers to judge the appropriateness of films for a young audience; no further orders were issued.[9]

The censorship orders did not only vary among the separate German states. There were differences between the various cities and governmental jurisdictions. In Prussia there were a total of 24 film censorship centres, of which Berlin was the most important. Within that centre, film censorship was annexed to the theatre department, which was also responsible for variety shows and circus performances. In Bavaria, all films had to be presented to a censorship centre in Munich. Paragraph 2 of the Bavarian film censorship law determined that the local centres in Munich could ban films that had been censored, 'if the local situation should so demand'.[10]

Wolfgang Mühl-Benninghaus is professor in the department of theatre and performing arts at Humboldt University in Berlin. His article on the German Film Credit Bank, Inc. appeared in *Film History* vol. III, no. 4. Correspondence c/o Humboldt Universitat zu Berlin, Institut für Theaterwissenschaft/Kulturelle Kommunikation, Unter den Linden 6, d–10099 Berlin, Germany.

On the national level, the Undersecretary of the Interior asked the Foreign Office on 25 May 1911 for their ambassadors to provide papers on film censorship policies for the various countries in which they were accredited, 'for eventual steps to be taken by the Empire in the battle against dirt in word and image'.[11] After a short debate in the *Reichstag* 'Mumm and Co.' offered a resolution with the goal of forced concessions for cinemas and a 'tougher and more stream-lined surveillance of cinematographic theatre'.[12] Despite considerable efforts on various sides, by August 1914 not only had all attempts to enforce film censorship failed in each German state, but the attempt to come up with a unified film law for the entire Reich had failed as well.

Independent of these legislative efforts, a comparison of the films shown in Munich and Berlin between 1912 and 1914 shows that the number of movies generally banned for those under age had reached its nadir by 1914. The comparison also shows that we can only speak conditionally of a homogeneous German film market for the period immediately preceding the war: movies that could be shown in Berlin were forbidden in Munich and vice versa, just as in the prior years.[13]

On 1 July 1914, without further explanation, the Berlin police issued an order raising censorship fees by 1,700 per cent. In response, many filmmakers refused to submit new films for censorship review in order to avoid paying the fees.[14] After much protest, the Prussian Minister of Finance signed a new order, which was at first limited to one year. However, the lowered censorship fees were still higher than before 1 July 1914.[15] In April 1915 this fee ordinance was made effective for the duration of the war.[16]

At the same time cinema reformers such as Karl Brummer[17] were unsuccessful in banning films using court orders.[18] The Higher Administrative Court in Berlin took the position that it is not the task of the police 'to march in with police orders whenever doubts are raised from a pedagogical standpoint'.[19] Despite the relatively low actual number of censorship cases in Bavaria and Berlin, public attacks from opponents of cinema, the Württemberg censorship law, and the raising of censorship fees and entertainment taxes for cinema immediately before the outbreak of the war, gave the impression that the economic existence of cinema was seriously threatened. To this extent film censorship remained one of the unsolved problems of the prewar period.[20]

During the War the number of censorship interventions increased. The ensuing difficulties affected not only the film industry, but also military and governmental positions, which used film as a medium for propaganda especially during the second half of the war.

The legal basis of film censorship in time of war

The imperial decree of 31 July 1914 placed the entire Empire except for Bavaria under martial law. With the order for mobilisation in accordance with Article 68, the laws of 4 June 1851 for a state of siege also went into effect in the German Empire. This meant that 24 military commanders from the army corps, as well as the 33 governors and commandants, assumed power of enforcement within the territories assigned to them. The army areas were not identical with governmental districts, that is, with province and state borders. Thus the military areas overlapped with the civil government creating a break in the traditional administrative technical structures.[21] This also affected the previous organisation of film censorship. The Reich's plans for mobilisation did not include any specific measures for the press or for film. Immediately prior to the onset of the war the commander in chief of the army dispatched an instruction sheet for the press in a state of war.[22] After 1 August 1914, public governmental work of the Reich was limited to a conference of the general staff with representatives from the press. At this meeting in the Reichstag the governmental representatives guaranteed a generous interpretation of censorship regulations. Press conferences held several times a week in Berlin served as a source of further information about war events in the following weeks. Representatives from various ministries and from the highest command ranks of the army participated. These conferences were meaningless for film production. This publicity, which was limited to written media, is typical in that it makes apparent that the use of pictures for reporting was far from the minds of leading military and ministerial bureaucrats at the beginning of the war. Like the later establishment of a department for censorship,[23] this example demonstrates that film only received a marginal role alongside other performing arts and that primary attention was focussed on the press during the entire war. As for the majority of the public, the press was the decisive medium in war reportage and the propaganda efforts which went into effect later. During the war, film was increasingly important as a publicity medium, especially for German domestic and foreign propaganda. Yet during the Reichstag discussions on cinema concessions in 1918, many of the delegates were still unaware that film censorship was even being practiced in Germany.[24]

Fig. 1. Handbill for *Messter Woche* military newsreel, 1916. [*Der Film*, no. 22, 1916.]

Official reportage of war events was initially limited to reports from the army.[25] First eight[26] and then fifteen rigorously selected war reporters from the press took care of further information.[27] After a corresponding order of the general staff,[28] several film companies were allowed from late September and early October 1914, to do front reportage: Messter-Film, Eiko-Film GmbH as well as a film company from Freiburg and Münich.[29] All remaining film companies and newspaper reporters were barred from direct war reportage.[30] Department IIIB of the acting general command was responsible for the censorship of texts, pictures and films.[31] Occasionally pure 'marine films' were censored by the press division of the naval staff.[32] In the various orders and guidelines on censorship contents of the acting general staff, military films were still treated in the second half of the war as part of picture (and thus press) censorship.[33] That is, film was considered by military leaders to be a conditionally independent medium of information.

Apart from the decisions made by the general staff, the military commanders, who were responsible in their respective divisions for 'insuring public order', also took over press and film censorship. On the basis of an order of the military commander and by order of the acting general command the state and municipal cinema censorship centres continued their activity from August 1914 onward. A specified film censorship was now introduced in all of those states which had previously done without. Due to the military subordination of the censorship centres, the Higher Administrative Court could only conditionally be called on to mediate as a decision-making power in legal differences between the censorship office and film producers.[34] Many general commanders did not feel bound by the censorship decisions of Division IIIB of the deputy general staff, in Berlin, which was reponsible, among other things, for military censorship of press and film. Thus the first censored war footage which came into the moviehouses in October of 1914 was banned in Hannover, Halle and Bremerhaven out of fear of espionage.[35] Since from the start only a few cameramen were allowed to take pictures at the front, and even those were strictly censored, the moviehouses were unable to provide the up-to-date war pictures which viewers were expecting.[36] The few pictures which could be shown were 'completely damaged'. They 'increasingly lost the right ... to be considered as such, since they were only harmless genre scenes, which had no drawing power'.[37] Beyond this they were missing the reality which moviegoers wanted due to lengthy censorship decisions.[38] These additional interventions in military censorship first changed when, in April of 1917, the highest censorship office under General Quartermaster Erich von Ludendorff became the enforcing organ of the highest army command, and the Chief of Division III B, Major Walter Nicolai – who had assumed this function since the beginning of the war – had directive power over the deputy general command. Already in the first days of the war the military commanders issued bans on film production which were later partially raised. From 3 August to mid-September 1914 it was forbidden to film departing troops in Dresden; and in Hamburg[39] and Berlin[40] it was forbidden to take pictures of squares and streets without police permission. In Lübeck, musical performances were forbidden as unpatriotic and Munich moviehouses had to close for ten days in observation of mobilisation day.[41] In Strasbourg all movie houses were closed in August for almost two months. A ban on photography was generally in effect.[42] War coverage was forbidden in all moviehouses in Berlin.[43] On 11 August, the President of the Police gave the following order: 'With respect for the present time of war, it must be expected that performances can only take place which are in keeping with the seriousness of these times and with the patriotic sense of the public. Further, performances are to be avoided which could have the effect of inciting the public to do violence to unarmed foreigners living here. Entrepeneurs who do not abide by this order and create irritation or disturbances to the public order through their performances can reckon with a retraction of the postponement of curfew, and that the closing of their premises will be considered'.[44]

Fig. 2. Major Walter Nicolai, Chief of Division III B of the general staff (signal section and counter-espionage). [Bildarchiv Preussischer Kulturbesitz.]

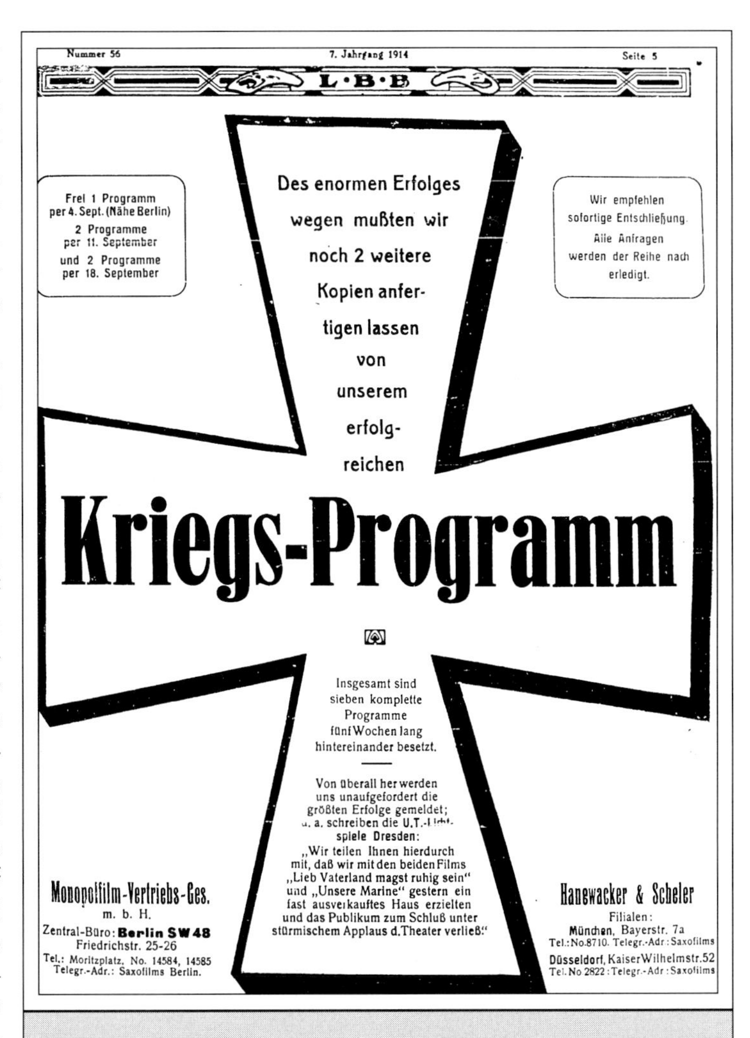

Fig. 3. War film advertisement, *Licht-Bild-Buhne*, 7 October 1914.

In as much as film censorship did not affect military subject matter, the following writ from the Prussian Ministry of War served the relevant offices during the war as a basis for decision-making: 'Feelings have been voiced here that [the] cinematographic theatre presents many pieces which, because of their superficiality and shallowness, are unsuited for the seriousness of our times, and that many of these are French and English films deserving of the same description which can only be seen as trash of the lowest sort. How much of the people's healthy common sense is destroyed by such poison? On the other hand, by presenting pictures of the fatherland and other noble images of a serious or humorous nature, these well-frequented theatres could contribute to the cultivation and preservation of a love for the fatherland and valuable morals in general. The Ministry of War can only subscribe to these ideas, making a humble plea to the royal commander in chief and the royal general command to bring their influence to bear on the responsible authorities so that these outgrowths can disappear.'[45] This circular was sent in Mid-December 1914 to all deputy general commands, the Chancellor of the Reich, the Prussian Minister of Interior and to the commander in chief in Mark Brandenburg province. The commander in chief answered the Minister at the end of December that this writing corresponded fully with his views, continuing: 'I have been influencing the censorship boards in this direction since the beginning of the war and the insititutions within my jurisdiction are under surveillance in this regard'.[46] He also forwarded this ministerial letter to the appropriate police headquarters, who reacted against the cinema. The Chief of Police in Berlin issued the following order on 4 January 1915: 'An ordinance issued by the Minister of War sent to me in the Mark Brandenburg mandates that all films not in keeping with our earnest times due to shallowness or banality should not be shown in our cinemas'. A notice for movie theatres dated 13 January 1915, continues in this vein: 'This is where, above all, the so-called trashy backstair novels belong, presentations of events from the lives of whores and criminals (all detective films as well), further films with humourous contents which are either offensive to the heart or mind of the viewer, or, for want of any larger idea, comprise a chain of crazy, outlandish, exaggerated and often meaningless scenes. Recommended, in contrast, are the presentation of solid pictures of a serious and humourous character which are suited to maintain high morals and to cultivate love for the fatherland. Non-compliance with this order can lead to coercive measures leading ultimately to a closing down of the movie theatre.'[47] The commander in chief in Altona strictly interpreted the mandate of the Minister of War.[48]

In the summer of 1915, the Berlin censorship ruling was rendered obsolete for the VII Army Corps (Düsseldorf) and its jurisdiction. It was replaced by local censorship. Officials as well as literary and pedagogical advisers were employed there as censors.[49]

The various orders from the General Command based on interpretations made by the Minister of War could not be translated into legal action because the specifications placed a focus on very general qualitative moments. Since corresponding criteria could not be described more precisely and there was no consensus about transposing conceptual contents into film, film censorship was based more and more on questions of taste. This meant that subjective ideas about morals and conventions determined the nature of prohibitions and partial prohibitions. Under these conditions, arbitrary decisions could not be ruled out, thus adding to the already reduced viability of the German film market before the war. Valid film censorship laws from before the war only remained in effect in Bavaria[50] and Württemberg.[51] There only supplementary specifications for the censorship of war pictures were issued.

Censorship measures were extended not only to films submitted for review during the war, but also to old films. For example, in Berlin all films censored before August 1914 had to be censored again.[52] By adding regulations for young viewers, film censorship became even more nebulous. The local variance from state to state in viewer age-limitations had an effect on the development of cinema.[53] An ordinance in Hannover ordered the separation of sexes for one group of viewers.[54] Under penalty of school disciplinary measures, young viewers in Württemberg up to the age of 18 were required to see films specified for children or young audiences, regardless of the fact that such showings were rare.[55] An ordinance in Rhineland Palatinate and Westphalia demanded 'the honorary cooperation of voluntary forces', to prevent youth and children from going to the movies.[56] Visits to the movies were forbidden for those under sixteen years of age unless school officials or the police gave special permission.[57] In Munich shows for young audiences were forbidden. Occasional special shows with 'programs arranged by teachers themselves' were allowed.[58] The First Bavarian Army Corps issued a decree on 7 March 1916 forbidding all viewers under 17 from going to the movies. As a protective measure, cinema owners were only allowed to display written announcements. Offenders could be sentenced to up to a year in jail.[59]

Following the Berlin ordinance of the end of April 1915, all films which had been approved for young audiences before 31 December 1912 had to be censored again by 1 October 1915 if they were to continue to be shown to this age group. Due to the acute lack of such films, a cost-free re-censorship on the part of the Berlin police expedited the process. At the same time the rigorous surveillance of movie houses was further intensified.[60] Beyond the qualitative moments contained in general film censorship specifications, the initiator of the ordinances issued especially for young viewers also attempted to establish pedagogical guidelines for the medium itself, which were not only limited to the age group in question. The Berlin Youth Censorship explicated the ordinance further: 'It has been repeatedly observed in recent times that owners of movie houses in greater Berlin have ignored police ordinances. Some of the movie house concessionaires in greater Berlin have recently been actively engaged in making the children's shows more attractive to unsupervised youth by showing forbidden pictures. In parts of the city with a high population of children these shows do in fact draw large numbers. Countless movie house owners are able to prevent observation by adults who would like to protect our youth from moral danger and the threat to their safety in overfilled rooms by preventing adult admittance to shows for younger audiences. Such inappropriate transgressive action will be met in the future with harsh measures. In order to enable authorities to move forward with more weight, police headquarters has been empowered by Higher Command in the provinces to close violating movie houses temporarily or permanently if necessary.'[61]

The German press was allowed to print army

reports during the entire war without censoring. Furthermore, all larger German newspapers were allowed to regularly publish reports of events in enemy territory. In addition, with the increased duration of the war, articles appeared about war events from the distant past, which at first could not be printed for fear of espionage. In contrast to all the larger newspapers, which regularly reported various events in foreign states, the showing of all films from countries with which Germany was at war was strictly limited. This self-isolation was a result of the impression made by the 'August experience'[62] and hefty attacks from a broad spectrum of the population against all French and English films[63] which were initially instigated by the cinema owners themselves.[64] Movie house owners, who had joined the Deutscher Filmbund founded after the beginning of the war, hung up a coloured placard with the text: 'No films from enemy countries will be shown here and no posters will be displayed which come from such countries. This movie theatre is a member of the German Filmbund.'[65] At a conference of the Society for the Protection of Common Interests of Cinematography and Related Branches, called in October 1914, many of the members debated, whether films brought from England and France prior to August should still be shown or not.[66] The Minister of War had already expressly referred to the negative influence of French and English films in October 1914,[67] yet had not specifically forbidden them.[68] During the period after the ban on all movies from allied nations which were not in Germany by August 1914, these were made a solid part of film censorship in agreement with many movie goers themselves.[69] As a result, old English and French films were shown in many parts of Germany due to a lack of films.[70] Thus, the deputy commanding general in charge in Münster placed special emphasis in his ordinance issued on15 February to keep the ban on English, French and Belgian films.[71] The verbal disparagement of films from the *entente* states on the part of broad segments of the German population shows that the historical significance of these films for the development of the medium was ignored due to the influence of the war. At the same time the import embargo issued in 1914 meant that the German Reich could not participate internationally in the development of the medium for almost an entire decade.

In November1915 the deputy general command extended its censorship domain to cinema advertising. After August 1914 advertising was done by artists and caricaturists, who, as a result of the war, had no more work in their own field.[72] Against the guidelines of the Press Law, on 8 November 1915, the Leipzig Police Department subjected all newspaper announcements, posters and advertising pictures for films to censorship before and after, threatening them with fines and imprisonment.[73] In Baden an ordinance of March 1916 limited the announcements of film showings to 'a simple announcement of the title of the piece to be shown without any reference to its content and without the addition of advertising pictures'.[74] After colour film posters in Stettin, Coburg, Düsseldorf and other cities gave in to censorship and were no longer allowed, almost all other cities in the German Empire followed suit.[75] The VIII Army Corps established for Koblenz that film adverstising posters with pictures be subject to pre-censorship. Furthermore, these were only to be allowed if the corresponding films were also approved for young audiences.[76] A police ordinance issued on 11 July 1916, established that cinema and variety shows were to be limited to dimensions 'typical for theatre'. 'Renditions of crime, violence and other such shocking things as well as morally offensive pictures were forbidden'. In addition, the letter print size for posters, with a maximum of 10 cm for large and 6 cm for small letters, was precisely stipulated.[77] As with many other censorship specifications, this one also used the term 'morally offensive,' that is, 'a thing about which not even a hundred people have ever been able to agree on'.[78] In September of 1916 poster censorship in Düsseldorf became more strict. Coloured posters, which enjoyed particular popularity on the front, were fundamentally banned during the second half of the war.[79] Press releases were no longer allowed to use scenes from movies for advertisements. Despite pre-censorship, advertising posters were only allowed to be hung on bill posts and theatre entryways.[80] In some Corps areas not only posters but even advertising photos were forbidden.[81] Some cities had to rescind poster bans in practice on the basis of court rulings, since the police could not prove 'their detrimental moral influence'.[82]

The uncoordinated interventions of the second

Fig. 4. Traugott von Jagow, Berlin police chief from 1909–1916, was responsible for motion picture censorship in that city during the first years of the war. [Bildarchiv Preussicher Kulturbesitz.]

commander in chief were not only limited to film and to the press. Berlin censors banned the Sarrasani Circus which had just held 75 performances in Dresden.[83] Between August 1914 and the end of 1916 around 2,000 censorship orders for the press were issued altogether.[84] 311 films during the same time were banned in Berlin, 244 of which were banned for the duration of the war.[85]

The implications of these figures are significant in as much as 'no film was shown in Germany during the war which did not pass Berlin censorship'.[86] Since it was not possible to show all the films approved in Berlin in the provinces as well, a divided movie market arose between the capital city and censorship practices in the provinces. Within Berlin that division existed between the larger theatres showing two long films at a time [87] and the smaller movie houses which showed one long film and several short ones.[88]

The dissatisfaction with these disparate censorship practices on the part of the press and film producers led to numerous extra sessions and debates in the German Parliament. The *Reichstag* alone spent some 20 controversial sessions on press censorship.[89] During these debates, the plenum also addressed issues concerning film censorship in May/June 1916 and in October 1917 and in March/April 1918. On the state level the Prussian House of Representatives dealt with the same topic in February of 1916 and 1917. The opinions on film censorship diverged considerably between the individual parties of the different parliaments. Thus on 4 May 1916, in a plea to the Chancellor of the German Empire, Representative Ferdinand Werner demanded of the German Social Economic Unification 'to successfully avert the escapades of the cinema which were especially shocking at the time'.[90] The Minister of the Interior answered to a similar demand from the Reich Chancellory with the request, 'that it be emphatically conveyed to Representative Werner that his description of the situation contains gross exaggeration and unacceptable generalisations about specific negative situations, whose rectification should be entirely left up to the individual states, who have been giving these problems their attention for sometime'.[91] The newspaper *Vorwärts* responded critically to the enterprising nature of the film producers and those running the movie houses.[92] During a censorship debate in the Reichstag, social democratic delegate Gustav Noske pointed out 'how ruinous the effects of censorship and the state of occupation had been for the cinematographic theatre'. He continued further: 'the deputy general commanders have further aggravated the situation with the cinema by extensive limiting of viewing time, and disallowing young viewers from going to the movies after 6 o'clock.'[93] Representative Georg Gothein of the German Progressive Party elaborated before parliament:

> The incommodation due to film censorship is really unheard of and we are in dire need of uniformity and a reduction of the inconvenience, if we are going to keep this film censorship at all.[94]

During the same session, Gustav Streseman, later Chancellor of the German Reich and Foreign Minister, sided with demands for uniform censorship throughout the Empire made by representatives of cinema concessionaires in cooperation with those affected in the corresponding committees.[95] All of these discussions had no effect whatsoever until after the war because of legal rulings regarding the state of war and the various notions of censorship.

Independent of these discussions, the *Bundesrat* attempted on 3 August 1917, to circumvent the *Reichstag* by introducing compulsory business for movie houses 'according to need' and declaring this order as a war time measure.[96] The concept of 'need' however was not defined in the law. Initial steps taken by the states toward enacting this law show that this lack led to very different interpretations. The proposed law was turned down on 11 October 1917 on formal grounds.[97] It was maintained that the present version of the parliamentary order touched on areas governed by business law. These far-reaching consequences did not conform to the content of the empowerment law from 4 August 1914 giving the *Bundesrat* far-reaching competence in war-related and economic issues. As a consequence the Bundesrat had to lift the law regarding compulsory business at the end of October 1917 once more. A second version of the law presented by the *Bundesrat* was also vetoed by the Reichstag in the summer of 1918.

In addition to the censorship boards installed by the deputy general commanders, local communities also attempted to place limitations on film consumption. The municipal office of Angermünde determined that it was a criminal act for war-supported wives of servicemen to go to the movies.[98] The Weida parish council in Saxony-Weimar threatened the same people with a withdrawal of support if they were found visiting the movies.[99] Due to the intervention of a pastor, two wives of servicemen with six children each lost their weekly support of two loaves of bread.[100]

Independent of concrete censorship ordinances and all other attempts to limit the population's film consumption, all measures demonstrated the attempt to enforce conformity with regard to expectations of relaxation and entertainment by making use of power politics and the consciousness of an elitist distance toward moviegoers. The political orientation for the conceptual shaping of the orders and all other measures was less a result of specific interests than of ideal purposes, which, at the same time, offered larger social guidelines for ordering thought and action.

Censorship interests of individual social groups during the war

Just a few days before the war started, the *Licht-Bildbühne* newspaper praised 'Die Waffen nieder' (Lay Down Your Arms), a film produced by the Nordic Film Co., based on a novel by the same name written by Margarete von Suttner.[101] The same newspaper declared on 1 August 1914, that now 'apparently all insignificant disruptions of business have naturally withdrawn totally behind the burning danger of war itself'.[102] There was little sign in the cinematographic press of the hawkish enthusiasm that was apparent during the first few days of the war in some segments of the population; rather, concern about the future predominated.[103] On the other hand, decisions to withdraw French and English films from schedules and considerations on the future of German film[104] showed that even the film industry had become caught up in the patriotic enthusiasm that struck Germany in August 1914, pushing, 'for the time being, all internal conflicts and tensions to the side'.[105] For a short time, this respite also implied that the film industry would refrain from encounters with state agencies such as the censorship board or local governments regarding entertainment taxes. No protests took place in Berlin against film censorship,[106] which was intensified at the start of the war, nor against the forced closings of movie theatres in various parts of the Empire. The ban on allied films, harsh censorship and insufficient transportation all contributed to an acute shortage of films in the early days of the war. At the same time, war recruitment efforts caused the number of movie house patrons to drop dramatically. Moreover, movie theatres as an institution and the films shown there were subjected to increased criticism during the first few weeks of the war. And finally, there was a shortage of projectionists since they were drafted, or even enlisted, for military service.[107] All of these reasons led to the closure of many cinemas, especially in August 1914.

Under the circumstances, some members of the film press and cinematographic associations feared the end of their industry. This is why they started defending themselves against new attacks as early as late autumn 1914. They declared an end to the truce that had meant deliberately refraining from public debate and pressure regarding differences of opinion in both the political and economic spheres. In late October and November, the *Licht-Bildbühne* had already printed numerous articles polemicising against the legal restrictions placed on film documentation from the front.[108] *Der Kinematograph* compared the manipulation of public opinion through the press in general and film in particular with the impact of the 42 cm cannon, one of the most powerful German artillery weapons, indirectly demanding the authorities approve more films.[109] On 16 February 1915, thirteen companies from a variety of branches submitted a several-page statement to the Prussian ministry of war, describing the circumstances facing German cinematography and requesting that measures be taken to improve the situation.[110] For the first time, the film industry was relatively unanimous in protesting the restrictions placed on motion picture advertising when it submitted a statement signed by approximately 70 companies and associations to the Prussian ministry of war, ministry of the interior and other departments.[111] Movie theatre owners in Saxony turned to the emperor, requesting that he mitigate the cinema decrees issued by the IVth army corps, which was responsible for their area.[112] In the course of the war, film industry representatives attempted to take preventive action to avert possible attacks. The Association of Cinema Owners of Greater Berlin and the Province of Brandenburg, for example, sent several letters of protest directly to the imperial chancellor in connection with a proposal for even more severe film censorship introduced on 4 May 1916 by Reichstag representative Dr. Werner.[113] During the second half of the war, the censorship board and the Society for the Protection of Common Interests of Cinematography proposed having regular meetings 'to initiate and preserve mutual understanding'.[114]

All the protest forms clearly show that the cinematographic associations and companies did not protest censorship in general. Despite many differences on specific issues, there was broad consensus that censorship was necessary, or at least inevitable. All existing documents reflect the associations' objection to excessive resolutions only. The respective authors demanded a uniform film censorship law within the territory of the German Empire and the right to participate in all decisions on censorship.[115] In addition, film producers tried to develop material that experience showed would just barely make it past the censors, since this promised the highest box office returns.[116]

'The World War brought in new elements. It was the first war that mobilised nations in their entirety, including the home front, and it was waged with massive armies, and set ... against a background of ideology'.[117] This also defined the relationship of different social groups to motion picture censorship. In particular, it was the harshest critics of cinematography and the staunchest supporters of film censorship whose attitudes were ideologically motivated. These people came from the ranks of the intelligentsia, including professors, teachers and artists who remained loyal to the system, and especially Church representatives.[118] The way these educated classes feared 'rising mass society ... verged on obsession. It served to strengthen aristocratic and exclusive traits, including dislike of any extension of egalitarian, democratic rights and institutions' and any pluralistic cultural offerings, as represented by cinemas and other popular entertainment establishments. This educated bourgeoisie saw all forms of popular culture as inferior, since these did not spread the '"idealistic" ideals, elevated and lofty goals and norms, as cultivated and supported by the major institutions of socialisation: schools and the church'. 'The relationship of this group to politics, the power politics of the nation-state',[119] contradicted – especially in times of

Fig. 5. The Welt-Biograph Theater in pre-war Pritzkow, c. 1913. The posters are all in French.

war – the distance to politics that was normally exercised in other contexts. Power politics was considered legitimate as long as it served the implementation of the propagated goals.

In the prewar period, motion picture developments had neglected many of the reform efforts of the intelligentsia. Social as well as cultural polarisation seemed to be eliminated, not only by the apparently smooth integration of the 'army of workers' into the war machinery, but by the immediate willingness of movie house owners to stop showing French and English films once the war started.[120] The 'dull monotony'[121] and the 'superficial comfort'[122] of the prewar period seemed to have made way for a new 'community'.[123] The spiritual sense of mission was supposed to be carried beyond Germany's borders as a service 'to humanity' in the 'holy war'.[124] But domestically as well, it was supposed to reestablish the 'spiritual harmony' that was lacking before the war and eliminate mammonism. This group hoped the coming peace would bring 'a healthy national soul', just as the 'peace of 1871 [created] a healthy national body'.[125] Correspondingly, the most important task of politics, especially in war, was seen as 'leading the national soul'.[126] At the same time, the war as 'the most powerful of all bringers of culture', was supposed to 'awaken [everything] that exhibits inner health and is still worthy of existence to a new, rich life'.[127] 'German culture is moral culture ... If it relinquishes its moral purity, then it stops being German.' The task of the war and the postwar period was to re-establish 'its pure image', that 'was spoiled by the fever of an insatiable desire for wealth, degenerate sensual pleasure, sprawling lascivious sensation-seeking and a superficial presumption of knowledge and ability'.[128] In other words, this single-minded way of thinking about war and society, denying all change, did not only equate spiritual values with military ones, but also negated the diversity of sensory perceptions, needs and life plans.

German Party representative Reinhard Mumm, one of the most prominent critics of cinemas, also considered film to be 'un-German'. He referred to it as 'a first-class devastator of the people, destroying more of their moral values than a hundred educators could sow in quiet labour. The average film is capable not only of trivialising, but of destroying',[129] since 'from its very beginnings until the present day, the new industry ... is virtually in Jewish hands'.[130] Other critics saw the French influence as the primary cause for movies to be 'un-German':

> The war has been the greatest cinema reformer of all. It accomplished that which we hardly dared to dream of. It destroyed the magnificent business organisation based outside our borders that was the support and secret of success of trash cinematography – the organisation that achieved the miracle of keeping alive the artificial, even anti-natural demand for thousands of worthless meters of film in hundreds of thousands of movie theatres around the world, serving the interests not of movie theatres, but of film capital. This organisation, in the end tracing back to the Pathé model, has been broken, and if we know even the very least of what we want, then it shall never return again.[131]

Even regarding films he thought were outstanding, like *Bismarck* and *Andreas Hofer*, Mumm disputed their 'certain, very refined impact ... on account of the facial expressions and title links'.[132]

Basing his statement on this criterion, Mumm spoke out in the authorisation debates in the German Reichstag in March 1918:

> The strongest grounds of moral life of our people speak in favour of it. We cannot let the soul of the people be devastated by unbridled capitalism ... That which is offered here and there under the influence of certain capitalistic circles – pepper, strip scenes, over and over a mockery of marriage and family life in general – that is not German humour; that is un-German gutter humour, and if censorship proceeds there with a very distinct degree of severity and takes vigorous action, then such measures will doubtless find the approval of all members of our German people with healthy feelings.[133]

Centre Party representative Kuckhoff made a similar remark during the same session:

> It is true that movies are largely to blame for the rising incidence of crime among adolescents in war times ... When the war is over and the restrictions are lifted, the audience will be the sole decision makers, determining the movie schedules of the cinemas. Show business will be dependent on the whims of the movie patrons. Competition will force even highly esteemed businesses to give in to the wishes of the majority of the audience, opening the floodgates to sensationalism. The small movie houses in the towns and on the outskirts of the cities will rise again, and we will once again be confronted with the regrettable phenomena that represent a serious threat to the health of the nation – dangers that can also be brought on by movie theatres with poor technical management. On top of that, we will suffer further insult to our aesthetic sensibilities whenever we walk through the streets and are forced to see the dreadful movie advertisements. We will once again have to expect that, wherever we go, criers will harrass us and tell us to go to the cinema. This situation must be avoided at all costs.[134]

Despite the divergent political opinions expressed, both speeches show a clear tendency toward a strong state that stands above the individual, politically oriented toward ideal aims and paternalistic concepts in order to resolve existing conflict. At the same time, both politicians succumbed to an unrealistic line of reasoning. On the one hand, they did not want to do without movie theatres totally, since they wanted certain pictures to receive as broad circulation as possible, and also because the film industry employed several thousand people.[135] On the other hand, companies interested in commercial profit were asked to sacrifice that in favour of educating the country. Private companies were thus given the task that the intelligentsia had failed to accomplish in the preceding decades. Without expressing it explicitly, the reformers pursued the goal of transforming the cinema into a partial substitute for adult education centres. Attitudes toward films, such as the ones cited here, were essentially determined by conservative newspapers, in particular the *Tägliche Rundschau* (Daily Review) and the *Deutsche Tageszeitung* (German Daily), papers read primarily by the educated classes,[136] and various family newspapers.[137] In addition, in the initial years of the war they also influenced the movie descriptions in newspapers, such as *Vorwärts* (Forward), which at this time was oriented toward ideas of the movie reformers.[138] To this extent, even during the war, public opinion was essentially determined by the intelligentsia's interpretation of the cinema and its accompanying ideas regarding censorship.

During the reign of Wilhelm II, many members of the educated classes were 'very active in extra-parliamentarian associations that were nationalistic in nature; in the Pan-German League, for example, 50 per cent of the members in 1901 were from the educated professions – professors, lecturers, artists, civil servants and teachers'.[139] Reserve officers were also over-represented in these associations. They saw themselves as a whole 'as the embodiment of the state'.[140] The common ground of these two social groups in these associations was apparent, first of all, in their shared conservative identity: that is, in their dislike of political parties and parliamentarianism, their antipathy towards social democracy, their affinity for heroic mythology, monumentality and pathos, everything Spartanic and warlike, and the corresponding lack of contact with reality. Furthermore, both groups demonstrated particular loyalty to the emperor and nationalistic convictions. On the other hand, they complemented each other, making up for their respective deficiencies. 'The intellectual horizon of many officers before the war was very narrow'.[141] Everything relating to the military, battles and war enjoyed particularly high esteem compared with that which was 'merely' civilian, and the civilian virtues among the nationalistic supporters of public culture. Their common basic convictions and mutual respect were important reasons why film censorship was implemented essentially according to the wishes of cinema reformers, as was documented especially in the first half of the war.

Aims of the censors

Despite all objections, critics of the cinema did not intend to bring the trade to a total standstill. Even before the war, demands for German nationalistic films were made again and again. Theologian Konrad Lange, one of the most prominent cinema reformers, wrote the following in 1913:

> No one wishes to keep the cinema from photographically documenting all kinds of daily events according to the methods of a conscientious reporter. There have never been any objections to showing beautiful landscapes and travelogues from moving trains in the movie theatres. And who would have anything against presenting motion pictures of interesting movements such as maneuver scenes, technical manipulations, agricultural procedures and the like, not to mention using cinematographic techniques for scientific purposes.[142]

Mumm, continuing his previous line of argument, stressed in a Reichstag speech in the last year of the war that 'images can be used in the service of the nation. If for example, we were soon to see a wealth of pictures in the cinema of the oldest land of German colonisation, the German Baltics, then we would enjoy such presentations, and maybe the urban scenes of German Riga, German Mitau, German Reval, would show the masses that have been miseducated by the Left press that these are countries of old German culture ... In this regard cinema can do an important job. It can do good work when it steps in for a generous propaganda project on the idea of a war homestead, which warmed Hindenburg's and Ludendorff's hearts. Constructive strength could come out of a film for a change.'[143] Even before the war, the imperial army used cinematographers to train soldiers how to shoot.[144] Moreover, films on imperial maneuvers and other military events, and those on military technology were part of the standard repertoire of movie theatres.[145] The military was even requested to provide a greater selection, especially of technology films.[146] Teachers also used these films in the schools.[147]

It is conspicuous that both in military circles and among the intelligentsia, certain pictures of nature, industry, cities, landscapes and military subjects were not only permissible but expressly characterised as deserving support. At the same time all films with dramatic content were rejected if they did not deal with German history, as did *Bismarck* and *Andreas Hofer*.[148] After August 1914, the censors had no objections to the numerous sentimental films that showed war in the clichés of the theatre productions of the war in 1870–71,[149] such as *Fräulein Feldgrau – Ein heiteres Spiel in ernster Zeit* (Miss Feldgrau – A lively game in serious times), *Es braust ein Ruf wie Donnerhall* (A shout is roaring like thunder),[150] *Ruf der Fahnen* (Call of the Banners), or *Ich hatt einen Kameraden. Aus dem Tagebuch eines Kriegsfreiwilligen* (I had a comrade. From the diary of a war volunteer).[151] Common to all the films either sponsored or well-meaningly tolerated by the military or the intelligentsia was the fact that the audience was not allowed any room for autonomous feelings beyond that of a very narrow emotionality, and no other fantasies were permitted except for the one recognised as nationalistic and supporting the state. In other words, any emotional freedom was considered potentially threatening and thus rejected. This explains some of the reasons for censorship: 'A film could be permitted in which a cadaver with a smashed skull is clearly shown, whereas another film is banned because the funny heroine crosses her legs. A film showing an atmosphere of champagne and dancing might be allowed and the forward dive of an acrobat is banned for the duration of the war because of excessive burlesque features. A detective who fights with poison, daggers and boxing gloves might be permitted and another, who has a trap door in his house, will be banned.'[152]

Fig. 6. Friedrich Wilhelm von Loebell, Prussian Minister of the Interior (on the right), defended existing film censorship procedures in 1917. [Archiv der Landesbildstelle, Berlin.]

A scientific explanation for these views was offered at the end of the nineteenth century by Gustave Le Bon in his book, *La psychologie des foules* (The psychology of the crowd). His research findings had already been transferred to film before the war started. A physician, H. Duenschmann, declared in 1912 that 'the crowd thinks only in images and can only be influenced by images that have a suggestive impact on their imagination. Such images can, for example, be awakened by certain magically sounding words and stereotypical formulas ... Even though the written word can simultaneously have a suggestive impact on a greater number of people, the spoken word is generally superior. The most powerful of all rapid means of suggestion, however, is the example. If you want to motivate the crowd to a particular action, the best method is to show them what to do.' After a few comments on the significance of pantomime, Duenschmann came to the conclusion the 'we can thus see that cinematography, by suggestively influencing the imagination of the crowd, is not only on a par with theatre in a qualitative sense, but often must be considered superior to it. At the same time, it is quantitatively infinitely superior, since, numerically, a virtually unlimited increase in the mass impact is possible, namely, through mechanical reproduction.'[153]

Fig. 7. The wartime activities of the German film industry were praised by Major Georg Schweitzer, member of the general staff in charge of film censorship.

This theory of the weak-egoed consumer and the inferiority of the masses equated the statements and intentions of films with the reactions of the audience. At the same time it provided the intelligentsia with the necessary basis from which to argue their own intellectual superiority and the spiritual sense of mission they drew from that. They were not able to determine their intellectual qualities rationally, but they accepted nothing but their own opinions, nor did they attach any importance to material realities. Instead, representatives of these groups regarded their own views as universally valid and they tried to make all social needs and demands subordinate to their own standards and values. They attempted to disregard existing laws[154] and assumed they could control, according to their own views, the content of films through censorship and restrictions on subject matter and forms of presentation. Since this minority used the written word to definitively declare those basic social, political and aesthetic ideas they considered correct, they also lacked the necessary understanding for the specific qualities of the language of film. Their criticism of motion pictures remained correspondingly vague and indefinite.

The fundamental appraisal of the cinema hardly changed among the members of the intelligentsia. During the budget debates in the Prussian parliament, Minister of the Interior Friedrich Wilhelm von Loebell stressed that the existing laws on censorship had proven effective. Between the onset of the war and 1 December 1916, the Berlin Censorship Board had banned 311 films, '244 of which for the duration of the war'. In 1916 alone, 116 films had been banned. Nevertheless, Centre Party representative Linz and Conservative representative von dem Osten demanded at the same session that everything 'undignified should disappear' from the cinemas.[155] Their comments emphasised the efforts of the intelligentsia to counter the 1914 ruling of the Berlin Higher Administrative Court, using the military censorship board to push through their educational ideas. Despite the consistency of their protest, generalised opinions like 'the average movie is nothing more than a projected lesson in trash',[156] which had been commonplace at the beginning of the war, largely disappeared. Parallel to the changes in statements, the practical ways of dealing with censorship decrees were also different in the first and second halves of the war. Major Georg Schweitzer, the member of the General Staff in charge of cinema censorship, said that 'German cinematography, it must be said without reservation, under the difficult conditions of the present – doubly hard, since they were totally new – has done its job entirely'.[157] The Conservatives' monthlies,[158] which were harsh critics of film, declared in 1917, 'Up to now there has been an all-too-strong tendency in Germany to view film and the cinema under the aspect of a more or less dubious means of entertainment and, much to the detriment of our cause, the extraordinary cultural and economic significance of film and cinema in the lives of the peoples, especially now during the world war, has been overlooked'.[159]

Censorship and propaganda

Censorship as a negative way of influencing film content and propaganda, as its positive counterpart, were constantly combined during the first world war. The theoretical origin of all efforts to use the media for the propagation of a particular interpretation of the war and its goals was based – as was censorship – on clear ideas about the weak-egoed consumer. This led to belief in rather extreme possibilities for propaganda both inside and outside Germany. Especially in the second half of the war, this model of behavior and consciousness had to be able to explain the unsettling developments in the hinterlands and on the front. This is why, starting in 1916–17, propaganda, demanded increasingly by the state and various interest groups, was used domestically and in neutral countries.

At the time war was declared censorship had been solely the responsibility of the military, but as of September 1914 a number of partly or wholely state-run institutions and 'private institutions competed in this area, dealing with constant reorganisation and unclear, overlapping responsibilities. Domestic and foreign efforts increased, as did news acquisition, reporting and manipulation. Efforts to influence the German public joined similar efforts in allied, neutral and enemy states.'[160] The Central Department for Foreign Service within the Foreign Office took on a key role when it was founded on 5 October 1914. The Empire tried to use it in allied and neutral countries to pursue active cultural propaganda aimed at spreading a positive image of Germany and its allies. It was hoped that this would prove to be useful foreign policy for waging war; culture thus became a weapon in the war. The main task of the Central Department was to circulate books, brochures and pictures in neutral countries. It also started sending a weekly war-newsreel, the 'Messter-Woche', to neutral countries on a regular basis.[161] Germany thus became the first war-waging country to pursue active state-organised foreign film propaganda. In the years following, concerts, art exhibitions and theatre performances were organised in allied and neutral countries. Within Germany, it was primarily members of the intellectual elite that took on propaganda tasks in the first year of the war by holding lectures. In addition, numerous writings and poems were published that interpreted the war and tried to justify it. In the first few months, differences in views were already visible with respect to the use and political opportunity of certain films. This debate continued for the duration of the war. For example, a letter from Switzerland in spring 1915 charged that 'Messter-Woche' number 12 showed Germans torturing Russian prisoners of war. The responsible censorship board definitively opposed this view.[162] A letter of 4 July 1916 to the embassy in Bern reported the following: 'The "Messter-Wochen" are often very boring'. They need 'exciting, impressive pictures... that unobtrusively show our strength and greatness'.[163] On 9 January 1917, Bintz, the German officer for propaganda in Scandinavia, telegraphed the director of the military film and photography department of the Foreign Office, as follows: 'films for Sweden far too little plot ... Urgently recommend preparing effective feature films; otherwise I have no material'.[164] In a cinema report made in the summer 1917, all other films propagating German's greatness were rejected, suggesting instead that more films be shown that deal with German social welfare and care for the wounded soldiers and prisoners.[165] According to research conducted by the *Lichtbild-Bühne*, even staff members of the Central Department for Foreign Service appraised the war footage as 'so harmless and meaningless', that they were useless 'in spreading truth'. For propaganda purposes the staff demanded 'real war reports that show battles and not boring, peaceful scenes'.[166]

The manifold difficulties regarding foreign propaganda also show that blocked or damaged communication lines due to the war, excessive patriotism and nationalism, and the limited content in the media due to censorship all served to form an intellectual cage that made it increasingly difficult in the course of the war for the responsible persons to understand foreign views of Germany and respond accordingly.[167] As a result, once a concept was acknowledged as correct, its implementation usually continued unchanged until the end of the war.

On 28 August 1916, Hindenburg and Ludendorff took over the Military High Command. In contrast to their predecessors, the naming of Hindenburg and Ludendorff had plebiscitary qualities. Since they enjoyed such broad-based support within both the military and the population at large, they were able to quickly develop their command into the most significant military and political force in the Empire. At the same time, as the war proceeded it became obvious that not only a massive army, but the entire strength of society was necessary to end it. It was no longer appropriate to separate military and civilian sectors, as had been typical in earlier wars. Instead, the struggle took place among nations in their entirety, with all their military strength, scientific know-how, industrial production capability and ideological inclination to wage war. As the war continued, increased psychological and physical tensions intensified the need for entertainment expressed by a broad base of the public. Film could fill this need for three main reasons. First, movie theatres were among the few recreational facilities that had not been prohibited during the war, especially in the rural areas; second, films were a welcome diversion from the dreariness of daily events of the war, both at home and among all divisions at the front; finally, with cinema, it was possible to reach classes of the population that did not take advantage of other forms of propaganda, such as lectures or written statements.

Fig. 8. General Erich Ludendorff, who took over the military high command in 1916, saw film as a more important tool than written literature in the education of the masses. [Archiv der Landesbildstelle, Berlin.]

Increased censorship, also including propaganda, could be observed in Germany starting in the second half of the war. Ludendorff, for example, saw film primarily as 'a means of educating the masses' that, 'today, has a more insistent and concentrated impact on the masses ... than the written word'.[168] This attitude led to the founding of the Military Department of the Foreign Office in 1916. Through the efforts of seven film teams, it started shooting footage at the front. Since it was difficult to circulate the films that were made, the Photography and Film Office (*Bild- un Filmamt, BuFa*) was formed in January 1917. Together with the Balkan-Orient Film Co., Bintz's organisation of distribution in the north, and others, the necessary distribution companies for foreign film propaganda were thus established.[169] The main censorship board became the executive body of the army in April 1917, subject to the orders of the heads of Department IIIB of the General Staff. Because of the prestige of the High Command among the acting military commanders, this step was an essential prerequisite for creating uniform censorship standards for military content thoughout the Empire, the BuFa films would achieve the desired circulation.

After much preliminary work – going back as far as 1915 – the German Cinema Company *(Deutsche Lichtspiel-Gesellschaft,* DLG) was finally founded on 18 November 1916 by groups related to heavy industry. The DLG attempted to use a commercial basis to spread cultural propaganda domestically and abroad. Whereas the BuFa concentrated on war films, the DLG produced mostly short urban, industrial and landscape films.[170] At the same time, the 'Central Institute for Education and Curriculum' started using more and more educational films for lessons in schools.[171] Despite changing attitudes toward film as a result of the diverse activities and new companies, the subjects of the DLG films and those of the BuFa were oriented toward the ideas of the intelligentsia. Not until the negotiations for the founding of the Universum Film Company (Ufa) in late 1917 did it become apparent that narrow, cinema-reforming ideas had lost their dominating impact on the leading commercial institutions and the military.

As early as spring 1916, the Berlin Association for the Protection of Common Interests of Cinematography and Related Branches had intervened to have films re-evaluated that were banned either entirely or for the duration of the war. As a result, a number of films could be shown with a few edits or even none at all. The Association was also able to achieve, by referring to the propagandistic significance of the medium, that even several acting Supreme Commands authorised some films that they had previously banned.[172] Berlin film censorship data for 1917 shows that the number of banned feature film productions had declined considerably. There were two main reasons for this. First, many film companies based their films on family newspaper novels.[173] Due to the subject matter, the target audience was the entire family, therefore refraining from the outset from everything 'that could possibly have disturbed the peaceful and comfortable atmosphere within the circle of the family'.[174] Second, the number of one and two act productions banned for the duration of the war decreased from 1916 to 1917 by 20 per cent, and bans on longer films decreased by about 35 per cent.[175]

Changed social attitudes toward the cinema around the end of the reign of Wilhelm II were also reflected by the 1918 Reichstag debate on the issue of licensing. In the corresponding Cinema Committee, only the Centre Party, the Conservatives and the German Party voted for the law; all other parties opposed it.[176] Although this committee decision did not mean cinema opponents stopped verbally attacking the subject matter of the films,[177] all attempts were finally crushed to pass a law going beyond the existing film censorship law to restrict film content even after the war, or to reduce the number of movie houses through non-economic regulations.

On 1 October 1918, the Berlin film censorship law was already ten years old; a few days later, the revolution started. On 12 November the imperial government declared that 'there is no more censorship. The theatre censorship law is hereby repealed'.[178] Initially, however, the Berlin chief of police continued to enforce all ordinances enacted by the Supreme Command, including the poster ordinance and the 'child ban'.[179] The justification given was that the new government had not abolished the relevant theatre censorship department, but the departments of the political police. On 11 December, the Association of Cinema Owners and film distributors asked the imperial minister of the interior to rescind the relevant regulation.[180] In late 1918, the Prussian government passed a resolution to repeal the film censorship law. Censorship was also lifted in other states, but it remained in effect in Bavaria and Württemberg.[181] The Weimar national assembly confirmed the abolition of censorship in Article 118 of the constitution, but section 2 allowed for a special censorship law pertaining to film. At the 100th session of the national assembly in 1919, Representative Mumm referred to sex education films in proposing a reinstatement of film censorship, thus continuing the same line of reasoning he pursued before and during the war. In spring 1920 this was then instituted throughout the Republic. ♦

Notes

1. cf. Herbert Birett. *Verzeichnis in Deutschland gelaufener Filme. Entscheidungen der Filmzensur 1911–1920* (Berlin, Hamburg, Munich, Stuttgart 1980), 1.

2. Thomas Nipperdey. *Deutsche Geschichte 1916–1918. Bd. 1* (vol.1), *Arbeitswelt und Bürgergeist* (Munich 1991): 817.

3. On the cinematic reform movement cf. for example: Anton Kaes. *Kino Debatte. Texte zum Verhältnis von Lieratur und Film 1909–1929* (Munich, Tübingen 1978); *Prolog vor dem Film. Nachdenken über einneues Medium 1909–14,* Jörg Schweinitz, ed. (Leipzig, 1992): 55ff.

4. Bundesarchiv, Abteilungen Potsdam (Federal Archives, Potsdam) (BA) Auswärtiges Amt (foreign ministry AA), no. 33018 B. 28.

5. 'Weimar. Eine Ministerialverordnung über den Betrieb von Lichtspielunternehmungen'. *Bild und Film,* no. 2 (1912) vol. 13: 148.

6. Griebel, 'Die Kinematographenzensur'. *Das Land,* no. 14 (1913): 273.

7. 'Die bisherige landespolizeiliche Regelung des Kinowesens in Bayern'. *Bild und Film,* no. 12 (November 1912–13): 277f.

8. BA AA, no. 33018 B. 27.

9. W. Warstadt. 'Aus dem Kampfe um die Kinoreform'. *Die Grenzboten. Zeitschrift für Politik, Literatur und Kunst,* no. 3 (1914): 128.

10. BA AA no. 33018 B. 81.

11. BA AA no. 33018 B. 8.

12. BA Reichsministerium des Innern (Reich Ministry of the Interior RMdI), no. 14033 B. 28.

13. The corresponding information will be published in the forthcoming dissertation on film censorship before 1914, by Gabriele Kilchenstein (Humboldt University, Berlin).

14 'Der Berliner Filmkrieg zwischen Polizeipräsidium und Filmfabrikanten'. *Lichtbild-Bühne (LBB) (8 July 1914), no. 41.*

15. 'Filmzensur'. *LBB* (5 September 1914), no. 58.

16. 'Die Berliner Film-Zensur-Gebühren'. *LBB* (20 February 1915), no. 8.

17. cf. for example: Karl Brunner. *Der Kinematograph von heute – Eine Volksgefahr* (Berlin, 1913).

18. Wilhelm Hennicke. 'Bumke auf der Anklagebank. Ein neuer Zensurstreich des Professors Dr. Brunner' *LBB* (11 July 1914), no. 42, cf: 'Ein aufgehobenes Zensurverbot. Eine über die gebräuchlichen Mittel der dramatischen Kunst nicht hinausgehende Filmdarstellung kann nicht verboten werden. *Urteil des Preußischen Oberverwaltungsgerichts* vom 13. January 1914'. *LBB* (1 August 1914), no. 48.

19. BA Reichswirtschaftsministerium (Reich Ministry of economics)(RWM), no. 2005 B. 46, 23.

20. cf. for example: Denkschrift betreffend die Lichtbildtheater und die gesetzliche Regelung des Kinogewerbes. Überreicht vom Schutzverband deutscher Lichtspieltheater – Sitz Berlin. BA RMdI, no. 14033 B. 38.; 'Zur Lage'. *Der Kinematograph* (29 August 1914), no. 396.

21. *Quellen zur Geschichte des Parlamentarismus und der politischen Parteien. Second series: Militär und Politik,* Erich Matthias and Hans Meier Welker, eds., vol. 1/1 *Militär und Innenpolitik im Weltkrieg 1914–1918,* Wilhelm Deist, ed., part 1 (Düsseldorf, 1970): XL f.

22. Geheimes Staatsarchiv Stiftung Preußischer Kulturbesitz Rep. 77 Preußisches Ministerium des Innern (Prussian Ministry of the Interior) tit. 949 Nr. 1[m] Bd.1 B. 71 ff.

23. Herrmann Cron. *Die Organisation des deutschen Heeres im Weltkriege* (Berlin, 1923): 15.

24. 'Die Zensur ist tot – es lebe die Zensur!' *Der Kinematograph* (11 December 1918): no. 623.

25. Detailed: Walter Nicolai. *Nachrichtendienst, Presse und Volksstimmung im Weltkrieg* (Berlin, 1920): 51 ff.

26. Heinrich Binder. *Mit dem Hauptquartier nach Westen. Aufzeichnungen eines Kriegsberichterstatters* (Berlin, Stuttgart, 1915): 26.

27. Ludolf Gottschalk von dem Knesebeck. *Die Wahrheit über den Propagandafeldzug und Deutschlands Zusammenbruch. Der Kampf der Publizistik im Weltkriege* (Berlin, 1927): 44.

28. 'Das Photographieren auf den Kriegsschauplatz'. *Der Kinematograph* (14 October 1914), no. 407.

29. The LBB caimed that four companies had permission to do frontal exposures, however the Erste Internationale Filmzeitung claims seven on the western front and four on the eastern front. A. Mellini: 'Das Monopol der Kriegsaufnahmen', *LBB*, (31 October 1914), no. 74. 'Der große Generalstab und die Kriegsaufnahmen. Ein Wort zur Abwehr bedauerlicher Angriffe, ein Wort auch zur Verständigung', *Erste Internationale Film-Zeitung* (7 October 1914), no. 45.

30. Film companies which had gone to the front without permission, had to call back their crews in order to evaluate the pictures that had already been taken. Cf. A. Mellini: '*Das Monopol der Kriegsaufnahmen (II)*', *LBB* (14 November 1914), no. 78.

31. Special conditions issued for frontal exposures on 6 October 1914, corresponded to those of the press. Cf. Gertrud Bub. *Der deutsche Film im Weltkrieg und sein publizistischer Einsatz* (Berlin, 1938): 94.

32. BA Militärarchiv (Military Archiv)(MA) Reichsmarineamt (Reich Department of Navy) (RM 3), no. 9875 B. 64.

33. BA MA RM 3 no. 10297 B. 189 ff.; 264 ff.

34. Richard Treitel. 'Aufhebung eines Filmverbotes unter dem Belagerungsgesetz', *Der Kinematograph* (6 June 1917), no. 545.

35. 'Zensur-Schwierigkeiten der Films von den Kriegsschauplätzen', *LBB* (17 October 1914), no 70.

36. 'Der Mangel an Aktualitäten', *Der Kinematograph* (26 August 1914), no. 400.

37. 'Das Ende der Kriegs-Aufnahmen', *LBB* (20 March 1915), no. 12.

38. 'Die Hemmnisse bei den Kriegsaufnahmen', *LBB* (31 March 1915), no. 14.

39. 'Hamburg, Dresden', *LBB* (19 September 1914), no. 62.

40. 'Photographieren auf der Straße in Berlin', *LBB* (29 August 1914), no. 56.

41. 'Kriegszustand und Theaterpraxis', *LBB* (22 August 1914), no. 54.

42. 'Straßburger Kinos und der Kriegszustand', *LBB* (10 October 1914), no. 68.

43. 'Keine Kriegserläuterungen in Berliner Kinos', *LBB* (10 October 1914), no. 68.

44. Karl Brunner, 'Die Filmzensur in der Kriegszeit', *Der Hochwart*, no. 10, (1915): 180

45. BA RMdI no. 14033 B. 52; 69

46. 'Um das große Erbe'. Aufhebung eines Filmverbots', *Der Kinematograph* (4 July 1917), no. 549.

47. Ibid.; cf. also Karl Brunner. 'Die Filmzensur in der Kriegszeit', *Der Hochwart*, no. 10 (1915): 181.

48. 'Das General-Kommando in Altona veröffentlicht': *LBB* (16 January 1915), no. 3.

49. 'Verschärfte Kinozensur im Bereich des VII. Armeekorps', *Der Kinematograph* (8 September 1915), no. 454.

50. 'Vorführung militärischer Bilder in Bayern', *LBB* (20 March 1915), no. 15.

51. 'Zur Württembergischen Filmzensur', *LBB* (10 April 1915), no. 15.

52. 'Die Nachzensur alter Films', *LBB* (16 January 1915), no. 3.

53. 'Dritter ordentlicher Verbandstag des Verbandes zur Wahrung gemeinsamer Interessen der Kinematographie und verwandter Branchen zu Berlin E.V.', *Der Film (12 February 1916), no. 3.*

54. Verhandlungen des Reichstags. XIII. *Legislaturperiode, II.* Session (Reichstag Proceedings, 13th legislative period, 2nd session), vol. 307 (Berlin 1916): 1296.

55. 'Kultusministerium und Kriegszustand', *LBB* (29 August 1914), no. 56.

56. 'Verschärfte Kinozensur im Bereich des VII. Armeekorps', *Der Kinematograph* (8 September 1915), no. 454.

57. 'Verschärfte Kinozensur im Bereich des VII. Armeekorps', *Der Kinematograph* (8 September 1915), no. 454.

58. 'Münchner Notizen', *LBB* (20 January 1917), no. 3.

59. 'Nachrichtenteil', *Der Film* (11 March 1916), no. 7

60. 'Das neue Kinderverbot für die Kinos', *Berliner Börsen-Zeitung,* 21 September 1915, no. 441 cf. also 'Der 1. Oktober und die Kinderfilms', *LBB* (30 September 1915), no. 40.

61. Karl Brunner. 'Die Filmzensur in der Kriegszeit', *Der Hochwart*, no. 10 (1915): 182.

62. Detailed: Wolfgang Kruse. 'Die Kriegsbegeisterung im Deutschen Reich zu Beginn des Ersten Weltkrieges. Entstehungszusammenhänge, Grenzen und ideologische Strukturen', *Kriegsbegeisterung und mentale Kriegsvorbereitung. Interdisziplinäre Studien*, Marcel van der Linden und Gottfried Mergner unter Mitarbeit von Herman de Lange (ed.) (Beiträge zur Politischen Wissenschaft Bd. 61) (Berlin 1991), 78 ff.

63. 'Die Hetze gegen die deutschfeindlichen Films', *LBB* (3 October 1914), no. 66.

64. cf. for example, 'Aus dem Kampfe gegen französische Films', *Projektion* (20 August 1914), no. 32 – 33.

65. 'Der Kampf gegen die ausländischen Films', *LBB* (29 September 1914), no. 64.

66. 'Verband zur Wahrung gemeinsamer Interessen

der Kinematographie und verwandten Branchen E.V.', *LBB* (31 October 1914), no. 74.

67. 'Gegen das Film-Franzosentum', *Bild und Film*, no. 4–5 (1914–15): 34.

68. BA RMdI no. 14033 B. 59.

69. The showing of a film in the summer of 1915 with shots of French castles and beautiful scenes from nature led to tumultuous scenes in a Berlin moviehouse. 'Französische Filme in Berliner Kinos', *LBB* (28 August 1915), no. 35.

70. 'Kinematographie und Krieg', *Der Kinematograph* (21 July 1915), no. 447.

71. Karl Schüller. 'Das schlecht beratene VII. Armeekorps. Freimütig-sachliche Betrachtungen über das für den Bezirk des VII. Armeekorps erlassene Verbot der Vorführung von Films der Dreiverband-Länder und Konsorten', *LBB* (6 March 1915), no. 10.

72. Schmidl. 'Der Krieg, das Kino und die Karikaturisten', *Der Kinematograph* (10 February 1915), no. 424.

73. 'Die Plakat- und Inserat-Zensur in Leipzig', *LBB* (13 November 1915), no. 46.

74. 'Unhaltbare Zustände in Süddeutschland', *LBB* (7 October 1916), no. 40.

75. Alfred Leopold. 'Kinoreklame unter Polizeizensur', *LBB* (6 May 1916), no. 18.

76. 'Coblenz', *Der Kinematograph* (31 January 1917), no. 527.

77. BA RMdI no. 14033 B. 199 ff.

78. 'Das gebändigte Kinoplakat. Eine neue polizeiliche "Reinigung"', *Vossische Zeitung*, (14 July 1916), no. 356; cf. also 'Pädagogen-Urteil über die Bedeutung der Kinematographie', *Der Kinematograph* (21 February 1917), no. 530.

79. Alfred Rosental. 'Das deutsche Feldkino. Ein Kapitel aus der Kulturgeschichte des Weltkrieges', *Der Kinematograph* (7 March 1917), no. 532.

80. 'Nachrichtenteil', *Der Film* (9 September 1916), no. 33.

81. BA RMdI no. 14033 B. 135.

82. 'Aufgehobenes Plakatverbot', *LBB* (1 July 1916), no. 26.

83. 'Zensur-Verbote', *Berliner Morgenpost* (28 January 1915), no. 28.

84. Helmut Rathert. *Die deutsche Kriegsberichterstattung und Presse als Kampfmittel im Weltkrieg* (Heidelberg 1934), p. 40.

85. 'Kinorede des Minister des Innern v. Loebell. Zur Etatsberatung im preußischen Abgeordnetenhaus', *LBB* (17 February 1917), Nr. 7.

86. 'Die Filmstatistik. Die Nordische Film Co. beherrscht mehr als 1/3 des deutschen Filmmarktes', *LBB* (6 January 1917), no. 1.

87. 'Beratungen im Reichsamt des Innern. Zur Frage der kurzen Films', *LBB* (9 December 1916), no. 49.

88. Albert Hellwig. 'Krieg und Lichtspielwesen', *Konservative Monatshefte für Plitik, Literatur und Kunst*, no. 8 (1916): 638.

89. For the various political positions, compare, for example: 'Zensur und Belagerungszustand. Wiederaufnahme der Verhandlungen im Reichstagsausschuß' *Berliner Morgenpost* (11 January 1916), no. 11.

90. BA RMdI no. 14033 B. 90.

91. BA RMdI no. 14033 B. 104.

92. 'Kino-Schund. Ludwig Frank als Kino' held', *Vorwärts*, 10 August 1916, no. 218; Gertrud David. 'Die Reform des Kinos', *Vorwärts* (5 November 1916), no. 305.

93. *Verhandlungen des Reichstags. XIII. Legislaturperiode, II. Session* (Reichstag Proceedings, 13th legislative period, 2nd session), vol. 307 (Berlin, 1916): 1296.

94. Ibid., 1304 f.

95. Ibid., 1309.

96. 'Des freien Kinogewerbes Ende. Die Verordnung des Bundesrats vom 3. August 1917 betreffend den Konzessionszwang der 'Lichtspiele' nach Maßgabe des Bedürfnisses. – Ihr Inkrafttreten am 1. September 1917 und ihr amtlicher Wortlaut', *Der Film* (4 August 1917), no. 31.

97. *Verhandlungen des Reichstags. XIII. Legislaturperiode, II. Session* (Reichstag Proceedings, 13th legislative period, 2nd session), vol. 311 (Berlin, 1918): 3901, 3904, 3931 f.

98. Ludwig Brauner. 'Der Kino vor, während und nach dem Kriege', *Der Kinematograph* (19 January 1916), no. 473.

99. 'Kinobesuch als Unterstützungshindernis', in: *Vossische Zeitung* (16 August 1916), no. 418.

100. 'Die Strafe für den Kientoppbesuch', *Vorwärts* (27 January 1915), no. 27.

101. 'Die Waffen nieder!' *LBB* (25 July 1914), no. 46.

102. A. Mellini. 'Deutschland im Kriegszustand!' *LBB* (1 August 1914), no. 48.

103. cf. also 'Kino und Krieg. Mars regiert die Stunde'. *Der Kinematograph* (5 August 1915), no. 397; for Messter's statements at the beginning of the war, see Helga Belach. Henny Porten. *Der erste deutsche Filmstar 1890–1960* (Berlin, 1968): 45.

104. cf. also Malwine Rennert. 'Nationale Filmkunst', *Bild und Film*, no. 3. (1914-15): 53; 'Film und neue deutsche Form'. *Der Kinematograph*, (25 August 1915), no. 452; 'Kinematographie und Krieg'. *Der Kinematograph* (21 July 1915), no. 447.

105. Thomas Nipperdey. *Deutsche Geschichte 1866–1918, Bd. 1* (vol. 2), *Machtstaat vor der Demokratie* (Munich 1992): 779.

106. The Lubitsch production, *'Der Stolz der Firma'* (Pride of the Company), which premiered on 30 July 1914, was also banned. On 9 January 1915 the film had its public reopening.

107. Josef Aubinger. 'Die Kinematographie in Kriegszeiten', *Der Kinemato graph* (12 August 1914), no. 398; A. Mellini. 'Krieg und Kino. Der Pleitegeier. –Die Adressenliste –Die LBB als Feldpostsendung –Patriotismus und Geschäft –Der Schutzmann als Förderer deutscher Filmfabrikation. Die Feinde im eigenen Lager', *LBB* (26 September 1914), no. 64.

108. A. Mellini. 'Das Monopol der Kriegsaufnahmen'. *LBB* (31 October 1914), no. 74; cf. also A. Mellini. 'Das Monopol der Kriegsaufnahmen II'. *LBB* (14 November 1914), no. 78.

109. Horst Emscher. 'Der Film im Dienste der Politik'. *Der Kinematograph* (4 November 1914), no. 410.

110. A RMdI no. 14033 B. 52ff.

111. 'Eine Eingabe gegen das Verbot der Kinoreklame'. *Vossische Zeitung* (21 July 1916), no. 370.

112. '§ 9b ... Ein Notschrei aus der Provinz Sachsen! Immediatgesuch sämtlicher Lichtspieltheaterbesitzer an Seine Majestät den Kaiser um Aufhebung oder Milderung der militärischen Kinoerlasse'. *Der Film* (20 May 1916), no. 17.

113. BA RMdI no. 14033 B. 90; 94f.; 105 ff.

114. 'Die Kino-Tagung. Regelmäßige Aussprachen mit der Zensur.' *Vossische Zeitung* (15 February 1917), no. 83.

115. 'Förderung deutscher Filmkultur'. *Der Kinematograph* (2 May 1917), no. 540.

116. A. Lassally. 'Kinogewerbe und Kinoreform'. *Die Umschau. Wochenschrift über die Fortschritte in Wissenschaft und Technik*no, no. 18 (1916): 342.

117. Peter Grupp. 'Voraussetzungen und Praxis deutscher amtlicher Kulturpropaganda in den neutralen Staaten während *des Ersten Welkrieges*. In Wolfgang Michalka', ed., *Der Erste Weltkrieg. Wirkung, Wahrnehmung, Analyse*. Im Auftrag des Militärgeschichtlichen Forschungsamtes (Munich, Zurich 1994): 799.

118. cf. for example, Vorstand der Generalsynode. ed. *Verhandlungen der siebten ordentlichen Generalsynode der evangelischen Landeskirche Preußens* (Berlin 1916), 47f., 50ff.; 'Zensur im Abgeordnetenhaus'. *Berliner Lokalanzeiger*, (23 February 1916), no. 98; Heiner Schmitt. 'Kirche und Film'. *Kirchliche Filmarbeit in Deutschland von ihren Anfängen bis 1945. Schriftenreihe des Bundesarchivs 26* (Boppard, 1979): 21ff.

119. Thomas Nipperdey. *Deutsche Geschichte 1866–1918, Bd.1* (vol. 1), *Arbeitswelt und Bürgergeist* (Munich, 1991): 818.

120. cf., for example, 'Ausländische Filme'. *Der Türmer. Monatsschrift für Gemüt und Geist* no. 4 (1914): 296.

121. Paul Natorp. 'Deutscher Weltberuf.Geschichtsphilosophische Richtlinien'. Erstes Buch. Paul Natorp. ed., *Die Weltalter des Geistes* (Jena, 1918): 35.

122. Hans Krailsheimer. 'Huldigung'. Reinhold Buchwald, ed., *Der Heilige Krieg. Gedichte aus dem Beginn des Kampfes* (Jena, 1914): 4.

123. Adolf Deißmann. 'Der Krieg und die Religion'. Zentralstelle für Volkswohlfahrt, ed., *Deutsche Reden in schwerer Zeit* (Berlin, 1914):12.

124. Heiliger Krieg. *Ein Aufruf an deutsche Soldaten.Von einem Pfarrer* (Munich, 1915): 17.

125. Reinhard Mumm. *Der Christ und der Krieg* (Leipzig, 1916): 21f., 28.

126. BA RWM no. 14127 B. 264.

127. Otto von Gierke. 'Krieg und Kultur'. Zentralstelle für Volkswohlfahrt, ed., *Deutsche Reden in schwerer Zeit* (Berlin, 1914): 7.

128. Ibid., 23.

129. BA Nachlaß (unpublished works) (NL) Mumm, no. 22 B. 2.

130. Reinhard Mumm. *Die Lichtbühne. Ein Lichtblick aus den Verhandlungen der Deutschen verfassunggebenden Nationalversammlung* (Berlin, without year): 3.

131. Hermann Häfker. 'Kinematographie und Krieg'. *Bild und Film* no.1. (1914): 1.

132. BA NL Mumm, no. 22 B. 2.

133. Verhandlungen des Reichstags. XIII. Legislaturperiode, II. Session (Reichstag Proceedings, 13th legislative period, 2nd session), vol. 311 (Berlin, 1918): 4418.

134. Ibid., 4409.

135. 'Berliner Kriegsfragen im Abgeordnetenhaus'. *Berliner Lokalanzeiger*, (25 February 1916), no. 102; cf. also 'Minister v. Loebell gegen die Schliessung von Kinos'. *Vossische Zeitung* (14 February 1917), no. 81.

136. cf., for example, Wilhelm R. Richter. 'Deutsche Art im Lichtspiel wesen'. *Der Türmer* no. 15 (1915): 177f.; Wilhelm Heinz. 'Kino im Kriege', *Kunstwart* no. 23 (1915): 152f.; 'Vaterländisches Pflichtgefühl und Lichtspielhaus', *Die Hochwacht* no. 6. (1915): 117f.

137. cf. for example, Alfred Geiser. 'Der Film als Waffe im Völkerkampf'. *Daheim* no. 51 (1917).

138. 'Kinos Offenbarung'. *Vorwärts* (21 September 1914), no. 258.

139. Klaus Vondung. 'Zur Lage der Gebildeten in der wilhelminischen Zeit'. In Klaus Vondung, (ed.) *Das wilhelminische Bildungsbürgertum. Zur Sozialgeschichte seiner Ideen* (Göttingen: 1976), 31.

140. Quellen zur Geschichte des Parlamentarismus und der politischen Parteien. Second series: *Militär und Politik,* Erich Matthias and Hans Meier Welker, eds., vol. I: 1. *Militär und Innenpolitik im Weltkrieg 1914–18,* Wilhelm Deist, ed., part 1 (Düsseldorf, 1970), XIX.

141. Erich Otto Volkmann. 'Das Soldatentum des Weltkrieges'. In Bernhard Schwertfeger and Erich Otto Volkmann, (eds.) *Die deutsche Soldatenkunde*, Bd.1 (vol. 1) (Leipzig, 1937): 154.

142. Konrad Lange. 'Die "Kunst" des Lichtspieltheaters'. *Die Grenzboten*, 24 (1913): 509; cf. also Erwin Ackerknecht. 'Lichtbild und Bildungs pflege'. *Illustrirte Zeitung*, no. 3889 (10 January 1918): 40.

143. Verhandlungen des Reichstags. XIII. Legislaturperiode, II. Session (Reichstag Proceedings, see note 133), vol. 311 (Berlin, 1918): 4418; cf. also: *BA NL Mumm*, no. 214: 167.

144. Walter Thielemann. 'Schießausbildung durch den Kinematographen'. *Bild und Film* no. 11–12 (1913–14): 282.

145. *Der Kinematograph* wrote the following at the onset of the war, when there was a shortage of current footage due to the censorship: 'Every factory could use its older, stored material to put together a film about the equipment and organisation of the Austria, Serbian, Russian, or French armies'. Josef Aubinger. 'Die Kinematographie in Kriegszeiten'. *Der Kinematograph* (12 August 1914), no. 398.

146. Oefele. 'Kinematographie für Heereszwecke'. *Frankfurter Zeitung* (10 March 1913), no. 69; cf. also Hildebrand Freiherr von Clas, Friedrich Swoboda. 'Kinematographische Aufnahmen von Geschützprojektilen während der Bewegung bei Tageslicht'. *Sitzungsberichte der mathematisch-naturwissenschaftlichen Klasse der Kaiserlichen Akademie der Wissenschaften*, vol. CXXIII (1914), dept. IIa (Vienna, 1914): 757ff.

147. Max Wilberg. 'Schulfeiern im Kinematographen'. *Bild und Film* no. 2 (1912–13): 34ff.

148. Malwine Rennert. Nationale Filmkunst. *Bild und Film* no. 3 (1914–15): 53.

149. cf. Roswitha Flatz. *Krieg im Frieden. Das aktuelle Militärstück auf dem Theater des deutschen Kaiserreichs* (Frankfurt/Main, 1976): 248ff.

150. This film title, taken from the first line of the song 'Die Wacht am Rhein', was also cited as the eighth subject in the first 'Messter-Woche'. (Friedrich von Zglinicki. *Der Weg des Films* (Hildesheim New York, 1979): 338) This line also appears in contexts other than the film, such as the poem written in August 1914 by Rudolf Herzog: *'Das eiserne Gebet*'. Reinhold Buchwald ed., *Der Heilige Krieg. Gedichte aus dem Beginn des Kampfes* (Jena, 1914): 16.

151. BA RWM no. 8031 B. 18.

152. 'Die Film-Zensur'. *LBB* (15 December 1917), no. 50.

153. H. Duenschmann. 'Kinematograph und Psychologie der Volksmenge. Eine sozialpolitische Studie'. *Konservative Monatsschrift* no. 9 (1912): 924; cf. also Albert Hellwig. 'Schundfilm und Filmzensur', *Die Grenzboten* 6 (1913): 142; Ferdinand Avenarius. 'Von Suggestion und Massenseele als zweien der "aktuellsten" Fragen'. *Deutscher Wille des Kunstwarts* no. 1 (1st quarter 1918): 1ff.

154. cf. for example, Konrad Lange. 'Die "Kunst" des Lichtspieltheaters'. *Die Grenzboten* no. 24 (1913): 511f.; *Verhandlungen des Reichstags (Reichstag Proceedings) 13th legislative period, 2nd session,* vol. 311 (Berlin, 1918): 3904.

155. 'Kinorede des Ministers des Innern v. Loebell. Zur Etatsberatung im preußischen Abgeordnetenhaus'. *LBB* (17 February 1917), no. 7.

156. Wilhelm Heinz. 'Das Kino im Kriege'. *Kunstwart* no. 23, 1915, 152; for an exception, see the following essay: 'Die Kino-Seuche'. *Kreuzzeitung* (17 October 1916), no. 531.

157. Major Schweitzer. Die Kinematographie im Kriege. *Der Film* (29 January 1916): no. 1.

158. cf., for example, Oertel. 'Kinematographenrecht'. *Konservative Monatsschriften* no. 12 (1912): 1278 f.; Albert Hellwig. 'Krieg und Lichtspielwesen'. *Konservative Monatsschriften* no. 8 (1916): 636ff.

159. 'Film und Kino als Waffe im Weltkriege'. *Konservative Monatsschriften* no. 10 (1917): 794.

160. Peter Grupp. 'Voraussetzungen und Praxis deutscher amtlicher Kultur propaganda in den neutralen Staaten während des Ersten Welkrieges'. Wolfgang Michalka, ed., *Der Erste Weltkrieg. Wirkung, Wahrnehmung, Analyse.* Im Auftrag des Militärgeschichtlichen Forschungsamtes (Munich, Zurich, 1994): 804.

161. BA AA, Zentralstelle für Auslandsdienst (Central Department for Foreign Service) (ZfA) no. 1744 B. 169.

162. BA RMdI no. 14033 B. 71.

163. Aktenauszüge über Filmpropaganda während des Weltkrieges unter besonderer Berücksichtigung der Feindpropaganda und der Organisationen von Bufa, Deulig, und Ufa. Excerpts from the Reich Archiv and the Military Archiv in Potsdam by Hans Traub, part 1 (Berlin, 1938): 34.

164. AA ZfA no. 947 B.161.

165. AA ZfA no. 949 B. 38.

166. 'Die Hemmnisse bei den Kriegsaufnahmen'. *LBB* (31 March 1915), no. 14.

167. cf. also Theodor von Bethmann Hollweg. *Betrachtungen zum Weltkriege, part 2, Während des Krieges* (Berlin, 1921): 58.

168. Erich von Ludendorff. *Meine Kriegserinnerungen 1914–1918* (Berlin, 1919): 300.

169. BA AA ZfA no. 1030 B. 142ff.

170. BA Reichspostministerium (Reich Postal Ministry) no. 4727 B. 34ff.

171. 'Die Neuorientierung des Films'. *LBB* (5 May 1917), no. 18.

172. BA RWM no. 2005 B. 46 26ff.

173. 'Was die Zensurstatistik verrät'. *LBB* (2 March 1918), no. 9.

174. Dieter Barth. *Zeitschrift für alle. Das Familienblatt im 19. Jahrhundert. Ein sozialhistorischer Beitrag zur Massenpresse in Deutschland* (Münster, 1973): 178.

175. 'Was die Zensurstatistik verrät'. *LBB* (2 March 1918), no. 9.

176. 'Die Kino-Verhandlungen im Reichstag'. *Der Kinematograph* (18 July 1918), no. 600.

177. cf. for example, 'Rhode kontra Hindenburg'. *LBB* (14 September 1918), no. 37; T. Behme. 'Der Krieg als Abendunterhaltung'. *Deutscher Wille des Kunstwarts* no. 23 (4th quarter 1918): 151 'Der "Amüsier" – Teufel'. *Deutsche Tageszeitung* (29 October 1918), no. 551.

178. 'Die Zensur ist tot – es lebe die Zensur!', *Der Kinematograph* (11 December 1918), no. 623.

179. Die Filmzensur bleibt. *LBB* (30 November 1918), no. 48.

180. Theodor Zimmermann. 'Zur Lage in der Zensurfrage'. *Der Kinematograph* (18 December 1918), no. 624.

181. 'Die Zensur'. *LBB* (28 December 1918), no. 52.

Film History, Volume 9, pp. 95–115, 1997. Copyright © John Libbey & Company
ISSN: 0892-2160. Printed in Australia

African American extras in Hollywood during the 1920s and 1930s

Charlene Regester

The decade of the 1920s was the earliest period in which records were provided on African Americans working in white Hollywood. During this decade a Central Casting Bureau office was established as an employment agency to place actors and to curb the growing number of reports that extras were being exploited due to the casual nature of their work and abusive employment practices.[1]

However, while the number of African-American actors working in white Hollywood increased, the roles assigned to them more often than not confined them to the status of extras. In fact, white Hollywood in the pre-1950 period utilised the screen to transfigure its construction of race, to project its own ideological complexities regarding racial otherness, and to transform an endless variety of representations deemed racially different – representations that more often than not were parodic constructions and that were manifested in the African-American extras' screen representation. The increased visibility that African American extras received forced the black press to assume a watchdog role in reporting on those motion picture studios. What the press saw and reported was that while African Americans had made gains in employment, these gains did not subsequently translate into improved status. African American extras were continually marginalised in American cinema and this marginalisation became the subject of press reports, particularly in two periods – the silent era and the introduction of sound.

Extra-roles were distinguished from other roles in that actors were required to provide the 'human backdrop' for pictures, to serve as supporting players to their more illustrious stars, and to lend authenticity to a picture's atmosphere.[2] According to Murray Ross, extras were required to assume a variety of roles including being cast as 'Eskimos and Fiji Islanders, infants and bearded men, ice skaters and soprano singers – all [of whom] must be available at a moment's notice ... The reservoir of extra players from which the studios draw their human atmosphere must be vast and of a polyglot character'.[3] Extras working in Hollywood managed to obtain assignments through their affiliation with the Central Casting Bureau; however, when studios needed what was referred to as 'unusual types or ... a large number of Orientals, Negroes or other "racials"'[4] special calls were made specifically for these types. Once African Americans responded to

Charlene Regester is co-editor of the *Oscar Micheaux Society Newsletter* and a visiting assistant professor at the University of North Carolina. Correspondence c/o African and Afro-American Studies, CB #3395, 401 Alumni Bldg., UNC, Chapel Hill, North Carolina 27599-3395, USA.

these casting calls they were hired primarily to 'create atmosphere in jungle, South Sea Island and African scenes as natives, warriors and the like'.[5]

The roles assumed by African American extras, arguably, were not to be envied. In comparison to its treatment of other ethnicities, Hollywood's racial othering of African Americans was pervasive and all too apparent. Film historian Thomas Cripps contends that by the 1920s:

> ... immigrants, Orientals and Indians developed into stock figures, irrelevant to industrial America except as romantic icons. Each had been a part of the American experience, but in turn each had atrophied in the hands of screenwriters into wooden figures of assimilationist sentimentality, tragically vanishing aborigines and inscrutable menace. During the decade Indians disappeared from westerns ... Compared with Negro imagery on the screen, Orientals suffered from redundancy, melodramatic convention and eventually the tackiness of the Bs.[6]

African Americans were certainly not cast in redeeming roles and occupied a degrading range of gradations in employment. For example, those hired to assume domestic roles were relegated to 'bit' roles, while those employed in individual or what was referred to as 'mammy' roles were characterised as landing 'parts'. Parts were distinguished from other roles because they allowed actors to be photographed in close-ups and remain prominently visible in the film. Part actors were usually hired on contract with individual studios and, therefore, records regarding their contracts were generally kept by the studios and not the Central Casting Bureau office.[7] Generally, however, African American extras depended on the Central Casting Bureau office whose efforts resulted in laws to regulate earnings and to insure that some accommodations to which they were entitled were provided.[8] For African Americans, being employed in white Hollywood meant being employed as an extra.

Black extra employment patterns in the silent period

Reports on such extra work by the African American press first began in the mid-1920s. From that time on, records on the total number of African Americans employed as extras were consistently reported. To attest to the large number of African Americans employed by white Hollywood studios in 1924, the Baltimore *Afro-American* reported that:

> Coloured screen actors are being kept busy by the various companies at Hollywood. A glimpse at the list printed by a Los Angeles exchange shows that more than two hundred and fifty are employed in the studios. The largest number is engaged in the Keaton Studio, 120 members of the Cinema Auxiliary are working in [films] there. Fox is next with 60. Vitagraph, Metro, Goldwyn, Lasky, Hal Roach, Mack Sennett, Thos. H. Ince, Christie and Berwilla Studio all employ an appreciable number of race artists.[9]

In the Hollywood of the 1920s, African American actors continued to gain employment with the motion picture studios, if generally as extras. But merely being employed, regardless of the capacity, was considered an advancement in this period of American cinema history. In December of 1924, the African American press reported that Art Collins, L. Lamar (a newspaper theatrical columnist), Ernest White and Eli Reynolds were working at the Fox studios, while J. W. Swan and Virgil Owens were employed at United Studios. Hayes (Fat) Robinson was hired at the the Mack Sennett Studio and Tom Blackalle, Gertrude Howard and Robert Frazier, along with some 18 members of the Cinema Auxiliary, were working at both the Lasky and Goldwyn Studios.[10] Lamar, Reynolds, Owens and Howard were actually establishing reputations (as extras).

While applauding the motion picture studios with guarded praise for employing African American actors in greater numbers, the African American press must also have viewed with distaste Hollywood's practice of employing white actors in black face as was the case with Lloyd Hamilton in *His Darker Self* (Hodkinson, 1924) and Al Jolson in *The Jazz Singer* (WB, 1927).[11] However, Hollywood did abandon the practice of hiring white actors to appear in black face, while transferring black actors to these roles. The Baltimore *Afro-*

Fig. 1. Lloyd Hamilton and Irma Harrison in *His Darker Self* (Hodkinson, 1924). Al Jolson turned down the role. [Museum of Modern Art/Film Stills Archive.]

American, complimentary of the motion picture studios for their employment practices, stated: 'In the dramatic productions the coloured actors had one of the best years on record, with not a single day in 1924 in which some race actor was not at work.'[12]

The year 1924 witnessed both gains and losses for African Americans in the cinema world. Cripps observes that in the mid-1920s the Hays office taboo on 'darkskinned heavies' and miscegenation, provided few arenas in which African Americans could be cast as Other on the screen.[13] Yet African Americans, despite such industry trends, continued to be hired, albeit also being transformed on the screen. The fact is, the motion picture industry was in a period of overall expansion; the average budget had increased from some US$20,000 in 1914 to US$300,000 by 1924.[14] There were also greater pressures applied by the African American press for increased visibility on the screen. When African Americans' gradual gains in the industry did not translate into improved status off the screen, some African American filmmakers decided to launch their own ventures. Thus it was that Oscar Micheaux that year, produced *Body and Soul* (Micheaux, 1924), featuring African American actor Paul Robeson in his first screen role.

Two years later, in 1926, 750 African Americans were hired to assume a wide variety of roles as pirates, soldiers, slaves, flower girls, coachmen, footmen, 'mammies' and other character parts in *Eagle of the Sea* (Paramount, 1926). These roles were played by well known African American actors such as Inez Anderson, George West, Ora Tuggle, Alice Nichols and Lola Mackey.[15] During the same year *Ladies First (1926)* hired some 30 black extras, including Sam Baker (a former boxer) and Floyd Shackleford.[16] The Tarzan episodes, and more specifically, *Tarzan and the Golden Lion* (FBO, 1927) in 1926 interviewed some 100 African American actors, including Zack Williams,

Floyd Shackleford, Eli Reynolds and Reginald Siki (a.k.a. Battling Siki, a former champion boxer).[17] These parts called for African Americans to appear as 'jungle natives', roles for which, in the opinion of their employers, they seemed well suited. *Tarzan and the Golden Lion* was the quintessential example of the imposition of colonialism on black Africa, where whiteness was associated with superiority and blackness with inferiority.

By 1926 fourteen leading motion picture corporations were employing African American extras. These included Metropolitan, United Artists, Hal Roach, Christie, FBO, Mack Sennett, Educational, Universal, Pathé, Warner Bros., William Fox, First National, Paramount and Metro-Goldwyn-Mayer. The Central Casting Bureau agency registered some 11,000 applicants.[18] In 1924, confirmed reports reveal that some 3,464 were employed; 1925 (3,559); and 1926 (6,816).[19] Arguably, African American extras had arrived in white Hollywood and were there to stay. The end of the silent era coincided with the indisputable fact that African American extras had established themselves as marketable commodities within the Hollywood ranks and they could expect continued visibility in subsequent decades.

Black employment patterns in the first phase of the sound era – prior to 1930

The year 1926 signalled the end of the silent era; the industry was catapulted into sound with the introduction of *The Jazz Singer* (1927) – a film that featured white actor Al Jolson who appeared in black-face. Particularly after the advent of sound, white Hollywood would capitalise on the widely held view that African Americans possessed remarkable vocal and musical talent.

In 1927, as sound was being perfected in cinema, the industry continued to employ African Americans in extra roles. For example, *Louisiana* (1927) employed a significant number of African American extras, casting Sam Baker along with Everett Brown, Mary Curry – who was featured in a 'mammy' role – Nathan Curry, Margaret Jones, Arthur Leuin, Oscar Morgan, Alice Nichols, Hattie Richards and Henry Smith.[20] Such gains were considered advancements as African Americans penetrated white Hollywood, despite the fact that many of the roles maligned African Americans and marginalised them in cinema in much the same manner that they had been marginalised in American life. However, it is also argued that their acceptance of such roles should not imply that they were oblivious to their marginalisation or distortion; in fact they were fully aware of the travesty that was being inflicted upon them, but many felt that before they could argue for improved screen roles, they first had to gain visibility.

Reflecting white Hollywood's fascination with colonial rule in black Africa, *Jungle Love* (believed to be *Jungle Gods*, 1927), was set in Africa; it was reported that ' Only one white man, a dwarf, who will evidently don black-face makeup, will be the only white character used'.[21] This film, which featured African American actors Cliff Ingram (a.k.a. as Rex Ingram) and Spencer Williams,[22] signified Hollywood's desire to explore its racial fantasies. *Jungle Love* (a.k.a *Jungle Gods*) in much the same manner as *Tarzan and the Golden Lion* signified the ideological complexities of white Hollywood regarding race, as it formulated constructions of blackness and whiteness on the screen, while providing spectators with the voyeuristic gaze and allowed them to vicariously experience exerting power and control over black 'savages' through identification with the white male coloniser.

A similar ideological position was reflected in *The Missing Link* (WB, 1927), a film that featured Everett Brown in the role of an African chief, along with some 153 other black actors, while Sam Baker had been hired for the gorilla role. During the production, it is noteworthy that the studios raised the salaries of twenty-nine black actors cast in the film, a gesture believed to have been designed to compensate these actors for the exploitation they endured.[23] A similar gesture was employed by the makers of *Tarzan and the Golden Lion* as some 300 black actors earned a total of US$2,250 per day collectively, or US$7.50 per day for each actor.[24] These payments were considered high for that period, but they elicited a harsh response from the African American press who regarded such payments as purely compensatory measures for the exploitation these black actors endured. Exploited or not, the fact is that these roles must have had devastating consequences for both black and white spectators if spectators internalised such representations and projected them on to African Americans off the screen.

During 1927, additional motion picture studios joined the ranks of those employing African American extras including California, Charles Chaplin, Columbia, De Mille, Fine Arts, Buster Keaton, Metropolitan, Tec-Art, Hal Roach and Stern Film Corporation.[25] However, this visibility did not come easily. African American extras were often assigned to physically challenging feats. African American actors disproportionate in numbers to whites in the role of extra, accepted the physical challenges and unpleasant conditions associated with their roles. Risking their health and even their lives, they felt they were perfecting their craft and increasing their visibility in the cinema industry. For example, in 1927, a number of African Amerian extras in *The River* (1928), including Joseph Banks, Ben Browder, Nathan Curry, Henry Harrison, Ernest King, Charles Milton, G. B. Morrow, Clark Moore, Curtis Nero, Jack Prayer and Spencer Williams (later himself a filmmaker), were required to brave the icy waters of the Colorado River.[26] That same year, African Americans were cast in *The Wedding March* (Paramount, 1928). 'Twelve of the most perfectly formed coloured performers of Hollywood, six men and six women, worked all night' in roles casting them as Nubian slaves.[27]

Most African Americans were denied opportunities to land major roles. At the same time, the African American body was commodified as an object of danger and desire because of its blackness. Even an extra such as Zack Williams was described as 'an unusually large physical type which enables him to enjoy quite a wide range of parts', yet these actors were rendered as unimportant, expendable, and merely embellishments to the enhancement of the white stars with whom they shared the screen.[28] A year later, well over 100 African American actors were cast in *Diamond Handcuffs*, (MGM, 1928) including Sam Baker, Everett Brown, Floyd and Lloyd Shackleford and George Turner.[29] Production on this picture prompted the *Opportunity* magazine to turn its attention to Hollywood and report that *Diamond Handcuffs* and an earlier film, *The Road to Mandalay* (MGM, 1926), had used more than 200 African Americans as natives for atmosphere.[30] According to the Central Casting Bureau in 1927 some 3,754 were employed and an appreciable number of African Americans were similarly employed in 1928.[31]

Table 1. *Placement of African Americans by central casting corporation from 1 January 1928 to 31 December 1928.*

Aggregate month	Placements	Aggregate wages (US$)
January	308	2,906.65
February	240	2,268.38
March	773	6,690.17
April	152	1,546.78
May	212	2,075.75
June	272	2,343.27
July	1,270	11,859.38
August	278	2,915.00
September	748	5,692.50
October	4,502	34,054.38
November	882	8,188.00
December	1,279	9,162.63
Total	10,916	89,702.89

Provided by 'The Negro Invades Hollywood' , by Floyd C. Covington, *Opportunity* 7 no. 4 (April 1929).

Such success may be attributed to the fact that in 1927 an African American component of the Central Casting Corporation, originally organised in 1925 by the Association of Motion Pictures Producers, was established.[32]

With the advent of sound African Americans gained increased visibility on the screen albeit in the role of extra. This paved the way for more substantive screen roles in all-black cast films and for the explosion of two-reel all-black talkies. Cripps asserts that:

> These [two-reel] films brought the best of Afro-American vaudeville, vernacular dancing and the more commercial forms of jazz to film. Also, because they required little investment and because the risk of failure and its impact on their careers was borne almost exclusively by the black performers, the studios could grind them out regularly.[33]

Central casting bureau

In October of 1927, reports circulated in the African American press that the Central Casting Bureau office established in Hollywood would place African-American actors seeking employment as extras. Charles Butler had been hired as a casting director, one of the salaried employees of this agency designed to fulfill the steady demand for African American actors. Butler's duties included 'collecting, classifying and distributing' African American extras, not an enviable position. It was reported that during the production of *Hallelujah* (MGM, 1929), in order to recruit 340 extras to report to the studio on a Sunday morning, Butler had to draw upon the talent provided by area churches.[34]

Capitalising on the belief that African American actors possessed unique musical talent, King Vidor, white producer, was inspired to make his film *Hallelujah*. This film was initially regarded as a 'godsend' because with the production of *Hallelujah*, African Americans were transformed into screen stars. At first Vidor was rejected by studios afraid to produce this all-black cast picture lest Southern theatres found it objectionable. Vidor finally convinced studio officials to proceed with his project after providing 'a list of scenes suitable for an all-Negro sound film – river baptisms, prayer-meetings accompanied by spirituals, Negro preaching, banjo playing, dancing, the blues'[35], and after forfeiting his salary as an investment for the project. It seems that Vidor was driven to make the film to resolve his own ideological racial views. Vidor reveals that:

> I wanted to make a film about Negroes, using only Negroes in the cast. The sincerity and fervour of their religious expression intrigued me, as did the honest simplicity of their sexual drives. In many instances the intermingling of these two activities seemed to offer strikingly dramatic content. The environment of my youth in my father's east Texas sawmill towns had left many indelible memories of the coloured man; and I had heard my sister rocked to sleep each night to one of the best repertoires of Negro spirituals in the South.[36]

With the production of *Hallelujah*, Vidor demonstrated that African Americans were a viable reservoir of talent for sound films. Cripps adds that 'the new sound film that had intruded upon silent film ... stirred a myth in Negro circles that Negroid voices recorded with higher fidelity than white' – a myth that was fueled even by African Americans such as musical composer James Weldon Johnson.[37]

Arguably, because of the advent of sound, African Americans could expect to be accepted into American cinema in increasingly greater numbers, and given that the Central Casting Corporation had now created an office to manage the employment of African American actors, African Americans would have a significant impact on white Hollywood. The Central Casting Corporation, originally created by motion picture czar Will Hays as an extension of the Association of Motion Picture Producers, established a separate division to control the employment of black extras working in white Hollywood. This division is believed to have been an offshoot of an earlier effort launched by African Americans who had established their own Cinema Auxiliary, referred to as 'filmland's coloured casting bureau'.[38] The leader of this auxiliary was Jimmie Smith, an African American who as early as 1915 had served as the casting director for the Lincoln Motion Picture Company (a black film company) and later 'made special castings for scores of Hollywood film companies'.[39] According to Cripps, Smith had imported black actor James Lowe to Universal studios during the filming of *Uncle Tom's Cabin* (Universal, 1927) where Lowe replaced black actor Charles Gilpin in the central role. Referring to the establishment of the Central Casting Bureau office as a power struggle, Cripps contends that Smith took 'his protegé [Lowe] to England in search of fortune rather than cling to the fringes of power'.[40] Butler, also formerly associated with the Cinema Auxiliary, then was hired as the black casting director of the Central Casting Bureau office.[41]

When the office was established to control the employment of African Americans in white Hollywood, the African American press viewed its development with some degree of suspicion, and many felt that it was a deliberate attempt to keep the black extra from having 'personal contact with the casting or employment heads of each individual studio'.[42]

Cautious in its report, the Baltimore *Afro-American* stated:

> Eliminating in one day the beneficial results of four years work on behalf of the coloured film extras, Will Hays, czar of the movies, thru his personal representative Fred W. Beetson ... has placed the coloured film extra under the absolute control of his Central Casting bureau. He appointed Charles Butler, former office manager of the Cinema Auxiliary, filmland's coloured casting bureau, as the Central Casting Bureau's head of all Negro employment.[43]

Cripps contends that both Jimmie Smith and Charles Butler had initially worked outside of the motion picture studios to recruit black extras along Central Avenue for white Hollywood. Others such as Oscar Smith of Paramount and Harold (Slickem) Garrison of MGM, both of whom were bootblacks for the motion picture studios, worked inside the studios to recruit black extras. Smith came to Hollywood while serving as the personal servant to white actor Wallace Reid.[44] By the late 1920s, Smith, who worked not only as a bootblack in Hollywood but also as an actor, had reportedly landed some 200 screen roles.[45] On the other hand, Garrison, referred to as 'Slickem' because of his ability to provide a brilliant shine as a bootblack, climbed the ladder on the motion picture studio lot and was hired as assistant director to King Vidor during the filming of *Hallelujah*.[46] Cripps asserts that:

> Both Smith and Garrison held flimsy power over blacks because of their modest influence among whites. But, like everything black in Hollywood, their power was quickly eroded at the end of the 1920s when the studios turned to the new Central Casting Corporation and their black agent, Charles Butler, for players.[47]

Garrison was later hired to assist in the production of *Going Hollywood* (MGM, 1933) and *Hollywood Party* (MGM, 1934), thereby making him the first African American assistant to work on two pictures at the same time.[48] As Garrison and Smith worked with the major motion picture studios to recruit black extras, Zack Williams (who rose from extra to actor) often worked in cooperation with Oscar Smith to provide black extras for independent filmmaking enterprises or companies not affiliated with the Motion Picture Producers Association.[49] Williams, while recruiting blacks actors, earned a reputation in Hollywood as being the champion lion tamer of the Pacific Coast. 'Whenever a director had an unruly lion and wanted him tamed a bit, he would always send for Zack Williams'.[50] Williams, like Smith, landed a number of extra roles and acting parts in Hollywood pictures.

The Central Casting Bureau office ultimately was responsible for the employment of a tremendous number of black extras in white Hollywood. In fact, the Central Casting Bureau's office was commended shortly after its inception: 'Over 100 coloured actors were called out by Charles Butler, coloured manager of the Central Casting Bureau Office for this scene [in an unnamed film], the finest and most elaborate cabaret scene of coloured actors screened in Hollywood.'[51] Actors cast in this unnamed film included: Mildred and Mona Boyd; Nathan Curry; Kid Herman; Hazel Jones; Pearl Morrison; Virgil Owens; George Reed; Hayes Robinson; Raymond Turner and Ernest Wilson.[52]

One year after the establishment of the Central Casting Bureau, such a large number of blacks were placed in roles, particularly in the all-black cast productions *Hearts in Dixie* (Fox, 1929) and *Hallelujah* that the *Opportunity* magazine reported that 'In the wake of this new experiment in all-Negro pictures comes the Negro's chance to be articulate on his own behalf. Greater still, the success of these pictures shall erect the foundation of the Negro's permanent place in the cinematographic industry in California.'[53]

With the establishment of the Central Casting Bureau office, African Americans were not only increasing their cinema visibility, they were also increasing their earnings. For example, some two years after the Bureau was established in 1929 it was reported:

> With the unusual demand for coloured extras during the year, mostly for talking pictures, 10,916 placements were made in Hollywood with 5,854 jobs given at US$7.50 a day. Of the number placed, 1424 got tickets ranging from US$20 to $35 a day and made a total of US$11,700. Total amount of money paid coloured extras was US$89,702.89, with the

Fig. 2. James Murray rehearses the floor show at the Black Bottom Cabaret in Tod Browning's *The Big City* (MGM, 1928). [Museum of Modern Art/Film Stills Archive.]

daily placement on year being 30 and the average daily earnings US$8.22.[54]

Finally, some African Americans received substantial earnings and long contracts, and some actors were elevated from the status of extra to featured player, as was the case with Hazel Jones who reportedly obtained a contract 'both fat and long to play the big shot in a new Tiffany-Stahl production.'[55] Some two years earlier, in 1927, Gertrude Howard was considered one of the highest paid black actresses working in white Hollywood, a period when she was competing with black actresses such as Madame Sul-Te-Wan, Daisy Buford, Carolyn Snowden *et al.*[56] Charles Butler reported that the earnings of black extras working in Hollywood exceeded that of any other extra working in the industry except for Chinese extras.

Perhaps the black extras' earning potential could be attributed to an unusual fact: blacks were often cast in a wide range of roles representing a wide variety of ethnicities on the screen. For example, it was reported that:

> In Mr. Chaney's current picture *East is East* (MGM, 1929), where Negroes are being used with a few Chinese and Filipinoes as natives of Siam. Lon Chaney has been willing to demonstrate the racial versatility of the Negro by using them in his pictures for Eskimos, Chinese, Malays, Africans, and many other types of Oriental character ... He expressed the opinion that Negroes are natural actors and easier to handle before the camera.[57]

That African Americans, already designated as Other, then masqueraded as Other invokes debate regarding how otherness was constructed by white Hollywood and how Hollywood was perhaps reconstructing its own identity of itself through its continual appropriation of the Other.

Black marginalisation

Although African Americans became increasingly more visible on the screen, unfortunately they could not escape being marginalised. Such marginalisation is well reflected in the commentary of an unnamed black actor who was quoted in the *Chicago Defender*:

> I appeared in several motion pictures; one was coloured and the others were white, and I acted the part of a coloured butler in one and in the other I appeared as a slave. I received less money for my work because I was coloured, and I am ... disgusted, as every profession is open to the whites and few open to us. I am thinking what an advantage I would have if I were white instead of coloured. I hope that you will keep on encouraging the people in the picture line in the paper. While I am disgusted, it might encourage others.[58]

Reports of such attempts to marginalise black actors by confining them to subordinate and demeaning roles proliferated. Three such examples include the reports that Elias English herded a drove of elephants in *The Man Who Laughs* (Universal, 1927), Katherine Garrett was employed as a maid in *Sailor's Wives* (First National, 1928) and 'Snowball' Henry was cast in a comic role as a boarding house janitor in *Save the Pieces* (Paramount, 1928).[59] African Americans were marginalised not only by being relegated to demeaning roles that cast them in subservient or comic capacities, but also they were marginalised by having their contributions considered less valuable than those of whites and therefore, were paid less money for those contributions.

As an example of their tenuous status, African-American actor Raymond Turner's supporting role in *The Patent Leather Kid* (First National, 1927) might have seemed an advancement for an African American, yet he was assigned the stereotypical name of 'Molasses'.[60] Thus, even when African Americans received significant screen roles, they still were marginalised, even down to uncomplimentary or degrading names.

Roles accessible to African-American actors often automatically stigmatised them, relegating them to subordinate status. In some instances, they were coded with multiple inscriptions, as was the case in *The Love Mart* (First National, 1927), Raymond Turner, cast as a slave, was also characterised as comic in the same film. To add insult to injury, marginalisation of African American actors was furthered in reviews, as: 'Raymond Turner, the "dark spot", in the picture, is nevertheless the lightest spot in the picture. His natural comedy is refreshing and despite the fact that the story is designed to make him a character of no importance this young player stands out prominently ...'[61] Even compliments to these African American extras were often laced with subtle insults. The *Pittsburgh Courier* reports that Tod Browning, director of the MGM production, *The Big City* (1928), a film that used a number of black extras, observed that 'the Negro player worked ... as if he were an individual with the full responsibility of the production on his shoulders ... the Negro as a race has the gift of pantomime in the highest degree. They feel keenly and respond to direction quickly, being about the most plastic material I have ever worked with.'[62] Marginalisation, manifested in a variety of ways, was just another form of racial othering that African Americans endured on American screens.

In some instances, when African Americans of light complexion were perceived as not being dark enough to photograph as black on screen, they were denied opportunities to act despite their talent. But in 1931 Harry Levette reported:

> 'For the first time since coloured actors and extras began work in the movies, a call came for players of very fair complexion. Heretofore, to the chagrin of some of our prettiest and most charming high-yellows, they could not get a break. Brown colours were preferred, because light complexioned people photograph white. But MGM called for twenty-five fair women and men for Hawaiian dance scenes in *Never the Twain Shall Meet* (MGM, 1931).'[63]

Brown-complexioned African American actresses were replaced and told they could not recreate the native dances satisfactorily.[64]

Far too often, small advances for African Americans were viewed as somehow a denial or infringement of the rights of whites, ignoring the systematic and historic exclusion that African Americans had endured. Thus, African Americans were made to feel guilty about their success as though such success was undeserved, and they were forced to feel they should apologise for their success. Harry Levette reported that:

> Once at Warner's after watching Edward Thompson, Lawrence Criner, John Lester Johnson, Virgil Owens, Arthur Ray, yours truly and a half dozen other 'sundowners' present call passes and prepare to pass through the buzzer wicket for interview, a handsome rosy complexioned young white fellow came close to the group. 'You fellows are sure lucky', he exclaimed, 'I have been reporting at all the studios the whole three months I have been in town and never got a break.[65]

Levette relates this experience to expose the dilemma that African American extras faced. Even when they managed to land employment, they were still subjected to the resentful attitudes of whites – many of whom were unwilling to acknowledge the subordinate status that African Americans had been relegated to both on and off the screen. Whites seldom took that factor into consideration.

African Americans were further marginalised by the roles in which they were cast. Among these were films that reflected upon the moral decay of American society. Expressing his concern, Harry Levette stressed the fact that African Americans were featured in films that bordered on being immoral. A significant number of blacks were cast in gangster dramas, and in films that depicted them as outlaws, as was true of Clarence Muse's role in *The Last Parade* (Columbia, 1931). In *Women of All Nations* (Fox, 1931) it disturbed Levette that black males were cast as guards to a harem, as their presence was believed to have reflected upon the morality of the entire African American community. Levette was concerned that *Are These Our Children?* (RKO, 1931), a film that focused on high school students involved in 'sky limit petting and hip flask parties', would have dire consequences for African Americans. *Union Depot* (First National, 1932), a film that employed a number of black actors, was condemned for 'showing for the first time in film history a men's washroom of a large railroad station complete in every detail'; Levette was disconcerted, fearing that such representations would reflect negatively upon African Americans.[66] White Hollywood evidently felt it both necessary and natural to cast African Americans in such films, as if blackness was somehow a natural extension of immorality.

Additionally, African Americans were far too often marginalised by being cast in unredeeming roles. In *Nagana* (Universal, 1932), African Americans found employment as savages. Casting call advertisements to recruit African American actors emphasised that those to be recruited had to 'resemble savages'.[67] A greater tragedy that than the insult itself is the fact that some 400 black actors responded to the call, indicating that black actors had to accept as the harsh reality that they would either assume such characterisation to acquire these 'savage' roles on the screen or remain unemployed.[68] For the filming of *King Kong* (RKO, 1933), a jungle film, Nathan Curry served as a talent scout to recruit black actors to portray savages.[69] As many as 3,000 black extras responded to a call by Charles Butler of the Central Casting Bureau for 'savage' roles in *Tarzan and His Mate* (MGM, 1934).[70] *Invisible Ray* (Universal, 1936), a film that starred white actor Boris Karloff, again recruited black extras for roles that cast them as 'savages'.[71]

African Americans found an abundance not only of 'savage' roles but subservient roles as well. Examples include John Larkins as a valet in *Gabriel Over the White House* (MGM, 1933) and Clinton Rosemond as a butler in *The Toy Wife* (MGM,1938).[72] *The Life of Chinese Gordon* (title could not be identified), may have been another picture that employed a larger number of 'coloured thespians', who this time were cast in slave roles – roles that reminded African Americans of a painful and not too distant past.[73] The black actor was presented as a prison convict in *San Quentin* (First National, 1937), a film that employed between 30 and 40 black actors.[74] And even when they managed to land roles and were given speaking parts there were problems. Aside from being reduced to speaking in dialect, African Americans were maligned because they were often forced to recite lines that were offensive to African American audiences. Such was the case in the *Torch Singer* (Paramount, 1933); a tiny, ebony hued girl named Sally, replying to Claudette Colbert, asks: 'Was your Sally black like me?' At this period, the word 'black' was

Fig. 3. Producer/director Merian C. Cooper, flanked by stars Bruce Cabot and Robert Armstrong, poses with extras during filming of the Skull Island scenes of *King Kong* (RKO, 1933). [Museum of Modern Art/Film Stills Archive.]

offensive to many African Americans and a direct insult to African American spectators.[75] Such dialogue was characteristic of the language and roles assigned to African Americans; they could not escape the one dimensional portrayals that reflected how they were being marginalised.

African Americans continued to be marginalised even after the completion of a picture, because many deserving recognition were ignored in the publicity materials and even denied screen credit. Such exclusion was deliberately designed by the motion picture industry so these films would not offend Southern audiences.[76] In fact, Spencer Williams was maligned by the studios, forcing the *Pittsburgh Courier* to express it's disapproval of such practices by stating, 'Spencer Williams is said to have lost a golden opportunity at Christie Studios by kicking too soon for screen credit for pictures he claims to have helped scenarise. He is said to have forgotten that we have to abide our time.'[77] Rather than offend the South, Hollywood would erase African Americans from publicity materials or screen credits, rendering them unimportant and insignificant, despite the fact that they had contributed to a film. Such shameless treatment was one of the many forms of marginalisation. This attempt to erase the black image from the Hollywood sphere was considered an American tragedy that, according to *Pittsburgh Courier* correspondent Earl Morris, had been inflicted by some Jews who operated white Hollywood.[78]

Such attempts to marginalise African Americans in cinema were often challenged by Levette, who took exception to the weak African-American response: 'We scoff at the fact that most of the parts portrayed by Negroes are those of menials instead of letting the studios know that we honor them as artists'.[79] However, it is also true that some African Americans responded to their marginalisation and resorted to resistance in a variety of ways.

Black extra employment patterns in the second phase of the sound era – throughout the 1930s

Following the advent of sound, Cripps contends, 'the motion picture industry would leap ahead of its audience's tastes and opinions. Blacks on the screen would become whole and rounded. Some studios would consult them with the care and politesse formerly reserved for organised Catholics and Jews'.[80] Although advances did occur, these years were often charcterised by a series of gains and losses. According to Eric Rhode, 'By the spring of 1930 at least four million Americans were unemployed: by 1931 this figure had risen to eight million, and by 1932 to at least twelve million ... Hollywood ... through sound, [was able] to provide a wide spectrum of response to the Depression'.[81] African-American extras were of course also affected by the social, political and economic factors that plagued the industry.

Nonetheless, in 1930, Harry Levette reported that on 5 April some 6,264 black extras were employed, 12 April as many as 5,887 had been hired, 19 April nearly 5,208 were working, and 26 April 5,662 were being cast in roles. In May, Levette reported that 'the coloured extras received a pretty fair break, much more than the previous month'.[82] But months later he wrote that there were 'no large number of coloured actors and extras in the current productions', though this trend was not expected to last.[83] With the onset of fall, Paramount, Universal – a studio that had been applauded for hiring black extras during the silent era – RKO, Fox and many of the larger studios were preparing to produce pictures that would require the use of hundreds of black extras. Even the smaller studios such as Tiffany, Harold Lloyd, Christie's, Pathé, *et al.* would provide roles for 'the "John Gilberts" and "Nancy Carrolls" in sepia'.[84]

The year 1931 was far from prosperous as the gains previously witnessed in employment had diminished. By February the depression had taken its toll, allowing only some 3,109 extras to be employed, the lowest number for all races in several years at the studios.[85] Three months later, the industry had apparently rebounded, as some 3,748 extras were called by the Central Casting Bureau. This increase was a welcome change, since the average number of extras previously employed was some 3,500.[86] The following May, 308 extras had been hired as atmosphere players and were paid as much as US$2,645. But in July of 1931 the number of black extras working for the studios had again declined. In fact, there were only 3,949 of all races working as extras – a pattern repeated in June, with some 4,359 extras of all races employed.[87] These lows would last for only a short time because within one month an increase in black extras working in Hollywood had again been observed.[88] This increase would continue well into September with the employment of 4,659 extras, who according to Levette, were considered the future 'Ira Aldridges and Charles Gilpins'.[89] By October of 1931 the number of extras working for the studios more than doubled to some 7,513.[90] Black extras who worked on *Arrowsmith* (Goldwyn, 1931) earned some US$7.50 a day, an amount which was considered a 'Godsend' for black extras.[91] As the year neared an end in November some 6,000 extras of all races were employed, thus representing an increase in the number of black extras hired by the studios.

With the begininng of 1932, Harry Levette was predicting that the spring would 'see one of the greatest seasons for the coloured actors and extras since the advent of the talkies. But this is not meant as a tip-off to start a gold-rush stampede of brown Gloria Swansons and John Gilberts to Hollywood. There are enough of them here now to take care of all the jobs that will materialise.'[92] Despite this deliberate attempt to discourage additional would-be black actors from seeking employment in the turbulent world of white Hollywood, by May of 1932 some 4,351 extras had been employed, a significant increase over the previous average of 3,500 extras.[93] The end of 1932 was considered a bitter sweet experience because although extras had limited roles available to them, they had managed to appear in the ten best pictures of the year, including *Arrowsmith* and *Wet Parade* (MGM, 1932). Being featured in the ten best pictures of the year was considered an accomplishment for African Americans, because it was felt that such exposure would translate into more opportunities in white Hollywood.[94]

That same year Floyd Snelson, *Pittsburgh Courier* correspondent, accused many African-American extras of participating in their own exploitation and marginalisation. Snelson argued that many black actors rambled around the studios making themselves a 'nuisance' and when provided with the opportunity to promote themselves, often undersold their services and made condescending remarks about one another, thereby losing the respect of studio officials. Disgruntled with such behaviour, Snelson stated,

> Another decadent evil, to my way of thinking, which is truly a disgrace to the race, is the fact that when some fortunate Negro happens to 'edge-in' to a little favour at a certain studio, he is the worst task master of his own people they have to contend with. He often goes so far as to tell the white employer just what handicaps to place in the paths of his brothers and what burdens to place upon their shoulders. He is often a typical 'Esau, who sold his brethen for a mess of porridge' ... The situation at Hollywood should be cleared up, but it will never be cleared up by broke, penniless and hungry actors and would-be actors, hovering around the studios, willing to take anything, to catch the crumbs from the table.[95]

Snelson resented the fact that some African Americans internalised the racial oppression that devalued blackness and, thereby, devalued themselves. Pleading for a show of self-respect and self-esteem among African American actors, Snelson insisted that 'Hollywood needs high class, intelligent, self-respecting men and women, who possess fine qualities of character, deportment and integrity. People who are welcomed upon the lots because of their serenity and affable competence.'[96] African American actors in the sound era took heed of Snelson's recommendations and proved themselves indispensable to the white Hollywood studios.

As 1933 debuted, the African American press predicted a good year for employment among black extras, expecting renewed interest by Hollywood in animal pictures and pictures laid in the South Sea islands or Africa, which would require a visible black presence. However, although by March of 1933 as much as $55,000 had been paid to black extras, there was actually a paucity of screen roles available.97 Levette revealed that according to the Central Casting Bureau:

> ... 34,201 coloured extra players [have been] employed through Central during the past five years. They received in hard cash US$306,785. This number and the cash received is only 85 per cent of those who really worked, the remaining being near stars, feature players and players who through starting as extras, became contract players. The poorest year was in 1931 when the 85 per cent only totaled 3,993, they receiving only UA$22,096.[98]

Levette implies that while these increases in visibility and earnings appear on the surface to reflect an advance for black extras, real growth was another issue because there were only a small percentage of actors who were reaping the greatest profits. In fact, only those who had been elevated from the status of extra to featured player or near star were really experiencing a significant growth in income. A case in point was John Larkin, an extra who received some US$66.60 per day for his role in *Forever Faithful* (1933); this amount was less than what he normally garnered for his services.[99] By August of 1933, the Central Casting Bureau had paid US$8,005 to some 1,186 black extras. This amount excluded payments to contract actors, bit players, or what was termed 'part actors'.[100]

In September 1933, employment again began to increase. During the first week 1,872 extras of all races were employed, followed by 2,907 the next week.[101] As the year closed, 1933 was described as 'a much bigger year than the previous year'. However, those employed were on a lower pay scale and earned some US$1,800 less than those in the previous year. According to Charles Butler of the Central Casting Bureau, 7,090 were employed in the year of 1933 and received a total of US$49,139.30 for their services.[102] In this period African-American extras were cast in gangster dramas and films that celebrated the jazz age but these films provided them meagre roles. Westerns similarly relied on the black extra. It is Cripps' argument that 'Westerns, indeed, provided a surrogate for Dixie because of their reliance on similar codes of single combat – the code duello and the shootout. So black sidekicks and bar-room flunkies

Fig. 4. Louise Beavers and Fredi Washington were featured players, not simply extras, in Universal's *Imitation of Life* (1934), directed by John Stahl. [Richard Koszarski Collection.]

took on the values of the antebellum servants, with illiteracy replacing servility as the caste mark ... By the decade's end the flagging genre perked up because of singing cowboys, such as Gene Autry, who varied their fare with occasional exotic settings where they took their blacks.'[103]

Cripps adds that by 1934, while African Americans landed a few bit roles, there remained a void in terms of an African American voice in white Hollywood and particularly one that allowed the cinema to explore African American life with any kind of depth or scope.[104] However, 1934 commenced with some degree of optimism for employment among African American extras. Reports circulated that January represented one of the highest paying months for black extras in the past three years. In fact, a total of 164 extras received US$4,197.50 for this month. In February, 539 extras received US$4,027.52 in wages, while in March although these wages were not officially reported, 436 were employed. These totals did not include black actors who were working on contracts or who had their own agents.[105]

In September, reports surfaced that the film *Imitation of Life* (1934) exceeded all other films in the employment of African Americans. Some five hundred extras were employed by Universal studios.[106] In the aftermath of *Imitation of Life*, African Americans were optimistic that they could expect continued visibility in white Hollywood, particularly, when Carl Laemmle publicly acknowledged African Americans and claimed that the studios were actively recruiting blacks for the motion picture screen. Laemmle stated, 'We are out to cast the foremost stars in our new films and to give opportunity to deserving new screen personalities, regardless of colour'.[107] Similarly employing an appreciable number of African American actors was Cecil B. DeMille's *Cleopatra* (Paramount, 1934). Such hopes of prosperity were soon dimmed when in October, only one month later, the Central Casting Bureau announced its plan to cut its work force by half, a work force that included some 9,000 extras. Campbell MacCulloch, recently appointed director of the Bureau, revealed that 'the state department of industrial welfare had been studying registration rolls containing names of 17,606 extra workers for the last two months. The film code committee intends a reduction of the list to about 8,000 at this time with further reductions later to prune the number of those who can make film work a regular livelihood ... '[108] Despite such reports, in October 1934, 206 players were paid US$1,340, while in November black extras earned as much as US$1,550. It was also noted that about 15 per cent of the black actors secured employment through agents, as opposed to utilising the services provided by the Central Casting Bureau.[109]

Cripps asserts that in the mid-1930s, 'Throughout the depression decade moviemakers attempted to capture Afro-American life on the screen in some format outside of show business circles, but whether in two-reel form or as bits of feature films the Negro segments rarely gave a fully rounded appearance to their subject'.[110] Subsequently, in 1935, black extras experienced a lull in employment due to weather conditions that interfered with production and due to script changes that delayed production. February of 1935 was considered one of the worst months in some seven years for black extras. The Central Casting Bureau distributed 178 checks to those whom they classified as atmosphere players and who received a sum of US$1,550.[111] Despite their vulnerability to the economic instability of the industry, African Americans were not deterred from pursuing employment in white Hollywood. Continuing to experience a decline in earnings, in May 1935, 165 black extras received wages totaling only US$1,262.50. This amount was a substantial decrease in comparison to April of the previous year, which was regarded as 'much more remunerative as more plays using Race players were being made'.[112] Eight hundred and sixty-one extras had received US$5,866 in wages.[113]

The attention received by Universal studios, producer of *Imitation of Life* (1934), for what was regarded as a showing of commitment to the employment of black extras spurred other studios to compete with Universal for the talent of black extras. Thus began production of the Paramount film *So Red the Rose* (1935). This film was 'destined to be the big vehicle for Negro screen talent this season' as it employed a considerable number of African American extras and some well known African American actors such as Clarence Muse and Daniel Haynes.[114] Such films certainly increased the earnings of black extras; it was reported that while in July 1934 over $10,000 had been paid to extras and actors, July 1935 had surpassed that amount.[115] Reports that African Americans could expect to be employed in the cinema proliferated as the *New York Amsterdam News* noted, 'The nation's film capital is going bronze in a big way. All major studios there are planning films to include coloured performers.'[116] Hollywood's interest in featuring the African American on the screen was not deterred even by Southern theatres refusing to exhibit such films. Studios simply would offset resulting declines in their earning potential by tapping the foreign markets for the exhibition of their films.[117]

As 1935 neared its end, Harry Levette predicted that 'Negro film players [would] have a great year in front of them, barring elemental disasters or other acts of God, that would prevent the 14 major studios and eleven independent ones from carrying out their large proposed schedules'.[118] In January 1936, African Americans welcomed the report that white actor Al Jolson would use some 100 black dancers in the *The Singing Kid* (First National, 1936). The Baltimore *Afro-American* reported that 'This is the first time, for many years, that the mammy-singer has consented to have "genuine" coloured dancers in his pictures. Usually he takes great delight in having white players blacked, giving the illusion of coloured dancers'.[119]

By September 1936, the Central Casting Bureau placed 56 youngsters and 40 black males with Fox Studios, 24 at Paramount, three actors and 21 extras at Warner Bros., two at Universal and a large number at MGM.[120] Employment gains soon came to halt however, when black extras working in Hollywood organised and staged a strike for higher wages.[121] The Central Casting Bureau was especially disturbed by these actions, since the actors had not contacted the Bureau before the strike, and, predictably, it was the Bureau that was held responsible. In the following years few reports in

Fig. 5. George Sanders and Wallace Beery as renegade slavers in Tay Garnett's notorious *Slave Ship* (Twentieth Century-Fox, 1937). [Museum of Modern Art/Film Stills Archive.]

the black press credited the Bureau for the hiring of black extras. The strike had backfired on the Central Casting Bureau.

On the positive side, a status change was occurring for African American actors. As 1936 ended, the Academy of Motion Picture Arts and Sciences would for the first time honour black actors in its ninth annual awards of merit and awarded the following: Eddie (Rochester) Anderson, Myrtle Anderson, Louis Armstrong, Louise Beavers, Willie Best, Stepin Fetchit, Abraham Gleaves, Daniel Haynes, Rex Ingram, Clarence Muse, Oscar Polk, George Reed, Paul Robeson, Al Stokes and Frank Wilson.[122] The black press reported that 'The outstanding 'A' cinemas of the academy's roster are liberal enough this year to concede that the triumph of the saga in numerous cases was due to the characterisations of the Negro artists'.[123]

In the following years, although several films, such as *Artists and Models* (Paramount, 1937), *Slave Ship* (20th-Fox, 1937) and *In Old Chicago* (20th-Fox, 1938) employed large numbers of black extras, the Central Casting Bureau's status continued to wane. In the film *Slave Ship*, black extras received record earnings representing the largest amount paid for extras for a single day's work in thirteen years; wages increased from $5 to $7.50 to $15 per day.[124] However, in August of 1938 black actors working as extras again staged a strike at MGM during the production of *Too Hot To Handle* in protest of the low wages they were being paid.[125] Cripps contends that by the end of the 1930s 'Hollywood during the depression provided few new opportunities for blacks. Southern literary metaphor had eroded a bit, but no clear alternative emerged. So blacks were represented only by memorable bits in films not really dealing with their needs or problems. Black critics and audiences made do with a few "stars" and hints of "progress".'[126]

At the end of the 1930s, the sound era had been characterised as one that saw African American extras exhibiting pride in their accomplishments, yet expressing dismay at still not receiving wages commensurate with their talent and experience. Thus, while African American extras gained visibility and employment, this period was signified by a series of both highs and lows.

Black extras engage in resistance in the sound era

The sound era, unlike the silent period, saw African-American extras becoming much less tolerant of the injustices and exploitation endured while working in white Hollywood. Thus, African American extras began to engage in acts of resistance. For example, during the filming of *The Spirit of Notre Dame* (Universal, 1931), football players cast in the picture 'absolutely refused to put on the grease paint make-up'.[127] Being compelled to darken their already dark skin was viewed as too great an insult for African-Americans athletes, and they refused to defile their appearance.

In 1936, 75 African American extras reportedly staged a strike on the studio lot of MGM demanding higher wages. These extras were filming *Tarzan Escapes* (MGM, 1936), a jungle picture that depicted them in Safari roles. Following their performance in this film they were then asked to 'take parts as savage tribesmen in another jungle picture in which their heads were to be painted white, and inasmuch as this feature is costuming, and difficult to remove the paint, higher wages were demanded'.[128] When MGM refused to meet their demands, the extras walked off the studio set. Charles Butler of the Central Casting Bureau was disturbed that the black extras had not filed an official complaint with his office prior to staging this strike. He then went on record as attributing the difficulties that many of the black extras endured in Hollywood to their own behaviour.[129]

Extras who had been hired to work in Clark Gable's *Too Hot Too Handle* were to assume G-string roles or those of African natives, and were hired to provide a maximum amount of work for a minimum wage of $8.25 per day. The extras considered this salary inadequate and they demanded $16 per day for their work, despite the fact that when they interviewed for these roles, they had known the pay was minimal. When their demands went unmet, African American extras 'sat down and held up the production for an hour before studio officials could adjust matters'.[130] Jesse Graves, the African American council member of the Screen Actor's Guild and Audry Blair, executive secretary of the Junior Screen Actor's Guild, served as mediators between the two disputing parties. The conflict ended when the studio awarded African American extras $11 per day instead of the $8.25. However, the extras' actions were viewed as detrimental to the future relations between studio executives and the Screen Actor's Guild. Moreover, only 35 of the African American extras who worked on this picture were paid the $11 per day, and some 250 extras were still given only $8.25 per day.[131] While this action may have pacified some, it disenchanted others. The differential in the pay received for their services may have been a Hollywood divide-and-conquer technique.

The *Pittsburgh Courier* asserted that this dispute was symptomatic of a larger conflict that had erupted between studio executives and the Screen Actor's Guild, an organisation that studio executives resented because they felt that it was attempting to control the motion picture moguls. Reportedly, 'Before the guild came into being, extras received more than $8.25 a day for this type of work. The guild, with a view toward protecting these extras, set a minimum wage scale [that would] graduate into a maximum scale of from $16 to $100 a day depending upon the type of work.'[132] However, despite the benefits the Guild tried to provide, the organisation did not represent the interests of African Americans. Launching a direct attack on the Guild, the *Pittsburgh Courier* stated, 'Robert Montgomery, Joan Crawford, James Cagney and Chester Morris, all union heads, haven't made one peep about the African-American guild members. But the guild [had] been most active to bleed these unfortunates who work two or three times a year for dues.'[133] The African American press argued that many guild members had not extended themselves for the assistance of their own guild members, many of whom were African American. This critic charged, 'You must remember these people at the box-office. Help the guy that helps you. The condition of the Negro film actor is pitiful. These stars do nothing to remedy this situation. It isn't any wonder 75 Negroes struck. And you know conditions have to be very, very bad when 75 Negroes object to something. These 75 were ready to quit work, and haven't worked in months.'[134]

Concerned with the negative publicity that MGM had received in the African American press, a conference was held with Fred Daity, chief of the casting offices for MGM and Earl Dancer of the *Pittsburgh Courier*, to allow MGM to 'absolve themselves from charges of discrimination' by arguing that the wages offered were the standard wages generally offered to any Guild members.[135] While MGM vehemently denied charges of racial discrimination, they then recommended that such matters be handled by the Hays office.[136] Morris, the reporter for the *Pittsburgh Courier*, obtained a role as an extra in the film around which the controversy surrounded, *Too Hot Too Handle*, in order to have access to information that otherwise would have been unavailable to him. While applauding Clark Gable for his amiable personality, Morris contended:

> We are appreciative of the employment of our group in this film, *Too Hot Too Handle*, also for the US$35,000 that was given to Negroes. But these pictures are not made often enough to keep Negro actors in good meals throughout the year. For our money at the box office we should have more pictures using large numbers of Negro extras and pictures making Negro stars.[137]

African Americans, having become more intolerant of discriminatory practices, were willing to resort to strikes to demand higher wages for their services. They were also pressuring the Screen Actor's Guild to seek more employment of African Americans because, as Jesse A. Graves reported to the Guild in 1939, African Americans were systematically being denied screen roles in Hollywood. This was true even for crowd scenes, as was the case in a film that featured a prize fight for which producers refused to use African Americans in the crowd. Graves reported that while 82 white non-Guild members had been employed by Paramount studios, only one of some 480 black guild members had been similarly employed. Graves contended, 'This was the opportunity to employ off-types of Negroes (off-types are singers, dancers and light-complexioned Negroes) who rarely ever work in pictures'.[138]

Conclusion

The silent and sound era through the 1930s are two periods in which African American extras in Hollywood witnessed gains in employment and earnings. Part of this could be attributed to the efforts of Charles Butler who was employed by the Central Casting Bureau. However, despite their monetary gains, African-American actors still could not escape being marginalised in the industry. By the sound era, the employment of African American extras working in the industry was of course subject to the fluctuations witnessed by the industry at large. But regardless of overall advancement, African Americans still could not escape the discriminatory practices that proliferated in white Hollywood. Finally, African-American actors, finding these practices intolerable, began more vigorously and more effectively to resist the de-centering that they endured on American screens. ♦

Notes

1. Murray Ross, 'Hollywood's Extras (1941)', in Gerald Mast, ed., *The Movies In Our Midst: Documents in the Cultural History of Film in America* (Chicago: University of Chicago Press, 1982), 224.
2. Ibid., 221.
3. Ibid., 223.
4. Ibid., 225.
5. Floyd C. Covington, 'The Negro Invades Hollywood', *Opportunity*, 7 no. 4 (April 1929). Page numbers missing for this source.
6. Thomas Cripps, *Slow Fade to Black: The Negro in American Film, 1900–1942* (New York: Oxford University Press, [1977] 1993), 145–146.
7. Covington.
8. Ross, 226–228.
9. 'Spotlights-Colored Screen Actors', *Afro-American* (Baltimore), (27 June 1924): 5.
10. 'Who's Who – And Where', *Afro-American* (Baltimore), (13 December 1924), 6.
11. 'Demand For Film Actors Increasing', *Afro-American* (Baltimore), (20 December 1924): 6. It was noted that Al Jolson had turned down the role in *His Darker Self* for fear that he would not be as successful on screen as he had been on stage.

12. Ibid.
13. Cripps, 127, 133.
14. Eric Rhode, *A History of the Cinema From Its Origins to 1970* (New York: Hill and Wang, 1976), 230.
15. 'New Paramount Film to Employ Cast of 750', *Afro-American* (Baltimore) (21 August 1926): 4.
16. '30 Colored Actors Used in Paramount Production', *Pittsburgh Courier* (24 July 1926): 10.
17. 'Another Tarzan Picture Calls For Race Actors', *Pittsburgh Courier* (9 October 1926): 10.
18. Covington.
19. Ibid.
20. 'Filmland Amusement Notes', *Pittsburgh Courier* (8 October 1927): 3.
21. 'FBO Is Preparing All Negro African Picture', *Pittsburgh Courier* (3 December 1927): 2.
22. Ibid.
23. 'Warner Raises Pay of Twenty-Nine', *Afro-American* (Baltimore), (16 October 1926): 13.
24. 'Colored Movie Actors Drawing Big Salaries', *Pittsburgh Courier* (4 December 1926).
25. 'Exhibitors Herald Production Directory', *Motion Picture Herald* (8 October 1927): 31–34.
26. 'Movie Actors Return From Location', *Afro-American* (Baltimore) (22 January 1927): 8.
27. 'Van Stroheim Uses Race Actors In Big Scene of His Latest Picture', *Pittsburgh Courier* (15 January 1927): 1.
28. Covington.
29. 'Actors Get Part In Diamond Handcuffs', *Afro-American* (Baltimore) (31 March 1928): 9.
30. Covington.
31. Ibid.
32. Ross, 224.
33. Cripps, 219.
34. Covington.
35. King Vidor, *A Tree is a Tree* (New York: Harcourt, Brace & Co., 1952), 175.
36. Ibid.
37. Cripps, 218.
38. George Perry, 'Hayes Centralizes Studio Employment', *Afro-American* (Baltimore) (15 October 1927): 9.
39. Lawrence Lamar, 'Jimmy Smith May Return to Casting', *Afro-American* (Baltimore) (6 December 1941): 13.
40. Cripps, 104.
41. Ibid., 166 and George Perry, 'Hayes Centralizes Studio Employment', *Afro-American* (Baltimore) (15 October 1927): 9.
42. George Perry, 'Hays' Organization Gets Race Casting Manager', *Pittsburgh Courier,* (15 October 1927): 2.
43. George Perry, 'Hayes Centralizes Studio Employment', *Afro-American* (Baltimore) (15 October 1927): 9.
44. Cripps, 103.
45. 'Bootblack Gets Contract', *Chicago Defender,* (2 March 1929): 8.
46. Covington, 131.
47. Cripps, 103–104.
48. Harry Levette, 'In Hollywood', *Afro-American* (Baltimore) (23 September 1933): 21.
49. Harry Levette, 'Coast Codgings as Doped by Harry Levette', *Chicago Defender* (10 December 1932): 7.
50. Billy Tucker, 'Coast Dope', *Chicago Defender* (21 October 1922): 6.
51. 'Filmland Amusement Notes', *Pittsburgh Courier* (5 November 1927): 2.
52. Ibid.
53. Covington.
54. 'Maurice Dancer, 'Stage Facts: Colored Movie Extras', *Pittsburgh Courier* (2 February 1929): 1.
55. Harry Levette, 'Gossip of the Movie Lots', *Pittsburgh Courier* (2 November 1929): 9.
56. 'Three Get Leading Roles in South Sea Film', *Afro-American* (Baltimore) (16 July 1927): 9.
57. Covington.
58. D. Ireland Thomas, 'Motion Picture News', *Chicago Defender* (19 July 1924): 6.
59. 'In Filmland', *Afro-American (*Baltimore), (26 November 1927): 9 and 'Negro Cast With Vernon', *Pittsburgh Courier* (28 January 1928): 3.

60. 'Race Actor Climbs to Fame in *The Patent Leather Kid*', *Chicago Defender* (5 May 1928):10.
61. 'Ray Turner – Big Star in *Love Mart,*' *Pittsburgh Courier* (17 December 1927): 3.
62. 'Tod Browning says Race Actors ... ' *Pittsburgh Courier* (12 November 1927): 3.
63. Harry Levette, 'Movie Gossip', *Afro-American* (Baltimore) (21 February 1931): 8.
64. Ibid.
65. Harry Levette, 'Coast Codgings by Harry Levette',*Chicago Defender* (29 August 1931): 7.
66. Harry Levette, 'Gossip of the Movie Lots', *Afro-American* (Baltimore) (14 November 1931), 9. Levette's charge that African Americans should be cautious in assuming roles that depicted them as immoral extended beyond the screen, as he advised that black actors similarly had a responsibility to conduct themselves in a respectable manner because their behavior was often a reflection of all of African Americans. He cautioned against the practice observed among some women who used their bodies to elicit the gaze of men working on the studio set. Levette even noted that 'Two lesbians caught by this scene peeper disgustingly caressing on the *Sea Bat* set at MGM [reveal] the sordid depths to which some women will stoop ... Of Gertrude Howard, Louise Beavers, Theresa Harris, Hattie McDaniel, Mildred Washington, Cleo Desmond and other veterans of the silent films, not the slightest whisper is ever heard of misconduct on their part' ('In Hollywood', by Harry Levette, *Afro-American* (Baltimore) (5 August 1933): 19.
67. 'Screen Director Asks For Extras; Gets Office Wrecked', *Chicago Defender* (31 December 1932): 6.
68. Ibid.
69. Harry Levette, 'In Hollywood', *Afro-American* (Baltimore) (27 May 1933): 11.
70. '3,000 Extras In *Tarzan and His Mate*', *Afro-American* (Baltimore) (22 July 1933): 10.
71. 'Hollywood Notes', *New York Amsterdam News* (9 November 1935): 12.
72. 'In Hollywood: John Larkin In Who's Who of Hollywood', *Afro-American* (Baltimore),(6 May 1933): 11 and 'Wanted in Hollywood: Hayes, Marian Anderson', *Afro-American* (Baltimore) (16 April 1938): 11.
73. Edward Long, 'Hollywood Chatter', *Afro-American* (Baltimore) (25 April 1936): 11.
74. Harry Levette, 'Thru Hollywood: *Follow The Movie Stars and Players Weekly*', *Chicago Defender* (31 October 1936): 12.
75. 'Say Torch Singer Film Had Insult', *Afro-American* (Baltimore) (25 November 1933): 18.
76. Harry Levette, 'Coast Codgings As Doped by Harry Levette', *Chicago Defender* (26 September 1931): 7.
77. Harry Levette, 'Gossip of the Movie Lots', *Pittsburgh Courier* (2 November 1929): 9.
78. Earl J. Morris, 'American Whites, Negroes Being Shoved Into Background In Movies by Jewish Film Owners', *Pittsburgh Courier* (27 August 1938): 20.
79. Harry Levette, 'Coast Codgings', *Chicago Defender* (1 December 1934): 7.
80. Cripps, 221.
81. Rhode, 270.
82. Harry Levette, 'Movie Gossip', *Afro-American* (Baltimore) (10 May 1930): 8.
83. Harry Levette, 'Movie Gossip', *Afro-American* (Baltimore) (12 July 1930): 9.
84. 'No More All-Colored Films In Sight', *Afro-American* (Baltimore) (27 September 1930): 8.
85. Harry Levette, 'Movie Gossip', *Afro-American* (Baltimore) (21 February 1931): 8.
86. Harry Levette, 'In Hollywood', *Afro-American* (Baltimore) (19 April 1931): 16.
87. Harry Levette, 'Movie Extras Find Tough Going On Hollywood', *Afro-American* (Baltimore), (25 July 1931), 7; and Harry Levette, 'Coast Codgings as Doped by Harry Levette', *Chicago Defender* (20 June 1931): 9.
88. Harry Levette, 'Gossip of the Movie Lots', *Afro-American* (Baltimore) (29 August 1931): 9.
89. Harry Levette, 'Coast Codgings As Doped by Harry Levette', *Chicago Defender* (19 September 1931), 7.
90. Harry Levette, 'Gossip of the Movie Lots', *Afro-American* (Baltimore) (3 October 1931): 9.
91. Ibid.
92. Harry Levette, 'In Hollywood', *Afro-American* (Baltimore) (23 April 1932): 19.
93. Harry Levette, 'Coast Codgings As Doped by Harry Levette', *Chicago Defender* (21 May 1932): 9.
94. 'Colored Actors Had Roles in 10 Best Motion Pic-

tures of 1932', *Afro-American* (Baltimore) (21 January 1933): 10.

95. Floyd G. Snelson, 'The "Low-Down" On the Negro in Hollywood: Snelson Reveals "Inside" Story of Noted Movie City,' *Pittsburgh Courier* (24 September 1932): 6.

96. Ibid.

97. 'Movies Paid $55,000 – Work For Extras Slim', *Afro-American* (Baltimore), (4 March 1933), 19 and 'In Hollywood', *Afro-American* (Baltimore), (14 January 1933): 10.

98. Harry Levette, 'Negro Players Drew $306,875 From Movies', *Afro-American* (Baltimore) (25 March 1933): 9.

99. Harry Levette, 'Coast Codgings as Doped by Harry Levette', *Chicago Defender (7 October 1933): 9.*

100. Harry Levette, 'In Hollywood', *Afro-American* (Baltimore) (23 September 1933): 21.

101. Ibid.

102. 'Race Film Players in Big Money', *Chicago Defender* (24 March 1934): 8.

103. Cripps, 273–274.

104. Ibid., 256.

105. 'Filmland's Pay Roll Is "Extra" Hot', *Chicago Defender* (31 March 1934): 8.

106. Lawrence F. Lamar, 'Universal Sets Record For Studio-Hired Sepians', *Pittsburgh Courier* (15 September 1934): 9.

107. 'Universal Partial to Race Since Imitation of Life, *Chicago Defender* (22 June 1935): 9.

108. 'Scores of 'Extras' May Lose Film Jobs', *Pittsburgh Courier* (6 October 1934): 9.

109. 'Race Players Given Plenty For Film Work', *Chicago Defender* (15 December 1934): 9.

110. Cripps, 258.

111. 'Your Hollywood Correspondent Reports', *Chicago Defender* (16 March 1935): 8.

112. 'Race Collects Large Sum For Film Work', *Chicago Defender* (18 May 1935): 9.

113. Ibid.

114. Harry Levette, 'Coast Codgings', *Chicago Defender* (13 July 1935): 7.

115. Harry Levette, 'Coast Codgings', *Chicago Defender* (10 August 1935): 9.

116. 'Hollywood Showing Interest in Negro', *New York Amsterdam News* (16 November 1935): 12.

117. Ibid.

118. Harry Levette, 'Coast Codgings', *Chicago Defender* (14 December 1935): 12.

119. Edward Long, 'Hollywood Chatter', *Afro-American* (Baltimore) (25 January 1936): 10.

120. '56 Youngsters To Be In Movie', *New York Amsterdam News* (12 September 1936): 8.

121. 'Motion Picture Extras "Strike" In Hollywood', *Pittsburgh Courier* (5 September 1936): 7.

122. 'Here Are Negro Actors Listed by Movies for Gold Awards', *Pittsburgh Courier* (30 January 1937): 7.

123. Ibid.

124. Bernice Patton, 'The Sepia Side of Hollywood',*Pittsburgh Courier* (24 April 1937): 19.

125. Earl J. Morris, 'Protest on Low Wage Scale Is Cause of Strike', *Pittsburgh Courier* (6 August 1938): 21.

126. Cripps, 268–269.

127. Harry Levette, 'Gossip of the Movie Lots', *Afro-American* (Baltimore) (5 September 1931): 9.

128. 'Motion Picture Extras "Strike" in Hollywood', *Pittsburgh Courier* (5 September 1936): 7.

129. Ibid.

130. Earl J. Morris, 'Protest on Low Wage Scale Is Cause of Strike', *Pittsburgh Courier* (6 August 1938): 21.

131. Earl J. Morris, 'Sit-Down Strike At MGM Ends', *Pittsburgh Courier* (13 August 1938): 20.

132. Earl J. Morris, 'Protest on Low Wage Scale Is Cause of Strike', *Pittsburgh Courier* (6 August 1938): 21.

133. Ibid.

134. Ibid.

135. Earl J. Morris, 'Sit-Down Strike At MGM Ends',*Pittsburgh Courier* (13 August 1938): 20.

136. Ibid.

137. Earl J. Morris, 'Earl Morris Becomes A Movie Extra "For A Day"', *Pittsburgh Courier* (20 August 1938): 21.

138. Earl J. Morris, 'Screen Actors Guild To Probe Race's Status in Film Industry', *Pittsburgh Courier* (11 March 1939): 20.

Film History, Volume 9, pp. 116–127, 1997. Copyright © John Libbey & Company
ISSN: 0892-2160. Printed in Australia

Ladies of the lamp: The employment of women in the British film trade during World War 1

David R. Williams

When moving pictures of the Boer War, in reality and in replica, were depicted on the screen, the cinematograph was still a mere music hall novelty. But by the start of the First World War on 4 August 1914, the picture house was an established part of every town.[1] It has been estimated that there were around 4,500 buildings being operated as full time cinemas, and there were many more giving occasional shows. A further estimate suggested that there were around 200,000 people employed in cinemas across the whole country.[2] No figures appear to be given for employment in the other areas of the cinema trade such as in film printing, film distribution, film renting, film sales and projector and ancillary equipment maintenance, so it is difficult to estimate the total work force in the industry

The Cinematograph Exhibitor's Association and the National Association of Cinema Operators were almost exclusively male preserves. Women found employment as cashiers, usherettes/attendants, film joiners and repairers and as office typists. The majority of suburban cinemas were proprietor-owned and a good number were run by husband and wife teams. But, by and large, as with most trades at the time, the key jobs were occupied by men. During the four years of the war, the manpower demands of the military and the munitions factories radically changed the situation.

As the first week of the war passed optimism was revealed in a survey of opinions about the possible effects of the conflict on the industry as published in *The Bioscope Weekly*.[3] Most interviewees in the film distribution trade were right to predict that it was too early to tell. Only James Williamson, suggested that 'dislocation of business during mobilisation must be considerable'. His business acumen in predicting some cinema closures also led him to ask firms to pay for films weekly rather than 'on account'!

The mobilisation of reservists was immediate. In a trade press letter,[4] the secretary of the largest cinema circuit, The Provincial Cinematograph

David R. Williams, B.A. (Hons), is the author of *Cinema in Leicester 1896–1931*. He was Head of the Film and Television Department of The College of St. Hild and St. Bede, Durham University. Now retired, he is a member of the Cinema Theatre Association and The Mercia Cinema Society, both dedicated to the preservation of cinemas and cinema history. Corespondence c/o 17 Wearside Drive, Durham City, DH1 1LE UK.

Theatres Co. Ltd. declared that they would be making a weekly allowance of 10 shillings [50p] to the wives of all employees called to the Colours, and 2s. 6d [12½p] for each child. They had over 100 reservists in their employment, 50 of whom had already been called-up. *The Bioscope* announced that it would be publishing a Roll of Honour listing trade draftees. By the middle of September the number of cinema employees listed was 85. The Oak Lane Cinema, London was reported to have lost four employees including their chief operator but a general surplus of labour enabled the gaps to be quickly filled.

Cinema attendance was generally reported as being fairly normal with obvious increases in places acting as military mustering points and grave concern in holiday resorts. The rumours of war, and the outbreak of war itself, had resulted in many vacation cancellations. Summer holiday resorts such as Blackpool reported poor business. The East Coast resorts facing on to the North Sea, and risking possible bombardment by the German Fleet, were even more affected. In the seaside resort of Cleethorpes, the Royal Picture House was 'invaded' by mustering Territorials in the middle of an afternoon performance! Hull Docks were at a stand still and 10,000 dock workers were laid off. Colliery closures had followed the cessation of exports from the East Coast Coaling Wharves. Thousands of men were idle and cinema closures soon followed as money shortages ate up any savings.

A leading article entitled 'No Panic' in *The Bioscope* of 13 August had assuredly predicted that 'the picture theatre which is the basis of the industry, is likely to be the last form of entertainment to suffer by the war since it is the cheapest, the most easily carried on, and, under current conditions, the most attractive to the public'. The editor of the other trade journal, *The Kinematograph and Lantern Weekly* in his predictions for 1915[5] saw no need for misgivings: 'The year will be one of prosperity for the prudent and skilful exhibitor if his business acumen is tempered with fairness.' But within a few months, he was penning notes of caution.

> It certainly seems that there are cinema managers and proprietors who are not alive to the labour problems created by the praiseworthy rush of kinema employees to follow the drum. One has but to scan the situations vacant columns of the daily press to discover the dearth there is in the labour market. Mere striplings of 15 are being offered what before August last was considered a living wage for a married man with a family. Managers and others advertising for attendants of the male sex, who are expected to do all the inside work, are being offered the princely sum of only 25/- [£1.25p].[6]

The increased employment of women in theatres is not yet seen as a solution, though legislation for this eventuality in other trades was already occurring. In October 1914, Government training schemes for women in market gardening and poultry rearing had begun. In March, a Women's War Service register had been opened and The Shells and Fuses Agreement allowed the use of unskilled labour and women in munitions factories. In June 1915, 46,000 women enrolled in the first week after the Munitions of War Act was passed.

When Mrs. Calvert Routledge took over the running of The Coliseum and His Majesty's Theatres in Barrow at her husband's call-up to the Royal North Lancashire Regiment, the event was given celebrity status in the Trade Topics column.[7] As a keen business woman it was expected that 'nothing will suffer in her hands'. Women managers, of course, were not unknown in the industry. Mrs. Edith Black had been manageress of The Belgrave Cinema, Leicester, in fact, though not in registered name, since its opening in 1913, and Mrs. L. Wright's tenure at Hibbert's Central Hall, Nottingham had for some time drawn the description of 'that energetic lady' in reports from the area.

Ladies were an essential part of the reviewing scene, though renters were often critical of their presence at trade shows. *The Kinematograph Weekly* reported that they had met Mrs. Longford of Swinton at a recent show and been 'quite surprised by her acumen and penetration'. Mr. Cass, also of Swinton, promoted her role by saying that if he heard commendation from women in his audience, he knew he was 'on the right track'. 'At all events', continued the report, 'some of the most successful exhibitors owe their positions to the friendly aid of a sister or a wife'.[8]

But, the advent of women doing anything un-

Fig. 1. From *The Bioscope*, 17 June 1915.

usual in the cinema trade provoked mirth and satire. 'We have heard of the advent of the lady commissionaire who presents an imposing appearance before some of the picture palaces in northern districts', commented the writer of *The Bioscope's Trade Topics*. 'This should relieve the minds of any film operators of military age, who are debarred from donning the khaki from a conscientious fear that the projection of pictures may suffer from their absence abroad. We feel sure that their female admirers will be only too willing to supply their places for so laudable an object, and with the adaptability of their sex will speedily master all the essentials of an honorable calling.'[9] The thumbnail sketch featuring a smart lady commissionaire and a classy operator only goes to emphasise the patronising nature of the final statement. The 'handle-turner' demonstrates her ignorance of the rules and the danger by smoking in front of a 'No smoking' sign, and she reads from a novel, thus avoiding the need to observe the quality of the projected images.

An entry in the Northern section of *The Kinematograph Weekly* for the same date is equally negative concerning 'Women in the Trade'. '[This] is a new question for the North, and from what I hear appears to cause some little stir amongst exhibitors. A new departure has been that women have been engaged on film travelling. A lady called upon my friend the other day and said 'Can I book a film for you?' My friend, who is a man of the world, said, 'Certainly not. You are entering upon a trade not fitted for a woman.' The writer, whilst accepting that opinions might differ upon the employment of women in a travelling capacity, felt that 'more suitable work might be found for those ladies anxious upon entering the industry'.[10]

The mirth was extended the following week with a strip cartoon satirising the possible consequences of the employment of women in various parts of the industry.

The commissionaire has not been replaced by a lady because there is a decrepit old man still available; the lady film agent vamps her way to an order; the aged and unglamourous bill-sticker spills the paste; the female attendant diverts the attention of the strangely all-male audience; the operator, in a sketch echoing the earlier cartoon, rests in an armchair, handle in one hand, and novel in the other, her chocolates nearby and the manager exhorting her to turn the handle occasionally. The film producer is portrayed as a hen-pecking harridan. In its contemporary setting, it is humourous, but it betrays the fact that the trade has yet to accept its potential dependence upon the un-tapped skills of women.[11]

An article in the the same edition further indicates the phenomenon without accepting the need. In some North Country papers, there had been advertisements from a company seeking to train women as projectionists. 'Apparently', the writer explains, 'the idea has gained ground that trained mechanics such as operators will be required for national purposes in the near future, and the suggestion of the engagement of ladies is a purely patriotic move. Those members of the gentle sex who take up the work are to be taught at the expense of the company advertising until such time as they are competent to act as assistant operators.'

It seems that he cannot bring himself to even suggest that they might become chief operators, because he still has reservations about the ladies being there at all. 'Under normal circumstances', he goes on, 'one might be inclined to question the advisability of introducing feminine labour into the operating box, but special situations need to be met

Fig. 2. The caption for this cartoon reads: 'Women, during the war, are taking the places of men in so many phases of life that no doubt we shall see something like the above in the kinematograph business in the near future.'
[From *The Kinematograph and Lantern Weekly*, 24 June 1915.]

with special treatment, and the present may be a case in point.'

Lady cinematograph operators and proprietors had existed even in the early days of showground cinematographs. Vanessa Toulmin's researches have highlighted Mrs. Holland's Palace of Light and Mrs. Weir's Electric Cinematograph Empire amongst others.[12] Mrs Fearn in Derbyshire used to act as an operator in 1902. In 1908, she recalled,[13] she had projected a full two hour show to 600 people in Derby with a splendidly clear 12 ft. picture. She was a 'limelight' expert; a system of illumination that required delicate handling and long preparation. She related that on several occasions she arrived late at the halls but still managed to get 'a picture on the sheet' within half-an-hour.

The first trade advertisement from a Lady Operator seeking a post was in *The Kinematograph Weekly* of 13 May 1915. In the first week of June, three more were offering themselves as assistants. and by the autumn the situations wanted columns brimmed with applications. 'Engagement wanted as Assistant Operator [lady] in London. British Bioscope Diploma'; 'Assistant Operator [Lady] N.London preferred. Would keep place open to release man for War Service.' One lady obviously hedging her bets on permanent employment makes the offer 'Lady Operator, Selig Diploma. Relief Sunday engagements or Saturday 1 p.m.'

The writer of Trade Topics in the 2 September 1915 number of *The Kinematograph Weekly* describes his visit to The Cinema Palace on the Old Kent Road. 'Mr. A.C.True, the manager/proprietor introduced me to his two lady operators, and expressed himself in terms of satisfaction concerning the efficiency of their whole-hearted attention'. One thing which he particularly admired in their work was their careful spooling and, in that process, their examination of every inch of the film. As relief projectionist, he had a French lady. All three operators had come to him with the approval of the London County Council after their employment had been

Fig. 3. Miss Daisy Kingsbury Saltcoats, 'lady manager' of the Countess Cinema, Glasgow. From *The Bioscope*, 31 August 1916.

referred to the Home Office. The corollary to this story is that one of these operators, Miss C.Watkinson was the first lady to join the YMCA cinema organisation attached to the British Expeditionary Force in France in August 1917. She had been manageress at the Queen's Theatre, Brighton and cinemas in Shepherd's Bush and Shaftesbury Avenue after her time in the Old Kent Road.[14]

A number of advertisers clearly still not wishing to entertain the idea of ladies in the 'box' added the sobriquet 'male' to their requests of operators. But the writing was on the wall. The Electric Palace, Highgate had lost 14 members of staff to the Army. There were weekly announcements of managerial changes: 'Mr. G.T.Turnbull of the Empire, Whitley Bay has been succeeded by Miss Margaret Baxter, who is also a talented vocalist'.[15] 'Mrs. Jack is in charge of Ideals Glasgow Branch; she is the only lady renter in Scotland.'[16]

In July 1915, the National Registration Bill sought to record all people by their occupation in preparation for a Military Service Bill which would enforce conscription. Heavy losses on a number of fronts meant that the 5,031,000 service volunteers had not been enough. From 10 February 1916, all single men (and those who had been married since National Registration) between the ages of 19–30 were liable for call up. On 2 March, this was extended to men from 18–41. General conscription for all fit men was ordered to take effect from 13 June 1916.

A Restricted Occupations list had been published, but no job in the Cinema Trade was included. Military Tribunals were set up to hear pleas for exemption. Lord Derby was critical of the numbers of exemptions being granted and urged businesses to replace eligible men with women. The Hosiery Trade and the Wood-working Industry agreed to take women on at men's rates where they were doing comparable jobs. An Official 1000 ft. film 'Women Workers for Victory' was released in May 1916 with great aplomb and the usual humour. It was almost time for panic.

The editor of *The Kinematograph Weekly* addressed the problem of the Military Service Act with a long editorial entitled '29 May – and after'.[17] The employment situation had reached an impasse:

> Already many proprietors are bemoaning the loss of operators, doormen and managers, and in a number of cases the services of women have already been requisitioned to make good the vacancies created by the calling up of members of staff for military service. As in other businesses. women are demonstrating their ability to adapt themselves to the requirements of the picture theatre industry.

But, he still has reservations:

> It is questionable whether women will in the long run prove physically equal to the exhausting and highly technical work of operating. Apart altogether from the responsible character of such duties, the screening of pictures involves a knowledge of mechanism and the handling of electrical apparatus, such as few women possess.

Disabled soldiers and men over military age would be preferable. A system of substitutions was operated by the authorities by which men deemed unfit for military service were offered to fill the places of draftees.

> We would even suggest that in exceptional cases it could be wise immediately to engage substitutes to take the place of men as they are called up, and by this means it would be possible to thoroughly initiate the newcomers in their duties before the more experienced members of staff have to leave.

The editorial goes on to consider the plight of the small showman/owner-manager and the plight of the industry if closures might mean that patrons lose the 'picture habit'.

The suitability of women as managers was questioned by the managing director of an unspecified cinematograph company at a Military Tribunal in Leeds.[18] He declared that he had tried women as managers and that they had been absolute failures. They were quite incapable of dealing with crowds and would be useless in the event of panic in air raids or fire. Although his argument managed to defer the drafting of his manager for a fortnight, it failed fully to convince the board.

The reported appointment of manageresses at this time, however, is an indication that this manager's argument was one of expediency rather than fact.

> Even in these days of especial feminine activity, the Countess Cinema, Saltcoats [near Glasgow] has the very unusual feature of a lady manager, and what is probably still more unusual is that Miss Daisy Kingsbury is qualified by experience to act as an operator. At the end of last year when the manager was called up for military service, Miss Kingsbury volunteered to keep the place open and for a considerable time rendered efficient service at the lantern. Since taking over the duties of manager, Miss Kingsbury has conducted the business of the house in a manner eminently satisfactory [sic!] to its numerous patrons.[19]

At least one manager was able to convince a Tribunal that he should remain in charge. A 32-year-old married man in Hull proved to the court's satisfaction that he was practically everything in his cinema. He was granted exemption on condition that he should join the Volunteers and become a part-time policeman as a special constable. But, for the most part Tribunals were unsympathetic to these appeals. It was clear that any attempt to suggest that the work they were doing was of National Importance was doomed to failure. Two examples early in their operation should suffice to indicate the resolve of the Tribunal Chairmen.[20]

The Electric Theatre, Halifax asked for exemption for their chief operator and electrician. The manager, Mr. Courtney Crocker, held that it was expedient in the National Interest that places of amusement should be kept open to provide some form of relaxation for people engaged in munitions. He said that he had no one who could take the chief operator's place, and that there was a female operator to assist him. He had advertised in the London and local papers but had been unsuccessful in securing a man. The Tribunal granted exemption for one month.

A County Durham tribunal, 'which shall be nameless', listened to the case of a man employed in a picture theatre. Four members of the staff, including the original operator, had joined the Army. The current employee was looking after the gas, the electricity and the operating. He was doing the work of at least two men, and if he went the cinema would have to close. 'Would that be a serious matter from the National Standpoint?', asked the chairman of the tribunal. 'Yes,' replied the applicant, 'People must have some recreation, and women cannot do this man's work. The man, too is unfit for the army, and I have a doctor's certificate to prove it.' The Chairman: 'If we send this man forward – you will get him back if the Army doctors reject him.' Manager: 'Yes, but in the meantime, have we to close the place up?' A member of the tribunal: 'I don't think this board cares much whether the place is shut or not.' The application was refused.

The attitude of Officialdom to the labour shortages in the Cinema Trade so clearly upset the editor of *The Kinematograph Weekly* that, in the 29 June 1916 edition, he devoted the whole of a longer-than-usual editorial to the subject. 'Not of National Importance' declared his headline, but his discourse instead presented a case for the opposite view. The industry had given 'splendid proof of its patriotism', and had 'cheerfully paid its war-taxation'. If British filmmaking was run down it would have difficulty in recovering its market after the war. The cinema 'being the chief amusement of the people', represented 'a safety-valve for sorrow and

Fig. 4. Gaumont projector advertisement, from *The Bioscope*, 28 January 1915.

depression'. The Official films showing the army and navy at work had demonstrated the importance of cinema to the Government's publicity campaign, and the editor wished the tribunals to respect this opinion.

It was a theme taken up by Mr. A.E.Newbould, the President of the Cinematograph Exhibitors' Association, almost a year later at a meeting with Neville Chamberlain held at the St. James's Theatre in March 1917. He described how there were only a few C3 men left working in the industry, and how a considerable proportion of the unskilled labour in the cinemas was now done by women. He stressed the need for at least one, or at most two, skilled men to be retained for each theatre. He drew attention to the size of the Revenue payments made by the industry and the publicity value of the cinema screen to Government appeals. 'It is seen by everyone present, and does not depend upon its ability to catch the eye as is the case in the Press. Furthermore, if shown in every picture house, it can be seen by over 15 million people in one week.' Mr. Chamberlain's reply included the statement that though the amusement of the people was an essential part of National work, there were other considerations when it came to the need for essential manpower. Out of context, the central section of that sentence became the banner headline., 'The Amusement of the People is an Essential Part of National Work' – Mr. Neville Chamberlain.[21]

The King's praise for the cinema in 1916 had been given similar billing in the defence of the trade. George Maxwell, a picture theatre proprietor of Dabeattie in Scotland, appealed for exemption on the grounds that he was engaged in work of great national and educational importance. The Sheriff: 'You will require to go elsewhere to teach people that' [laughter]. The Agent: 'Well, I have the King's authority for the statement after he had seen The Somme film.' The Sheriff:'Yes, but he didn't say that the cinema should be worked by people who ought to be in the army, and he didn't say that the work was more important than winning the war. It may be only my ignorance, but I thought all the operator had to do was turn a handle.'

Projection boxes, by and large, still contained projectors that were turned by hand. Motorised projectors did exist and were fitted in many 'grand' cinemas, but lack of standardised film-taking speeds required fluctuation in projection speeds, often between scenes. Proprietors were also known to request a faster pace for their programs in order to ensure two houses in an evening. Though the complexities of projection were often stressed by appellants at tribunals, the manufacturers were constantly using simplicity of operation as a selling point. But, there was more to the job than turning the handle and the operation and trimming of carbon arcs and a variety of illuminants, and the maintenance of DC generators and 'gas' engines required training if not a full understanding of the circuitry. 'It now becomes clear', wrote the editor of the *1917 Kinematograph Weekly Yearbook*, 'that we should long ago have adopted some system of examining and licensing operators'.

In the North, Mr J.R. Millet opened a school for operators in April 1917 at 64 Victoria St, Liverpool.[22] In London, the Victoria Kinema College at 36 Rathbone Place, off Oxford Street, offered instruction to women and ineligible men with the promise of good salaries at the course's conclusion.[23] The 1916 pay and conditions agreement between the National Association of Theatrical Employees and the Cinematograph Exhibitors' Association in the London area divided Picture Houses and wages into two sections without distinguishing between male and female operators. In Class A Houses with continuous performances from 2 o'clock to 11 o'clock for a six day week of 8½ hours per day, the rate of pay was £3 for the Operator in charge, and £1.5s [£1.25p] for an Assistant with less than three months experience and £1.12s [£1. 60p] for an assistant with more than three months experience. This can be compared with minimum weekly wage of £2 for door keepers and attendants. The rate for Class B houses with only continuous nightly shows was £1.17s. 6d [£1. 87p] for chief operators, and a rate of 8d [3p] per hour for assistants with a daily minimum of 2s 6d. [12½p] A Doorkeeper's minimum wage was £1.1s. [£1.05p] per week for a 5 hour day. Boys or Girls were listed as assistants in the re-wind rooms. These were paid 3d per hour [1¼p] if they were under 15, and 6d per hour [2½p] between 15–18. Increasingly girls were being employed as 'Kinema Buttons' doing all the odd jobs around the projection room and tackling bill posting, since the boys could earn much more in the munitions factories.[24] In 1916, the London County Council prohibited anyone under the age of eighteen from assuming control of a projection box. But, age was not necessarily a recommendation for the task. There was concern that openings were being left for the 'inefficient or careless worker', and there was a realisation that an examining and licensing scheme for cinematograph operators should have been set up long ago.[25]

Surprisingly an article in the Kinematograph of 2 November 1916, entitled *Picture Theatre Music*, declares that Mr. Oswald Stoll [The Theatre entrepreneur] has defied tradition by admitting women to his music-hall orchestras, and surmises that other halls and picture theatres will doubtless follow. *The Bioscope* had already reported in February that Miss A. Lee had taken over the direction of the orchestra at The Picture House, Grantham,[26] and the article itself accepts that, for many years previously, instrumental trios and quartets, as well as pianists and relief pianists, were just as likely to be women as men.

The article written by Edith M.G.Reed, ARCO offers some quite weird comparisons between men and women musicians which seem to be socially oriented rather than musically accurate: 'According to one report women's string tone is much weaker and that of a man much sweeter'; and 'The wind department presents more difficulties for the reason not that women have insufficient breath supply, but that they have inefficient breath control'. In a somewhat convoluted argument, the writer in commenting upon the equal pay offered, declares that 'no manager will discharge a man ineligible for war service in favour of a woman unless the man is unfit for his musical duties as well as his military'. By this token, she suggests that the chances of available men being employed are not compromised because managers will no longer have the excuse of employing more women for the same outlay'. 'After the war', she adds ominously, 'matters will adjust themselves'. Reports of all-ladies orchestras soon followed at The Evington Cinema, Leicester and The Charing Cross Picturedrome, Birkenhead. [27]

The man-power situation in the industry was even more constrained by the new National Service Regulations of March 1917. Under these, all civilian males between the ages of 18 and 61 not required by the Military Services would not be allowed to fill vacancies without the consent of the Director of National Services unless the work was of National Importance. A certain vagueness in the regulations initially seemed to suggest that theatre chains could not move men around their picture houses to fill vacancies, but clarification indicated that the regulations did not permit increases in staffing. 'Nobody would be so foolish as to say, for example, that two men might have to do the work hitherto done by three, or that women may have to be brought in to do some of the work.' [28]

Situations Vacant advertisements, at this time,

Fig. 5. From *The Kinematograph and Lantern Weekly*, 22 February 1917.

however, clearly indicated that women operators were very much being sought after. 'Lady Operator and Assistant wanted. State Wages'. 'Chief Operator, lady, required. Must be experienced. Good Wages. High Class Theatre. No Sunday work. Picture House, Leyton.' 'Chief Operator required, lady, for first class theatre, N.E.London.' 'Wanted at once, Lady Operator, used to motor generator, Henderson, Grand Theatre, Coventry.' 'Operator (lady) and Assistant (lady) wanted for South London Hall, State wages and experience.'

Mr. Lionel Grant, the chief engineer of The Electric Pavilion, wrote to *The Kinematograph Weekly* in support of female operators.[29] He said that he was busily engaged in training girls as operators and was pleased to say that he was getting excellent results from them. In his opinion, if girls can be trained and supervised by experts and not by 'handle-turners' or 'prejudiced' persons they are as receptive as men, and in the majority of cases more conscientious.

A revealing but somewhat sad letter from Madge St. Hinton of the Theatre Royal, Rushden was published in the 21 March 1918 edition of *The Kinematograph Weekly* under the heading 'The Right Sort of Lady Operator'. Its personal detail and ambivalent content is worthy of quotation at length.

> I have been in the business with my husband for nearly ten years, and have seen more film repairing done during the last six months than ever I did. It wants all good old hands to come out on strike, then perhaps they would be appreciated. As for wages, well, they all knock you down if they can. The only way is, as someone said a week or two ago, demand the wage and give a good show. As regards lady-operators; well, I have had to work the show since the war, and with good experience, I am not like my husband. A lady operator has not got the nerve. Another thing, what good would be a lady operator or a would-be boy operator out of one of these schools if he or she were called upon to work a new kind of machine, such as an old Dog, or one where a spiteful operator (who has had the sack) has taken the machine to pieces, eh? As for wounded soldiers, by all means let them learn if they have the nerve. My husband himself has really only one hand. On the right hand, there is only one finger he can use, and I'll guarantee him against anyone. I do not think that a man with a left hand injured would be much good, or if his eye-sight were bad, but if he has the pluck he will do it. and all honour to him. I carried on when my husband went into the army, and if other operators taught their wives instead of having duds, there would be less room for any complaints whatever. Some will say, just like a woman, such a lot to say. Yes, to a few of the renters and the dud operators etc. I wish I could sometimes let you know all I say and think.

The Editor's comment on the letter revealed that he was still accepting the employment of women only as an expedient:

> Many women and even girls have nerve enough and to spare. The trouble is that those who have the nerve seldom have the imagination, whilst those who have the imagination are generally jumpy in their nerves. A man is not like that. He can know keenly the danger attendant upon a slip in handling the film and still keep cool and clear headed.

The editorial in *The Kinematograph Weekly* a month later suggests a more positive view of the long term involvement of women in the trade. Until the title 'Gentlemen! 'The Ladies'. Helping the Trade to Carry On in Wartime and After', the declaration is made that the cinema industry is too young to have developed an exaggerated respect for tradition. Innovation is central to the business. 'It can claim to have early shown itself alive to the possibility of women's co-operation.' The article further declared that women had occupied places in every department of the trade prior to the war, and the present employment of women was 'the result of a natural development rather than a revolution' ... Film houses found a use for women as managers, viewers and travellers and paid equal wages for equal work even before the war. The editor rebukes those who imagine that it will be 'just as before when the war is over'. The Nottingham and Derby Branch of the Cinematograph Exhibitors' Association had recently appointed Mrs. Beastall of the Premier Electric Theatre, Somercotes, Derbyshire as an elected trustee. She had opened her first cinema in Somercotes in a small hall which was later demolished and re-built in an enlarged form.[31]

It is clear that the article is only referring to the activities of the distribution and management sides of the business. There is not a single mention of projector operators. Even the observation of women being appointed to managerial posts is greeted with a certain surprise. FIRST LADY SALES MANAGER is the headline of a news item in *The Kinematograph Weekly* of 7 December 1917 detailing the appointment of Mrs Stanton to the post handling Famous French Films in The Fox Film Co. Declaring that her organising ability and powers of persuasion have been well tested as organising secretary and public speaker for various social and political activities, the report goes on to quote her opinions: 'I find the film trade a very jolly family. Of course there are lots of small squabbles, which are only a sign of healthy growth, but they are quite good humoured and there is no bad feeling or sex rivalry ... Of course, I want to prove that we understand a square deal and can be just as good sports as the men in the trade.'

Fig. 6. Mrs Stanton, 'first lady sales manager'. From *The Kinematograph Weekly*, 7 December 1917.

In the same edition, the headline 'The "Lady Publicity Chief" has arrived!' announced the appointment of Miss Agnes Haynes to that post with the Famous Players Film Company. The quotation marks and the exclamation mark register the tone of disbelief despite the fact that she was an accomplished member of The Institute of Journalists and had experience on a number of National Daily newspapers. The qualifications of Mr. H.W. Proctor, the draftee whom she was replacing are not declared.

Mrs J.D. Walker's appointment as Film Agent

to her husband's firm is not tipped as nepotism, for, as the report declares, 'she is a lady with a distinct personality of her own and a keenness for business that has already become one of her acknowledged features and has enabled her to make so many friends in the trade'.[32]

The lecture 'Women and Film' given by a Miss Irene Miller at the Stoll Picture Theatre Club in May also seems to be directed more to management than general employment.[33] She pleaded that the heads of the cinema industry should be more inclined to put their daughters into the business in the same way that their sons were apprenticed in days gone by.

The operator shortage was beginning to be alleviated by the employment of ex-servicemen and men who were also engaged on munitions production. In 'Sunderland Notes',[34] the reporter states that nearly every manager is plagued by 'box'-troubles.

> Operators were mostly young men and their transference to the Army is causing no end of inconvenience. Wounded or discharged soldiers are eagerly seeking the jobs, but, as one manager remarked to me, 'We cannot run the pictures until they know their job. It's not safe.' At several places, the ex-soldiers are 'getting their hands in' by doing 'the boys' work', though this has been in the hands of girls for some time.

In Leigh-on-Sea, a picture house was owned and managed by 'silver-badged' men in its entirety. From the managing director to the attendants, every man in the place had been invalided from the Forces during the war. Even the operator and the members of the orchestra wore badges for 'services rendered', whilst the women attendants were all widows of men killed in action.[35]

In July, it was reported at the CEA Conference that 300 disabled ex-servicemen had now been trained as operators. Future problems with this training had been voiced by *The Bioscope* in April.[36] At the classes, the trainees were given a thorough theoretical training as well as practical experience. It now transpired that when some of the trainees took up their posts, they revealed a better knowledge of optics and electricity than their more experienced chief operators. 'The result is', the report concluded, 'that some of them get an inflated idea of their value, and think that they might at once get the highest paid position'.

In December 1918, a month after the Armistice, *The Future of Demobilised Operators* was discussed in a brief editorial. Over 700 cinemas had closed their doors during the war years, and cinema building and alteration had been stopped by limiting regulations for three years.[37] However, 265 cinemas are reported to have been newly opened between January 1914 and July 1916 according to *The Kinematograph Weekly Yearbooks* for the succeeding years. A considerable amount of post-war unemployment was foreseen. Some men had gained a theoretical knowledge of electrical apparatus in the armed forces and they had used this to gain employment in the cinema trade. Many pre-war operators lacked this expertise and found themselves depreciated.

The advertisement columns of the trade press contained vacant situations for Lady Chief Operators throughout November, but then that specific demand was discontinued. With rare exceptions, ladies ceased to be employed as operators. Returning husbands replaced wives in the management seats. The cinema trade had returned to normal. A photograph of the annual dinner celebrations of a well-known distribution company in *The Kinematograph Weekly* of 5 December 1918 shows an all male group.

And yet, only months before, the following eulogy [quoted here in full] was printed in *The Kinematograph Weekly*.[38]

> **The lady manageress – her influence on the kinema:**
>
> There was once a kinema that was never full. It was always slightly dirty and its program seldom coincided with its day bill. The attendants were lackadaisical and the general atmosphere around the place was not inviting. That kinema just kept its head above water. In the theatre that we have in view, as the manager walked out to join the colours, his wife walked in – as manageress. At first there was a little tendency to nervousness. Would the operator obey the feminine order? Further, should the generating machine break down, what would the lady manager do? The burly door attend-

ant, would he toe the line to the new authority? And the powers that be in the shape of the police etc. would they take kindly to a lady? Today, that erstwhile shabby and disreputable kinema is a palais-de-luxe in reality. Woman has had her opportunity. She has fought hard in the struggle for kinema efficiency, and with her woman's wit, patience and sagacity, she has conquered. There are many kinemas today, brighter and better paying propositions, because woman has been offered the opportunity of proving her mettle. The industry is better for her influence, and may her good work last long after the war has brought home the men, whom the days of peace allowed to doze at their work.

The opportunities afforded to ladies in the World War One were repeated to a lesser extent in World War Two. By then, physical factor of moving the film through the gate had been totally eliminated by electric motor, and it was feasible to recruit non-eligible men whether they were in that capacity by virtue of disablement or age. But, women operators are still rarely found in the projection rooms of the nation, and their 1914–18 employment, whilst saving many picture houses from closure, failed to dent the male monopoly of the industry. ♦

Notes

The source of most of the text is either *The Bioscope Weekly* or *The Kinematograph and Lantern Weekly* [*K.W.*]

1. 'The Cinema : Its Present Position and Future Possibilities' 1917. page xxi quoted by Low, Rachel, *The History of the British Film 1914–18* (London: Allen & Unwin,1950).
2. Laurence Treveleyan 'Amusements and The War' *The Bioscope* (5 November 1914).
3. *The Bioscope* (6 August 1914.)
4. *The Bioscope* (20 August 1914). For comparison with 1996 prices, all sums of money given in this article should be multiplied by a factor of 31 for 1914–16, and a factor of 17 for 1916–18.
5. *K.W.* (7 January 1915).
6. *K.W.* (29 April 1915).
7. *K.W.* (13 May 1915).
8. *K.W.* (3 June 1915).
9. *The Bioscope* (17 June 1915).
10. *K.W.* (17 June 1915).
11. *K.W.* (24 June 1915).
12. *Film History* vol. 6 no. 2: 223.
13. *K.W.* (19 December 1918).
14. *K.W.* (15 December 1918).
15. *The Bioscope* (16 December 1915).
16. *K.W.* (24 June 1915).
17. *K.W.* (4 May 1916).
18. *The Bioscope* (20 July 1916).
19. *The Bioscope* (31 August 1916).
20. *The Bioscope* (23 March 1916).
21. *K.W.* (8 March 1917).
22. *Kinematograph Yearbook* (1918): 57.
23. *K.W.* (15 February 1917).
24. *K.W.* (17 August 1916).
25. *'A Technical Survey of 1916' Kinematograph Yearbook* (1917): 29.
26. *The Bioscope* (16 February 1916).
27. *K. W.* (27 October 1916), and *The Bioscope* (25 January 1917).
28. *K.W.* (8 March 1917).
29. *K.W.* (15 February 1917).
30. *K.W.* (25 April 1918).
31. *The Bioscope* (13 June 1918).
32. *K.W.* (2 December 1916).
33. *The Bioscope* (10 May 1918).
34. *K.W.* (20 June 1918).
35. *The Bioscope* (3 October 1918).
36. *The Bioscope* (4 April 1918).
37. *The Bioscope* (17 June 1917).
38. *K.W.* (3 October, 1918).

FILM HISTORY

Back issue and subscription order form

PLEASE SUPPLY:

.... Subscription(s) to *Film History*
at Institutional/Private rate (please specify)
Surface/Air Mail (please specify)
.... Back issues of the following volumes/issues
....
....

I enclose payment of £/US$ ....
Please send me a Pro-forma invoice for: £/US$ ....

Please debit my Access/Master Card/Visa/
American Express/Diner's Club credit card:
Account no..Expiry..........
Name ....
Address ....
....
....
.... Zip/Postcode ....

Signature ....Date ....
(This form may be photocopied)

SUBSCRIPTION RATES & BACK ISSUE PRICES

Institutional Subscription rates:

All countries (except N. America)
Surface mail £85/A$170
Air mail £95/A$190

N. America
Surface mail US$151 Air mail US$172

Private Subscription rates (subscribers warrant that copies are for their PERSONAL use only):

All countries (except N. America)
Surface mail £33/A$66
Air mail £44/A$88

N. America
Surface mail US$59 Air mail US$79

Back issues: All issues available – Volumes 1 to 7: £12/US$20/A$24 each number.

JOHN LIBBEY & COMPANY LTD,
Level 10, 15–17 Young Street
Sydney, NSW 2000, Australia
Telephone: +61 (0)2 9251 4099
Fax: +61 (0)2 9251 4428
E-mail: jlsydney@mpx.com.au

FILM HISTORY

An International Journal

Aims and Scope

The subject of *Film History* is the historical development of the motion picture, and the social, technological and economic context in which this has occurred. Its areas of interest range from the technical and entrepreneurial innovations of early and precinema experiments, through all aspects of the production, distribution, exhibition and reception of commercial and non-commercial motion pictures.

In addition to original research in these areas, the journal will survey the paper and film holdings of archives and libraries world-wide, publish selected examples of primary documentation (such as early film scenarios) and report on current publications, exhibitions, conferences and research in progress. Many future issues will be devoted to comprehensive studies of single themes.

Instructions to Authors

Manuscripts will be accepted with the understanding that their content is unpublished and is not being submitted for publication elsewhere. If any part of the paper has been previously published, or is to be published elsewhere, the author must include this information at the time of submittal. Manuscripts should be sent to the Editor-in-Chief:

Richard Koszarski
Box Ten
Teaneck
NJ 07666, USA

excepting for submissions to thematic issues directed by one of the Associate Editors.

The publishers will do everything possible to ensure prompt publication, therefore it is required that each submitted manuscript be in complete form. Please take the time to check all references, figures, tables and text for errors before submission.